Seek Ye First
The Kingdom
of God

Seek Ye First The Kingdom of God

By President N. Eldon Tanner

Compiled by LaRue Sneff

Published by
Deseret Book Company
Salt Lake City, Utah
1976

ISBN Number 0-87747-510-5

Library of Congress Number 73-91712

Lithographed by

DESERET PRESS

in the United States of America

Contents

INTRODUCTION vii

PART I.   A PHILOSOPHY OF LIFE

  1.   "Seek Ye First the Kingdom of God" 1
  2.   "I . . . Having Been Born of Goodly Parents" 7

PART II.   SEEK TO KNOW, LOVE, AND SERVE
          THE MASTER

  3.   The Divinity of Jesus Christ 21
  4.   "For Unto Us a Child Is Born" 32

PART III.   SEEK TO LOVE ONE ANOTHER

  5.   The Second Great Commandment: Love One Another ..39
  6.   Search for the Wanderers 48
  7.   "Judge Not, That Ye Be Not Judged" 53
  8.   "Woe Unto You . . . Hypocrites" 62
  9.   The Brotherhood of Man 71
  10.   Our Concern for the Lamanite 77

PART IV.   SEEK TO EXERCISE FREE AGENCY

  11.   "Thou Mayest Choose for Thyself" 83
  12.   "Choose You This Day Whom Ye Will Serve" 92
  13.   Reverence for Law 100
  14.   Our Civic Responsibilities 109
  15.   The Blessings of Obedience 116

PART V. SEEK TO KNOW AND KEEP THE
COMMANDMENTS OF GOD

16. "The Heavens Are Open" 127
17. The Gospel Our Bulwark 136
18. "Where Art Thou?" 144
19. The Power of Prayer 154
20. The Plan of Life and Salvation 165
21. Priviliged Priesthood Holders 174
22. The Word of Wisdom 180
23. Lead Them Not Into Temptation 190
24. In the Lord's Service 198

PART VI. SEEK TO KEEP FAITH WITH YOUR FAMILY

25. Keep Faith With Your Family 207
26. The Role of Woman in the Church 214
27. Preparation Begins in the Home 224
28. Vocational Training 228

PART VII. SEEK TO EMULATE THE LIVES OF
GREAT MEN

29. Joseph Smith, the Prophet 243
30. David O. McKay, the Man 254
31. David O. McKay: A True Exemplar of the Life of Christ..265
32. Joseph Fielding Smith: A Man Without Guile 273
33. President John F. Kennedy: A Memorial 280

PART VIII. SEEK ALWAYS TO SERVE AND TO
GIVE THANKS

34. A Pledge to Serve 285
35. A Privilege and a Call 287
36. "I Will Go and Do the Things . . . " 291
37. Rejoice, and Give Thanks 294

INDEX 297

Introduction

"In my office I like to maintain such an atmosphere that those who come to call will go out feeling better than they did when they came in."

These words were part of the conversation which took place on the occasion of the first interview I had with N. Eldon Tanner, who had recently been called as second counselor in the First Presidency. The secretary who had been serving with him had just been married, necessitating her replacement, and he had summoned me for consultation.

He went on to explain carefully that he did not mean to imply that he felt superior in any way to those who might visit, but by trying to build them up and lift their spirits, he would be building himself and improving his own character. Though he did not say so, I felt as I sat before him that he wanted nothing more than to devote himself as wholeheartedly as he could to the service of the Lord and his fellowmen.

During the intervening years I have been often reminded of his expressed desire as person after person, in passing my desk as each one has left our office, has paused to make some such statement as: "He has helped me in the solution of my problem. I feel so much better than I did when I came in." I feel sure, from the expression I have seen on his face as I have ushered people in to his presence, that he is thinking: "Now what can I do or say to make this person feel better?" Then he does or says it.

On those occasions when we would remind him that perhaps his schedule is too full for another appointment, or that he should not take on another responsibility, he will say, typically, "I am here to do all the good I can."

Modestly he accepts compliments and tributes paid to him. When some complimentary thing is said or some generosity extended, he will say in genuine surprise, "Now why would they say that about me?" or "Why would they want to do that for me?" He does not solicit or expect any special consideration or privilege for himself, but he does accept graciously those things people do for him out of respect for the position he holds.

Having spent most of his life in Canada engaged in government service and in industry, he is held in high regard there by Church members and nonmembers alike, and he became known as "Mr. Integrity" in many circles. A representative of Brigham Young University, returning from an assignment in Alberta, Canada, wrote President Tanner a letter in which he said: "Wherever I went, and as soon as it became known I was from Salt Lake City and a member of the Latter-day Saint Church, I was asked to bring greetings to you. Someone said to me that he supposed no one had ever made as much of a contribution to the economic, social, moral, and spiritual welfare of Canada as you."

One special tribute to him was paid by President A. Theodore Tuttle of the First Council of Seventy and, in my opinion, is as fine a sentiment as could be expressed about a man. Elder Tuttle was presiding over the South American Mission and had come home for general conference. President Tanner had invited him to have lunch with him and other special guests between conference sessions. As Elder Tuttle came through the Church Office Building on his way to the Tabernacle for the afternoon meeting, he opened the door to our office and made this brief comment: "That was a choice experience. That man is as common as an old shoe, and as noble as a prince."

This is in harmony with what his former secretary told me. She had served with President and Sister Tanner in the mission home when they presided over the West European Mission with headquarters in London, England. She said that in visiting around the mission they could enter the most humble cottage or the most lavish residence or castle and be equally at home and make everyone around them feel comfortable and at ease.

President Tanner is a most considerate husband to his lovely wife, who supports him so ably and devotedly. Together they visit the sick, comfort the sorrowing, help the poor, accept assignments, and minister to the needs of their children and grandchildren, all of whom are keenly aware of the great love their parents and grandparents have for them.

They are most charming and hospitable hosts, and much sought after as guests. They love and are loved by all with whom they associate. Their philosophy of life is the same, with family and the Church taking priority over other things.

As the writings of President N. Eldon Tanner are herein presented, it will be of worth to the reader to know that he reminds himself often of some of the scriptures he feels are the basis for the messages and testimony he bears to the world, not the least of which is: ". . . seek ye first the kingdom of God, and his righteousness; and all these things shall be added unto you."

LaRue Sneff

I

A Philosophy of Life:

"Seek ye first the kingdom of God,
and his righteousness;
and all these things
shall be added unto you."

(Matthew 6:33)

CHAPTER 1

"Seek Ye First the Kingdom of God"

As I look back over my life, I should like to pay tribute to and thank my father and my bishop—who was the same man—for the direction and help and guidance and example he gave me all the time I was growing up. He continually taught me: ". . . seek ye first the kingdom of God, and his righteousness; and all these things shall be added unto you." (Matthew 6:33.)

He explained to me that "all these things" meant everything that would be for my good, and I am very grateful for learning in my youth that it is not always good for us to have everything we want or think we want. Disciplining ourselves to want only those things that are right for us to have and discerning between the right and the wrong things are part of the training that every young person should experience. My father guided me along these lines.

Faithful always in his church duties, my father tried to instill this same desire in me to attend my meetings and perform my assignments. When I was a deacon we had to travel eight miles to attend priesthood meeting and the general stake priesthood meeting, which was held once a month on Saturday. We had no cars or trucks, but only wagons and buggies.

Father used to make those trips pay both ways. For

instance, he would drive a team and wagon full of wheat, and I would follow him with a team and wagon full of wheat, taking a little more than two hours to go eight miles. We went early enough to unload the wheat and load our wagons with coal to take home after the meeting. But we never missed the priesthood meeting.

As I think back over the experiences I had with that wonderful man, and my home training given by my father and mother, I can't help giving them practically all the credit for directing me and teaching me to believe that if I would seek first the kingdom of God and his righteousness, all other things for my good would be added unto me. That was a great lesson for me to learn.

I remember another thing my father taught me that was very important. As a bishop he was not able to spend the time at home that some men can who are not bishops. He left us one afternoon while he was going out to look after his flock in the ward, and my brother and I were assigned to do certain things. He came back sooner than he had intended, or than we had expected him to come back, and we hadn't accomplished what he had asked us to do. We had some calves in the corral we thought needed riding, and so we went about to accommodate those calves.

I will never forget what happened when my father came home and found we had not done the work which we had been assigned. He called me over to him and said, "My boy, I thought I could depend on you." That is all he said.

I made up my mind at that moment that Father would never have reason to say that to me again as long as I lived and as long as he lived. And I was happy that he gave me that experience. A trouncing wouldn't have done the good that "My boy, I thought I could depend on you" did. I made up my mind then that no one would ever have reason to say, "I thought I could depend on you." I vowed also that I would try to so live that the Lord would always be able to depend on me.

It is an interesting thing that neighbors expect one another to keep their covenants and to keep their agreements, and if a neighbor makes an agreement with another neighbor and he doesn't live up to that agreement, his neighbor immediately rates him way down. But this same neighbor might be and very possibly is not keeping his covenants with his Heavenly Father. And I wonder if his Heavenly Father is saying, "Son, I thought I could depend on you."

Again I wish to say, if you seek first the kingdom of God and his righteousness, all these things will be added unto you.

Let me relate a little story that I have told all over the Church. My daughter and her girl friend were at our house, and they were going to a party; then two young men came and called for them. I sat and talked to them. I love young people. I was talking to them about different things, and just before they were ready to leave, I said, "Now, have a good time, kids." But just as they were going out of the door, I stepped over to my daughter and said, "Now, behave yourself."

And she said, "Well, Dad, make up your mind."

Then I said to those young people so they could all hear me, "Have a good time, kids, the best time you will ever have in your lives, but the kind of time that tomorrow, next week, a month from now or a year from now, ten years from now, you can look back on tonight and say, 'I had a good time,' and have nothing to regret or be sorry about."

And I think they went out and had a good time.

That was my slogan for our missionaries in the West European Mission—to have a good time. One young man, after I had been talking to a group of missionaries over in Germany, came up to me and said, "President Tanner, I don't think it's right for you to tell these missionaries to have a good time. The only way they can do it is to do their work."

I said, "Then go and have a good time." He was right.

The story is told of another missionary over there who was discussing the gospel with a minister, and the minister wasn't making the progress that he thought he should, and finally he turned to the missionary and said, "Well, at least you will agree that we are both trying to serve the Lord." The missionary looked at him for a moment and said, "Yes, I think I would—you in your way, and I in His." Now, that might sound impudent, and maybe it was, if the story is true. But right there is a real lesson to me.

If I can serve the Lord in his way, then I am going along the path where I will have the greatest success and the greatest joy.

Too many of us would like to change the rules and would like to serve him in our way, not his way. Some of us wonder why we have to go to church and keep the Sabbath day holy. Some of us wonder about paying a full tithing. Some of us wonder about the Word of Wisdom. Some of us wonder about other things—moral living. In fact, a young woman came to me and said, "President Tanner, I have tried to live the gospel just as nearly as I could possibly live it, as I understand it. I am a little older now. I am a teacher. I am still single. But I think you should know that too many of our young men today are saying, regarding morality, 'Oh, what's the difference? What does it matter? That is a lot of nonsense.' And I know young men who are returned missionaries, young men who come from some of the best families, who are saying the same thing."

I should like to say to all our youth that such an attitude is just as far from right as it can possibly be. You cannot do those things and make progress and enjoy success and happiness nor have the Spirit of the Lord to be with you.

Let us never be ashamed of the gospel of Jesus Christ, for it is the power of God unto salvation (see Romans 1:16), and let us never hesitate to call upon the Lord. Let us be obedient to the Lord; let us be obedient to the priesthood. Let us magnify our callings so that they can magnify us. Let us not cheat as we go along and try to do it halfway, or serve in our way; but let us serve in his.

Let us each so live that we can say, with the poet:

> I have to live with myself, and so
> I want to be fit for myself to know,
> I want to be able, as days go by,
> Always to look myself straight in the eye;
> I don't want to stand, with the setting sun,
> And hate myself for the things I've done.
>
> I don't want to keep on a closet shelf,
> A lot of secrets about myself,
> And fool myself, as I come and go,
> Into thinking that nobody else will know
> The kind of man that I really am;
> I don't want to dress up myself in sham.
>
> I want to go out with my head erect,
> I want to deserve all men's respect;
> But here in the struggle for fame and pelf,
> I want to be able to like myself.
> I don't want to look at myself and know
> That I'm bluster and bluff and empty show.
>
> I never can hide myself from me;
> I see what others can never see;
> I know what others may never know;
> I never can fool myself, and so,
> Whatever happens, I want to be
> Self-respecting and conscience free.

—Edgar A. Guest, "Myself"*

I plead with all Latter-day Saints, wherever they may be, to live so that they can enjoy their own self-respect and the respect of others, and so that the Lord will be able

*From *Collected Verse* by Edgar A. Guest; copyright Reilly & Lee.

to say, "Here is a person on whom I can depend. He is a person who can be counted upon to live up to all the standards and commandments of the Church and be a real leader."

Let us go forward this day and always, seeking first the kingdom of God and his righteousness, knowing that it will bring joy, success, and all things for our good.

Chapter 2

"I...Having Been Born of Goodly Parents"

My people came to this, the American continent, in the *Mayflower*: three of them were on that boat. They came because of their convictions, because they were prepared to sacrifice anything they had—their lives, if necessary—to gain the freedom to live and worship God according to the dictates of their own consciences. I am so thankful that I can trace my genealogy back to them and know that they were that kind of people.

Now let us jump to 1832, just two years after the Church was organized by the Prophet Joseph Smith. That year two young men, Simeon and Jared Carter, went out to preach the gospel in Bolton, New York, and a man by the name of John Tanner heard that they were in the district. He was a very public-spirited man, a religious man, and when he heard that these Mormon missionaries were coming into his district, he wanted to be sure to put a stop to this and see that none of this nonsense was preached to the people.

Though he was a cripple and had been for months, and the doctors were not able to heal his leg, and he was in a wheelchair, he told his sons that he wanted to go to that meeting and to put those missionaries right. They took him to the meeting and wheeled him up to the front so that he could look the missionaries in the eye and question them, heckle them, and tell them where they were wrong.

One of the missionaries got up and told about the apostasy, the restoration of the gospel, and the story of Joseph Smith. John Tanner sat and listened without saying a word.

Then the other missionary told about the restoration of the priesthood and the establishment of the Church, the translation of the plates that are now the Book of Mormon, and some of that book's teachings. John Tanner sat and listened—no criticism, no corrections, no heckling.

When the meeting was over, he turned to one of his sons and said, "I'd like to meet those young men." So his son went up and brought them down and introduced them to his father. He said, "Would you men like to come and stay with me tonight?" They accepted his invitation.

At the insistence of their host, and to their satisfaction, they taught the gospel to him until the early hours of the morning, answering his questions, telling him the truths that had been restored, what the new church at that time had to offer the world, and that it was the same church organization that existed in Christ's church while he was upon the earth.

John Tanner said to those young men, "If I were well enough, I think I'd like to apply for baptism this morning." One of the young men said, "Do you believe the Lord could heal you?" He thought a minute and then said, "Yes, I think he could if he wanted to."

Then they told him that they were elders and had the priesthood of God, and they reminded him that Christ taught that "if there are any sick among you, let him call in the elders to pray over you." One of them said, "Would you like to be administered to?" John Tanner said, "I would." The young men administered to him, and that very day he left his wheelchair, walked three-quarters of a mile, and was baptized in Lake George.

Now to me that means a great deal. It is most important in my life to think that John Tanner had the courage when he saw the truth to take his stand and join the Church and accept the gospel of Jesus Christ, knowing that he would be ridiculed, knowing that he would be ostracized. But he had the courage.

In its early days the Church experienced great financial difficulty. John Tanner was fairly well-to-do, and he sold everything he had and let the Prophet Joseph Smith have the money to take care of the indebtedness of the Church. I am thankful for those missionaries who taught him the gospel; that he, my great-great-grandfather, remained true to the Church; and that his son, and his son, and his son, who was my father, remained true to the faith, knowing that God lives and that the gospel has been restored in these, the latter days. They lived according to its principles and teachings, and as a result I am a member of the Church and bear testimony to its divine origin. Those things mean more to me than I can express.

James S. Brown, my great-grandfather on my mother's side, also had great faith and served in the Church with devotion and distinction and was a member of the Mormon Battalion. His very illustrious life has been recorded in the book *The Giant of the Lord*, written by one of his grandchildren.

My own parents, when they were married, had a feeling of conquest and decided that for their honeymoon they would go to Canada from Salt Lake City by way of covered wagon. It took them six weeks to travel to the southern part of Alberta, near Cardston.

When they arrived, their financial situation was such that Father had to sell his horses in order to buy groceries and other things necessary for them to carry on. He didn't think of calling on the government or anybody else for a handout. He had sold his horses, but how could he farm without them? Of course there were no cars, no tractors. So he went to a neighboring rancher and arranged with him to break or train horses with the understanding that if he broke four horses, he could use two of them himself for the rest of the year. This is the way he established himself on a homestead.

A homestead is where you go out into the wide open spaces and choose a quarter-section of land and bet the government ten dollars that you can make a go of it. That is what he did. In order to win the bet, he dug out a hole in the side of a hill and got some logs for the walls and sides of the house, left the hill for the back wall, and put logs on the front. They started from the ground up; the floor was earth, and the roof was sod. This is the kind of place they lived in first, and where they started rearing their family.

Later we moved to nearby Aetna, a hamlet of about 100 persons. We had no plumbing, and we used to catch flies with flypaper hanging down from the ceiling. We had kerosene lamps—I never saw an electric light in the area where we lived. In the whole of that little place there was no indoor plumbing, no hot and cold water other than the hot water we heated on the stove in a boiler; no library, no newspapers, no telephones. Horse transportation was the only thing we had, except oxen that I drove when we were farming; but we didn't have any other type of transportation until I was twenty years of age.

I was given what education I could get in a two-room school. We had no furnaces, no central heating. A coal range and a heater were in our house, and a big heater in the school. In that area all the kids went barefoot in the summertime because they couldn't afford shoes. However, my parents wouldn't let me go barefoot, and I felt very disappointed, unhappy, in fact, because I was different from those who were going barefoot.

I attended Primary where I remember one thing in particular my teacher told me: *Whatever is worth doing is worth doing well*, and I have had that as a slogan—that the thing that is at hand is the thing that should receive your whole concentration and effort if you really want to succeed.

One early experience I recall was when my oldest sister, who was quite a bit younger than I, had spinal meningitis and she was very, very sick. This is the first time that I really felt the importance and the effect of prayer. We as a family knelt in prayer. That night Father said, "My boy, you are a deacon. We would like you to lead in prayer tonight and remember Lillie." I'll never forget the feeling that came over me as I prayed that she would be made well. I had that prayer answered. She wasn't made well immediately, but from that time she began to improve in health. She is now the mother of three children and enjoying life. That has meant a great deal to me and introduced me into an experience that is most important in my life. What a wonderful privilege it is, what a wonderful blessing, to know that you can go and call on the Lord. You don't have to make an appointment, but you get down on your knees in all humility and know that he stands ready to answer your prayer if you are just in tune. There is no greater privilege in this world than to be able to call on the Lord and know that he answers our prayers and has given us a plan of life and salvation because of his interest in us.

My father had me work when I was a young boy. When I was twelve years old, he sent me out with a team and wagon to haul grain seven and a half miles to the grain elevators, a two-hour trip. When I was fourteen he had me drive four head of horses with two wagons.

Father taught me many lessons. He used to say, "It is better to aim at the moon and miss it, than aim at nothing and hit it." In other words, set up your goals and strive to get there. If you just barely miss them or if you miss by quite a bit, it is better than aiming at nothing and hitting it.

Another thing he used to say was, "Now, if you want your dreams to come true, you'd better wake up." How true that is. We must be constantly alert and working if we want to accomplish or reach our goals. I would like to suggest to all young people everywhere that if you prepare yourselves to stand against and meet opposition, any temptation, anything serious, you can face it and overcome it. You know, it isn't the mountain you climb that gets you down; it's the sand in your shoes. The little things that come into your life have to be watched—that is where we have to be careful. If we really want to be successful, we have to see that the little things are taken care of.

I had some good teachers to help me learn these lessons. In our little town, they taught only through grade eight, so when I completed that, I said to Dad, "I would like to go to grade nine." We went to talk to the principal of that two-room school, and he said, "If you can get five kids to take grade nine, I'll teach it."

As fall approached, my father, though he was on the school board, said, "I need you to work on the farm." That was a little disappointing, but I went to the school principal and said, "If we come in after Christmas, will you teach us?" We had found four others who would be able to go also, and he said, "Yes."

So I took my grade nine after Christmas, and later grade ten. While I went to grade eleven, I worked in a butcher shop, in the slaughter yards, building fences, or doing anything I could get to do, for twenty-five cents an hour. But I enjoyed it, and it did get me through my high school. Then I wanted to go to Normal School so I could qualify as a teacher.

Father didn't have the money; I had no money. I couldn't save money at twenty-five cents an hour, not very much of it anyway. Father said, "If you can borrow the money, I'll spare you from the farm so you may go to Normal School." I went to the bank to see if I could borrow the money, and here I learned another great lesson.

I trembled as I sat in the manager's office, waiting to see if I could borrow $400 to go to Normal School. Although I think he knew who I was, I told him my name was Tanner.

He said, "Oh, are you so-and-so's boy?"

"No, I am N. W. Tanner's boy."

"N. W. Tanner's boy?"

"Yes."

"When can you pay this money back?"

"I would pay it out of my first earnings when I start teaching school," I said.

"Very well. If you are N. W. Tanner's boy, we'll let you have the money."

I thought what a wonderful thing it is to have a good name. You know, you make your own name. This is so important, and each day, each move, everything you do, leaves the person who is watching you and observing you with a definite feeling about whether or not you have a good name or are an individual on whom he can depend. After that I wouldn't let my dad's name down for anything.

I went to Normal School and came out with a second-class certificate. I was principal of a three-room school in Hill Spring, Alberta, when I was twenty years of age. The first year I taught grades seven and eight. The next year I taught grades seven, eight, and nine. The next year we established a four-room school, and I taught grades nine and ten, and the next year grades nine, ten, and eleven.

Students of these grades were required to take government departmental examinations, which were marked independent of myself by a government representative. All passed except one student in one subject in grade ten. The six young men in grade eleven passed all their subjects. Inasmuch as I had only gone as far as grade eleven myself, I joined with my six students and went on to take grade twelve in Cardston.

Being a married man with two children, it was necessary for me to do substitute teaching while I was taking grade twelve, as well as teaching English to fifty-six grade nine students. Besides this, I milked cows and sold the milk. Sister Tanner also did some teaching during this period to help the family finances during this school year. She was a constant source of help and encouragement to me.

I should mention how we met. I saw her for the first time at the Cardston High School where we had gone to register. She was at the far end of the room talking to a couple of girls, and I was talking to a couple of boys. I said, "Who is that beautiful black-eyed girl down there?" One said, "Why, that's Sally Merrill." Then I said, "You know, some day I am going to marry that girl!"

We didn't actually meet until two years later because that very day I got a phone call from my father telling me my brother was registering in another school in Raymond, and he felt my brother needed my company. So I left immediately and registered in the other school.

Two years later I went to teach at Hill Spring, where I met Sara Isabelle (Sally) Merrill, and we taught in the same school. Right away I knew she was the girl I wanted to be my wife and the mother of my children. I think that is most important—that boys and girls select the kind of mates they want as the parents of their children. She has been all one could hope for as a wife and mother, and I am very grateful for her love and companionship, and the help she has been to me through the years.

As the children came and our family increased I decided I couldn't make a living at teaching. Salaries were not good then, and times were not good either; in fact, one year when I taught school I had to take notes from the school board for my salary. For a whole year I collected less than $300.

When I found that I couldn't make a living at teaching, I decided to buy a store—a general store in the little town of Hill Spring. Well, I didn't have any money, so how could I buy a store? I made a down payment on a lovely Ford car; then I took the car to the man who owned the store and said, "I would like to put this car as a down payment on the store." He accepted it. Then I went to a wholesaler, because now I had a store, and said, "I would like to have credit here for $500." And he gave me the credit. I went to another wholesaler who dealt in dry goods and hardware and he said, "Yes, I'll give you $500 credit."

This is the way we got into business. I did my own trucking and freighting. I couldn't give credit because I didn't have any money to carry on if I did; I had to take cash for everything that I sold.

We later moved to Cardston where I was principal of the school, bishop of the ward, on the town council, and Scoutmaster—all at the same time.

Some of my most interesting and helpful experiences occurred while I was in the Alberta government. Three candidates were chosen in each constituency by members of the local party, and then a central committee representing the party interviewed those three people and chose the one they thought would be the best representative for the government. I was elected to serve in the legislature—and was doubly surprised to be named speaker, because I had never sat in the legislature before. It was a distinct honor and a fine experience.

Then late one night a year later the Premier of the Province called me and said, "How would you like to come into the Executive Council [the Cabinet] in the government?"

I said, "Well, I've never thought of it, Mr. Aberhart. I am happy where I am, and you've got a good Cabinet."

He talked for a little while and then said, "We need another man in the Cabinet. How would you like to come in?" I told him I had no ambition to be a Cabinet minister, but that I would do whatever he wished me to do. He replied that he would get in touch with me.

Two days later I received a wire that said "Kindly report to Edmonton as expeditiously as possible to take over the Department of Lands and Mines." Well, I had never been a miner; I didn't have an education or any experience in that field. At a dinner given for me by the oilmen of the Province, I said, "I don't know anything about this department. I have had no training, no experience; there is only one thing I do know for sure, and that is that I would like to serve my country the best I know how. I am going to set out first thing to see that we have no waste of our natural resources." That was all I could tell them.

My philosophy has been: Don't be afraid to accept responsibilities if others think you have the ability to do a job and have confidence in you. When you set to work, dedicate yourself to the thing at hand. All you can do are the things you are expected to do, putting first things first, and realizing that anything that is worth doing is worth doing well.

I have had many wonderful experiences, and I am grateful to the Lord and to those who taught me gospel principles and had great faith in me. I have had opportunity to meet many great people, to travel widely for the government and the Church and to speak to many groups. May I mention just one experience I had while I was in the government.

I was called down to Dallas, Texas, to speak to a group of oilmen. As I was to be introduced by the governor of Texas, he had his secretary write to my secretary for some information so he could introduce me to those people properly. At the meeting he got up to introduce me and said that I had five children, that I was in the government, that I had been a bishop in the Mormon Church, and so on. Then as he finished he said, "You know, a government is fortunate to have in it a man like Mr. Tanner."

I looked over at him and thought, "Now what does the governor of Texas want from me?" I couldn't think of anything that he might want, and so I wondered why he said the government was so fortunate to have a man like me. But anyway, I got up and spoke.

After I sat down, he said, "When I introduced Mr. Tanner, I told you that a government is fortunate to have a man like Mr. Tanner serving in it. Now I'll tell you why I said that. As I introduced him, I told you that he had been a bishop in the Mormon Church. I would like to tell you men that anybody who is worthy to be a bishop in that church needs no other introduction, as far as I am concerned."

I thought at that time that it would be a wonderful thing if any bishop, any stake president, anybody who holds an office in the Church could go and say to a man, "I am a member of the Mormon Church and am in good standing, living the principles of the gospel," and have that man and the world be able to say, "You need no other introduction as far as I am concerned."

Now, we can do that. Just as soon as every young man will honor his priesthood, stand by his standards, do that which is at hand and do it the way it should be done, seeking first the kingdom of God, knowing that all these other things for his good will be added unto him, and as soon as every young woman will honor womanhood and live a virtuous, clean, exemplary life, that is all the introduction we will need anywhere in the world.

People expect Mormons, more than anyone else in the world, to live up to their standards. The world has their eyes on this church. We are marked not by the world, but by the Lord. We are given great responsibility. It's a great privilege, and how important it is that we stand up, remember who we are, and act accordingly at all times! May we all live worthy of membership in the church and take our responsibilities seriously. I am grateful for my heritage, for "having been born of goodly parents," for the gospel of Jesus Christ and for my knowledge and testimony that it is divinely inspired today!

II

Seek to Know, Love, and Serve the
Master

CHAPTER 3

The Divinity of Jesus Christ

Because of the great doubt that exists throughout the world and that has been expressed in many places, even by influential men, including ministers of the gospel, regarding the real existence of God the Eternal Father and his Son Jesus Christ, some of our youth are experiencing doubt and are asking such questions as: "Was Jesus Christ actually the Son of God?" "Was he crucified and literally resurrected?" "Is the gospel more than just a moral code of ethics?"

Before dealing with these questions, I should like to emphasize this one fact: that those who are questioning the existence and power of God and his Son Jesus Christ and the purpose of Christ's mission here upon the earth readily accept the fact that man with his finite mind can put inanimate objects and even men into space and keep in touch with them, receive messages from and send messages to them, and control them, and that man has directed their courses even to the point of landing on the moon. Yet they doubt that God the Creator of all can speak to man, and that man's prayers can be and truly are answered regularly.

The scriptures have much to say about the coming of Jesus Christ, his mission, his crucifixion and resurrection, the message of peace and love, and the plan of life and salvation that he brought. All of the scriptures that we have are not accepted by all of the people in the world today. The Old Testament is accepted by the Jewish people as the word of God. The Old Testament and the New Testament are accepted by the Catholics and the Protestants as the word of God. We as members of The Church of Jesus Christ of Latter-day Saints, commonly called Mormons, accept both the Old and New Testaments as well as the Book of Mormon as the word of God, and also the Doctrine and Covenants and the Pearl of Great Price. These are known as the standard works of our church.

There is no conflict between the teachings of the Old and New Testaments or between the Bible and the Book of Mormon, the Doctrine and Covenants, and the Pearl of Great Price, all of which contain the gospel as given by God through his prophets from Adam down to Joseph Smith and by Jesus Christ himself as he visited the Old and the New Worlds.

One of the greatest evidences that he is the Son of God and that he was chosen by God as the Savior of the world is the fact that his coming was foretold centuries before his birth and mission here upon the earth. It was seen in vision and foretold by Adam, Enoch, Moses, Job, David, Zechariah, Isaiah, Micah, Lehi, Nephi, Jacob, King Benjamin, Alma, Abinadi, Samuel, and many others, including Mary, the mother of Jesus.

Moses tells us that after Adam and Eve had been turned out of the Garden of Eden into the lone and dreary world, they called upon the name of the Lord and offered sacrifice unto the Lord:

And after many days an angel of the Lord appeared unto Adam, saying: Why dost thou offer sacrifices unto the Lord? And Adam said unto him: I know not, save the Lord commanded me.

And then the angel spake, saying: This thing is a similitude of the sacrifice of the Only Begotten of the Father, which is full of grace and truth.

Wherefore, thou shalt do all that thou doest in the name of the Son, and thou shalt repent and call upon God in the name of the Son forevermore.

And in that day the Holy Ghost fell upon Adam, which beareth record of the Father and the Son, saying: I am the Only Begotten of the Father from the beginning, henceforth and forever, that as thou hast fallen thou mayest be redeemed, and all mankind, even as many as will. . . .

And thus the Gospel began to be preached, from the beginning. . . . (Moses 5:6-9, 58.)

Ever since that time this information has been handed down from father to son, and therefore the human family, whether pagans or Christians, have continued to look toward some kind of God and rely upon a Savior to redeem them from the evils of mortality. Because of apostasies and false teachings, men have had distorted views and beliefs regarding Jesus the Christ. However, because of God's interest in the immortality and eternal life of man, he has seen fit to inform his people through his chosen prophets in the different dispensations that Jesus is the Christ and that their salvation can come only in and through him.

Enoch saw the day of the coming of the Son of Man, even in the flesh, and he beheld the Son of Man lifted up on the cross, after the manner of men, and then Enoch beheld the Son of Man ascend up unto the Father. (See Moses 7:47-59.)

Several hundred years before Christ was born, Isaiah made this prophecy: "For unto us a son is born, unto us a son is given: and the government shall be upon his shoulder: and his name shall be called Wonderful, Counseller, The mighty God, The everlasting Father, The Prince of Peace." (Isaiah 9:6.)

He also predicted that Christ would be born of a virgin, that he would be despised and rejected of men, and that he would go like a lamb to the slaughter and make intercession for the transgressors, and said, "Surely he hath borne our griefs, and carried our sorrows: yet we did esteem him stricken, smitten of God, and afflicted." (See Isaiah 53:1-12.)

In the Book of Mormon we find that from six hundred years before Christ until the time of his coming, many American prophets from Lehi to the Lamanite prophet Samuel had foretold that he would be born of a virgin, that he was the Only Begotten Son of God in the flesh, that he would heal the sick and bless the poor, that he would minister among the people in power and glory, but that he would be judged and crucified by man; and they predicted that whosoever shall believe in the Son of God, the same shall have everlasting life. "And if ye believe on his name ye will repent of all your sins, that thereby ye may have a remission of them through his merits." (Helaman 14:13.)

And we all know, as recorded in Luke, that the angel said unto Mary:

... thou shalt . . . bring forth a son, and shalt call his name JESUS.

He shall be great, and shall be called the Son of the Highest: and the Lord God shall give unto him the throne of his father David:

And he shall reign over the house of Jacob for ever; and of his kingdom there shall be no end. (Luke 1:31-33.)

Many young people wonder how it was that the shepherds and the wise men were looking for and recognized the sign that would tell of the birth of the Savior. They expected a new star. This was because ancient prophets had foretold the signs that would appear. Those who had read of the prophecies were prepared for these signs when they came, and what a thrilling thing it is to know, as recorded in the Gospel of Matthew, that the wise men from the East followed the star to the place of his birth, and as they came to Jerusalem they asked: ". . . Where is he that is born King of the Jews? for we have seen his star in the east, and are come to worship him." (Matthew 2:2.) They were instructed to go to Bethlehem, where he would be born, as prophesied by Micah the prophet. When they arrived at

Bethlehem, they saw the young child with Mary, his mother, and fell down and worshiped him.

All the scriptures to which I have referred are testimonies of those who were told by angels or by God himself, many years before the birth of Christ, that he is the Son of God; that he would come and dwell among men; that he would be crucified and resurrected; and that all of this was done that all mankind may be saved.

We also have the testimonies of many of those who walked and talked with him while he was here on the earth among men, who testify that he is the Son of God. In fact, the New Testament gives its readers a beautiful and enlightening story of Jesus while in mortality and of his message of love and salvation and of his crucifixion and resurrection.

We have Peter's testimony as recorded in Matthew, when Christ, speaking to his disciples,

saith unto them, But whom say ye that I am?

And Simon Peter answered and said, Thou art the Christ, the Son of the living God.

And Jesus answered and said unto him, Blessed art thou, Simon Barjona: for flesh and blood hath not revealed it unto thee, but my Father which is in heaven. (Matthew 16:15-17.)

Then imagine Paul, who without fear, but with conviction, pleaded for himself as he stood in chains for trial before Agrippa, saying that he had persecuted the Christians, and when they were put to death he gave his voice against them. He then recited the vision which he received while he was on his way to Damascus to persecute the Saints, saying:

At midday, O king, I saw in the way a light from heaven, above the brightness of the sun, shining round about me and them which journeyed with me.

And when we were all fallen to the earth, I heard a voice speaking unto me, and saying in the Hebrew tongue, Saul, Saul, why persecutest thou me? it is hard for thee to kick against the pricks.

And I said, Who art thou, Lord? And he said, I am Jesus whom thou persecutest. (Acts 26:13-15.)

Paul then bore testimony that he was directed to tell the people that Christ had appeared to him, that they were to repent and turn to God and do the works meet for repentance. Then he said: "For these causes the Jews caught me in the temple, and went about to kill me." (Acts 26:21.)

As he proceeded to plead for himself he said:

King Agrippa, believest thou the prophets? I know that thou believest.

Then Agrippa said unto Paul, Almost thou persuadest me to be a Christian.

And Paul said, I would to God, that not only thou, but also all that hear me this day, were both almost, and altogether such as I am, except these bonds. (Acts 26:27-29.)

Paul, when released, continued to bear testimony to the Romans, the Corinthians, the Ephesians, and many others that Jesus is the Christ, the Savior of the world, and that he did appear to and instruct him.

So we have these irrefutable testimonies concerning the divine mission of Jesus Christ by men whom God raised up for this very purpose. They testified not only of his birth, death, and resurrection, but also of his ministry among the children of men. They told about the things he would teach that would make it possible for mankind to be saved and exalted in the kingdom of God.

Now let me refer to Christ's own beautiful Sermon on the Mount, in which he admonished mankind: "But seek ye first the kingdom of God, and his righteousness; and all these things shall be added unto you." (Matthew 6:33.)

Then he went on to say: "Not every one that saith unto me, Lord, Lord, shall enter into the kingdom of heaven; but he that doeth the will of my Father which is in heaven." (Matthew 7:21.)

Another touching evidence of Christ's love for mankind, even as he suffered on the cross, is found in these words: "Father, forgive them; for they know not what they do." (Luke 23:34.)

And when one of the thieves said to Jesus, "Lord, remember me when thou comest into thy kingdom," Jesus replied, "Verily I say unto thee, To day shalt thou be with me in paradise." (Luke 23:42-43.)

Finally, he said: "Father, into thy hands I commend my spirit: and having said thus, he gave up the ghost." (Luke 23:46.)

On the early morning of the Sabbath following his crucifixion the devoted Mary Magdalene and the other Mary came to the tomb, and the angel who had rolled away the stone said unto the women:

> . . . Fear not ye: for I know that ye seek Jesus, which was crucified.
> He is not here: for he is risen, as he said. Come, see the place where the Lord lay.
> And go quickly, and tell his disciples that he is risen from the dead. . . . (Matthew 28:5-7.)

Following his resurrection, the disciples were discussing the events that had transpired and the fact that the Lord had risen indeed.

> And as they thus spake, Jesus himself stood in the midst of them, and saith unto them, Peace be unto you.
> But they were terrified and affrighted, and supposed that they had seen a spirit.
> And he said unto them, Why are ye troubled? and why do thoughts arise in your hearts?
> Behold my hands and my feet, that it is I myself: handle me, and see; for a spirit hath not flesh and bones, as ye see me have.
> And when he had thus spoken, he shewed them his hands and his feet. (Luke 24:36-40.)

Thomas, who was not present, did not believe that Jesus had come to them, but after eight days Jesus appeared again to the disciples, and Thomas was with them.

Then saith he to Thomas, Reach hither thy finger, and behold my hands; and reach hither thy hand, and thrust it into my
side: and be not faithless, but believing.

And Thomas answered and said unto him, My Lord and my
God.

Jesus saith unto him, Thomas, because thou hast seen me, thou
hast believed: blessed are they that have not seen, and yet have
believed.

And many other signs truly did Jesus in the presence of his
disciples, which are not written in this book:

But these are written, that ye might believe that Jesus is the
Christ, the Son of God; and that believing ye might have life
through his name. (John 20:27-31.)

When Jesus had spoken to his apostles, and while
they beheld, he was taken up and a cloud received him
out of their sight.

And while they looked stedfastly toward heaven as he went
up, behold, two men stood by them in white apparel;

Which also said, Ye men of Galilee, why stand ye gazing up
into heaven? this same Jesus, which is taken up from you into
heaven, shall so come in like manner as ye have seen him go into
heaven. (See Acts 1:9-11.)

In the Book of Mormon also we have the testimony
that Christ appeared to the multitude on the American
continent following his crucifixion, and the multitude heard
a voice which said unto them:

Behold my Beloved Son, in whom I am well pleased, in whom
I have glorified my name—hear ye him.

. . . and behold, they saw a Man descending out of heaven;
and he was clothed in a white robe; and he came down and stood
in the midst of them; . . .

And it came to pass that he stretched forth his hand and spake
unto the people, saying:

Behold, I am Jesus Christ, whom the prophets testified shall
come into the world. (3 Nephi 11:7-10.)

And he invited them to come forth and thrust their
hands into his side and to feel the prints of the nails in his
hands and feet. (See 3 Nephi 11:14-15.)

All of these testimonies to which I have referred were made by men of integrity who had no reason to lie or deceive or mislead in any way, but who in spite of all threats and danger continued to testify that they had seen Jesus Christ before, at the time of, or following his crucifixion and resurrection. These testimonies then are of the resurrected Lord—not Jesus, the Teacher, nor Jesus of Nazareth, but Jesus the Lord, the Redeemer of mankind.

Why do men doubt the truthfulness of these irrefutable testimonies and deprive themselves and their families of the guidance of the Spirit of the Lord? I urge those who have any doubt to do as Moroni admonishes us to do, that is, ". . . ask God, the Eternal Father, in the name of Christ, if these things are not true; and if ye shall ask with a sincere heart, with real intent, having faith in Christ, he will manifest the truth of it unto you, by the power of the Holy Ghost." (Moroni 10:4.)

One of the most outstanding testimonies of all time regarding the divinity of Jesus is that borne by that young boy Joseph Smith just over a century ago, when he, only fourteen years of age, went into the grove alone to ask God in all humility which church he should join. From his own written record we read the experience of this young man:

I kneeled down and began to offer up the desire of my heart to God. . . .

. . . I saw a pillar of light exactly over my head, above the brightness of the sun, . . .

. . . When the light rested upon me I saw two Personages, whose brightness and glory defy all description, standing above me in the air. One of them spake unto me, calling me by name and said, pointing to the other—*This is My Beloved Son. Hear Him!*

. . . I asked the Personages who stood above me in the light, which of all the sects was right—and which I should join.

I was answered that I must join none of them, for they were all wrong. (Joseph Smith 2:15-19.)

As he left that grove he knew as he knew he lived that God and Jesus Christ live and that in answer to his

prayer they had appeared and spoken to him. As he told
ministers and others of his experience and the vision that
he had seen, though he was an obscure boy of only fourteen years of age, he was persecuted by the great ones
of the most popular sects of the day, and ridiculed and
tormented. In spite of all this persecution he continued to
bear testimony that he had seen a vision; that God knew
he had seen it and that he could not deny it.

Another vision to which I should like to refer is that
given to Joseph Smith the Prophet and Sidney Rigdon
over a year after the Church was organized, which bears
further witness that Jesus is the Christ:

> Hear, O ye heavens, and give ear, O earth, and rejoice ye in-
> habitants thereof, for the Lord is God, and beside him there is no
> Savior.
> By the power of the Spirit our eyes were opened and our un-
> derstandings were enlightened, so as to see and understand the
> things of God—
> And now, after the many testimonies which have been given
> of him, this is the testimony, last of all, which we give of him:
> That he lives!
> For we saw him, even on the right hand of God; and we
> heard the voice bearing record that he is the Only Begotten of
> the Father—
> That by him, and through him, and of him, the worlds are
> and were created, and the inhabitants thereof are begotten sons
> and daughters unto God. (D&C 76:1, 12, 22-24.)

And to our young people today I should like to bear
my own personal testimony that by the power of the Holy
Ghost I know as I know I live that God lives; that Jesus
is the Christ, the Redeemer of the world; that he came
and dwelt among men; that he willingly gave his life for
you and me; that he was literally resurrected; that he and
God the Eternal Father did actually appear to Joseph
Smith in answer to his prayer; that Joseph Smith and all
who have succeeded him as President of the Church are
indeed prophets of God.

If people throughout the world would accept Jesus

Christ as the Son of God and keep his commandments, there would be no more war, but peace and good will would reign in the world, and we would be assured of immortality and eternal life.

It is our responsibility as members of The Church of Jesus Christ of Latter-day Saints who have this testimony to bear it to the world and to keep the commandments of God so that we might all enjoy eternal life, which is God's greatest gift to man.

CHAPTER 4

"For Unto Us a Child Is Born"

"For God so loved the world, that he gave his only begotten Son, that whosoever believeth in him should not perish, but have everlasting life." (John 3:16.)

The birth of Jesus Christ was foretold by the angels to Adam, to Enoch, and to many other prophets. Isaiah foretold this great event in these words: "For unto us a child is born, unto us a son is given: and the government shall be upon his shoulder: and his name shall be called Wonderful, Counseller, The mighty God, The everlasting Father, The Prince of Peace." (Isaiah 9:6.)

Isaiah also saw in a vision that Christ would be born of a virgin; that he would be despised and rejected of men; and that he would bear the sins of many and make intercession for the transgressors.

Many of the early American prophets saw and foretold the coming of Christ. King Benjamin, just a hundred years before the coming of the Savior, saw an angel who said:

For behold, the time cometh, and is not far distant, that with power, the Lord Omnipotent who reigneth, who was, and is from all eternity to all eternity, shall come down from heaven among the children of men, and shall dwell in a tabernacle of clay, and shall go forth amongst men, working mighty miracles, such as healing the sick, raising the dead, causing the lame to walk, the blind to receive their sight, and the deaf to hear, and curing all manner of diseases. (Mosiah 3:5.)

And he shall be called Jesus Christ, the Son of God, the Father of heaven and earth, the Creator of all things from the beginning; and his mother shall be called Mary. (Mosiah 3:8.)

Prophets also foretold of the signs that would precede the birth of the Savior. An angel appeared to the Lamanite prophet Samuel and told him of the signs:

> . . . this will I give unto you for a sign at the time of his coming; for behold, there shall be great lights in heaven, insomuch that in the night before he cometh there shall be no darkness, insomuch that it shall appear unto man as if it was day.
>
> And behold, there shall a new star arise, such an one as ye never have beheld; and this also shall be a sign unto you.
>
> And it shall come to pass that whosoever shall believe on the Son of God, the same shall have everlasting life. (Helaman 14:3, 5, 8.)

It is because of the prophecies predicting his coming that the people were prepared to receive and understand the signs that would precede and accompany the birth of the Savior. In Faber's *History of Idolatry* (volume 2, page 92), we also read, in the words of Zoroaster, the Persian prophet:

> A virgin should conceive and bear a son, and a star would appear blazing at midday to signalize the occurrence. "When you behold the star," said he to his followers, "follow it whithersoever it leads you. Adore the mysterious child, offering him gifts with profound humility. He is indeed the Almighty Lord, which created the heavens. He is indeed your Lord and everlasting King."

What greater evidence could we have that Jesus is the Christ, the Son of the Living God, the Only Begotten in the flesh, than for God to give this information to the prophets which they could foretell even in the time of Adam, and all down through the history of mankind until an angel visited Mary and said unto her:

> Fear not, Mary: for thou hast found favour with God.

And, behold, thou shalt conceive in thy womb, and bring forth a son, and shalt call his name JESUS.

He shall be great, and shall be called the Son of the Highest: and the Lord God shall give unto him the throne of his father David. (Luke 1:30-32.)

Besides these predictions, we have the testimonies of Matthew, Mark, Luke, and John, who walked and talked with Jesus himself before and after his crucifixion; and of Paul, who received a direct testimony of Jesus Christ, who appeared unto him; and of others, testifying that Christ was the Son of God, the Savior of the world. And Peter, when asked, "But whom say ye that I am?" answered, "Thou art the Christ, the Son of the living God." (Matthew 16:15-16.)

How thrilling it is to realize that the wise men and the shepherds recognized the signs, and the wise men from the East visited Palestine at the time of the birth of Jesus. They followed the star to the place of his birth, and as they came to Jerusalem, they asked: "Where is he that is born King of the Jews? for we have seen his star in the east, and are come to worship him." (Matthew 2:2.)

They were instructed to go to Bethlehem where he would be born, as foretold by Micah, the prophet. When they arrived at Bethlehem they saw the young child with Mary, his mother, and fell down and worshiped him, and offered him gifts of gold, frankincense, and myrrh.

The account of the shepherds and the angels on the evening of the birth of Christ is so beautifully told by Luke in the following words:

And there were in the same country shepherds abiding in the field, keeping watch over their flock by night.

And, lo, the angel of the Lord came upon them, and the glory of the Lord shone round about them: and they were sore afraid.

And the angel said unto them, Fear not: for, behold, I bring you good tidings of great joy, which shall be to all people.

For unto you is born this day in the city of David a Saviour, which is Christ the Lord.

And this shall be a sign unto you; Ye shall find the babe wrapped in swaddling clothes, lying in a manger.

And suddenly there was with the angel a multitude of the heavenly host praising God, and saying,

Glory to God in the highest, and on earth peace, good will toward men.

And it came to pass, as the angels were gone away from them into heaven, the shepherds said one to another, Let us now go even unto Bethlehem, and see this thing which is come to pass, which the Lord hath made known unto us.

And they came with haste, and found Mary, and Joseph, and the babe lying in a manger. (Luke 2:8-16.)

The real meaning and spirit of Christmas is to commemorate the birth of Christ and to remind ourselves of the great message of joy and peace on earth, goodwill toward men, which Jesus brought to the world, and the great blessing he brought to all mankind. It is a time when families get together and enjoy one another's companionship and a happy family reunion. Love is demonstrated at Christmas more than at any other time of the year. We forget our differences with one another and endeavor to follow the example of Christ and his teachings, and in so doing we find real joy and happiness and can truly have a merry Christmas.

Christmas is a time for rejoicing and thanksgiving, a time of loving and giving, a time when we all stop and ponder in wondering awe that "God so loved the world, that he gave his only begotten Son, that whosoever believeth in him should not perish, but have everlasting life."

Because of his sacrifice, the greatest of all gifts to all mankind, we try at Christmas time to show our love for the Lord and for our fellowmen. In giving and sacrifice we find the greatest joy. As we accept and practice this spirit of loving and giving, a feeling of peace is brought to our souls, to our families, to our communities, and to the world.

Yes, if we all would determine this day to accept Jesus Christ as the Son of God and the Savior of the world, and to love one another as he has loved us, we would all enjoy peace on earth and goodwill toward all men.

This is the true meaning and spirit of Christmas. May we all strive to catch it and carry it with us throughout our lives, overcoming our selfishness and loving God and Jesus Christ and our neighbors as ourselves.

III

Seek to Love One Another

CHAPTER 5

The Second Great Commandment: Love One Another

As I contemplate conditions in the world that are causing so much unrest and unhappiness, I ask: What is our greatest need in order to meet these conditions and bring about a change so that we might enjoy peace and happiness?

My answer seems to center on these two messages, taken from the teachings of the Lord Jesus Christ: "Seek ye first the kingdom of God, and his righteousness; and all these things shall be added unto you," and "Love one another."

In these two statements can be found the key to the solution to all those problems which are causing such misery and trouble for individuals, communities, nations, and the world. By accepting and living according to these two doctrines, we could have joy unspeakable here and eternal happiness hereafter. These are the blessings for which we should all be seeking.

When the lawyer asked Jesus, "Master, which is the great commandment in the law?" Jesus answered:

Thou shalt love the Lord thy God with all thy heart, and with all thy soul, and with all thy mind.

This is the first and great commandment.

And the second is like unto it, Thou shalt love thy neighbour as thyself.

On these two commandments hang all the law and the prophets. (Matthew 22:36-40.)

From this statement it is evident that *love* is the greatest thing in the world. Then referring back to the early scriptures, I found, as recorded in Leviticus 19:16-18, this commandment given by the Lord in speaking to Moses:

Thou shalt not go up and down as a talebearer among thy people. . . .

Thou shalt not hate thy brother in thine heart. . . .

Thou shalt not avenge, nor bear any grudge against the children of thy people, but thou shalt love thy neighbour as thyself. . . .

In Deuteronomy we read:

And thou shalt love the Lord thy God with all thine heart, and with all thy soul, and with all thy might.

And these words, which I command thee this day, shall be in thine heart:

And thou shalt teach them diligently unto thy children, and shalt talk of them when thou sittest in thine house, and when thou walkest by the way, and when thou liest down, and when thou risest up. (Deuteronomy 6:5-7.)

When Christ came to the earth the law of Moses was in effect, an example of which was "an eye for an eye, and a tooth for a tooth." But the Savior said:

A new commandment I give unto you, That ye love one another; as I have loved you, that ye also love one another.

By this shall all men know that ye are my disciples, if ye have love one to another. (John 13:34-35.)

The Lord also gave us what is often referred to as the Golden Rule. It is found in Matthew 7:12: "Therefore all things whatsoever ye would that men should do to you, do ye even so to them: for this is the law and the prophets."

If we are to have this love of which the Savior spoke, and which he emphasizes as being the most important thing in life, it must begin in the home and then carry into our daily lives. A happy marriage is never handed to a couple on a silver platter, but it is something we have to build continually. If each will think of the other's convenience, comfort, needs, and happiness, and determine to see the best in each other, try to understand and express love for each other, there will be true love and harmony in the home.

Yes, the only slogan we need in order to be happy in our home is: Love Each Other—three simple words. Apply the ingredients of love. Sacrifice for each other. Make each other happy. If this were always uppermost in our minds, we would have very little trouble indeed. If there is love between the father and the mother, there will be love between the parents and the children and among the children. One cannot overemphasize the importance and value of being courteous, kind, considerate, and polite in the home.

Have you ever seen anything sweeter than the family that loves one another? Where there is true and perfect love in a family, such commandments as "honour thy father and thy mother," "thou shalt not steal," "thou shalt not bear false witness," are quite unnecessary. Love is really the fulfilling of the law.

As we look back over our life, whether it be short or long, we realize that the things that give the greatest joy are in doing something for someone else because we love him. Let us express our love to God and to our fellowmen now, while we can, by our every act and word, for "we shall not pass again this way."

The most difficult thing for us seems to be to give of ourselves, to do away with selfishness. If we really love someone, nothing is a hardship. Nothing is hard for us to do for that individual. There is no real happiness in having or getting, but only in giving. Half the world seems to be following the wrong scent in the pursuit of happiness. They think it consists of having and getting, and in having others serve them, but really it consists of giving and serving others.

I had an experience early one morning that really touched my heart, and was an evidence of great love. A woman called me to say that she had just received word that her grown son had been killed in an auto accident in the East, where he lived. She said that her husband, the father of this boy, was in another city carrying on some very important and serious business negotiations, and that she did not want to disturb him while he was thus involved. In our conversation I agreed to call someone who was with the father so that he might be informed as soon as the negotiations were concluded. To me her action was an outstanding example of love and unselfishness and interest in her husband's welfare to the extent that she was prepared to suffer alone.

We cannot apply or fulfill all at once the Golden Rule that the Savior gave to us, but by seriously trying, we will find greater joy, success, satisfaction, and friendship as we go through life, and enjoy the love of others and the Spirit of our Father in heaven. If we will always look for the best in others, in our friends, in our neighbors, in our wife, in our husband, in our children, to us they will be the most wonderful people in the world. On the other hand, if we are looking for their weaknesses and faults and enlarge upon them, these same people may seem even despicable.

When I was in the mission field interviewing missionaries I thought it was a very important thing for them to have love in their hearts if they were going to preach the gospel and be representatives, ambassadors, of the Lord Jesus Christ, and I asked those missionaries every time if they loved the Lord, and they said yes. And I said, "How does he know?" And they said, "Well, we have told him."

The Lord said, "If you love me, you will keep my commandments." (See John 14:15.) That's the way he knows. Then I asked those boys, "How many of you love your mothers?" There wasn't an exception. I said, "How many times have you told your mother you love her?" And on many occasions the answer was, "I don't know when I told her or how many times I have told her," or, "I don't think I ever told my mother I love her."

Imagine any young man, an elder, out representing this church, having never told his mother that he loved her. Do you know why he hasn't? Because his father didn't tell his wife that he loved her.

I felt like writing to the fathers of those boys every time, but each time I had that boy promise me that he would sit down and write a letter and say, "Mother, I love you," and tell her why he loved her. It is so important, brethren. Don't let another day go by without telling your wife you love her, how fortunate you are to have her, how much you think of her. And do what you can to make her believe it. Be the same with your children. "There is beauty all around when there's love at home." Be courteous. Be considerate. Be kind. I don't know of anything that is more important, and I think I am agreeing with the Lord when he says the same thing, "And the second is like unto it, Thou shalt love thy neighbor as thy self," and surely the most important neighbor is the one who lives with you in your home.

Sometimes as I move among people I am almost convinced that it is human nature to magnify the weaknesses in others in order to minimize our own. We sing these words in one of our hymns:

> Nay, speak no ill; a kindly word
> Can never leave a sting behind;
> And, oh, to breathe each tale we've heard
> Is far beneath a noble mind.
> Full oft a better seed is sown
> By choosing thus the kinder plan,
> For, if but little good is known,
> Still let us speak the best we can.
>
> Then speak no ill but lenient be
> To other's failings as your own.

If you're the first a fault to see,
Be not the first to make it known,
For life is but a passing day;
No lip may tell how brief its span;
Then, O the little time we stay
Let's speak of all the best we can.

—*Hymns,* no. 116

Let us always remember that men of great character need not belittle others or magnify their weaknesses. In fact, the thing that makes them great is the showing of love for and interest in their neighbors' success and welfare.

As we try to apply the Golden Rule we must realize that love will not permit us to hold grudges or ill feelings. These canker the soul and crowd out love. We hurt ourselves by holding grudges and ill feelings. We hurt and sometimes destroy the person about whom we are bearing tales. We would not think of stealing from or injuring physically one of our associates, friends, or neighbors, but we do even worse by stealing his good name. It is not uncommon to see people—clerks in stores, secretaries in corporations, individuals in clubs and in affairs of church and state—talking about and criticizing one another, trying to enlarge on their weaknesses with the idea of belittling them in the hope that their own weaknesses might be minimized or overlooked. If we really loved one another as the Lord loves us, there would be none of this friction, but confidence and happiness would reign.

I should like to join with each and every one of you in taking stock of ourselves to see if we are actually really striving to apply the principle of love toward those with whom we are associated. Are we patient, kind, generous, humble, courteous, unselfish, showing no temper, guileless, and sincere? Do we try to put ourselves in the other person's place, whether he be a merchant, a clerk, secretary, a caretaker, one of another religion or race, or a man in prison, and then act toward him as we would like to be treated were we in his place?

Let us never forget that the Lord gave us this commandment to love God and to love one another and apply the Golden Rule. We cannot love God without loving our neighbor, and we cannot truly love our neighbor without loving God. This applies to you and to me, and if each of us applies it to himself, we need not worry about the other.

Some time ago a friend of mine related an experience that I should like to pass on to you. He said:

My father's cousin and my father lived in the same community and were competing in the construction business. There grew up over the years a very keen and bitter rivalry between them. This was triggered in the beginning in the bidding of construction contracts, and later in our city political affairs where they opposed each other in very spirited elections.

Our immediate families inherited this situation upon the death of my father, for we boys seemed to take over where Dad left off. It was quite a strain on the members of his family and ours even to be civil to one another, even in our Church callings where he served as bishop of one ward and I in another, and later in the high council where we were both members. When we came together it seemed that Satan took over, and I am sure he did, for haven't we been told that where contention is, the Spirit of the Lord is not?

This situation continued to fester. Suddenly I found myself with a call to put aside all worldly things and go to preside over a mission. This was a thrilling experience to contemplate, and yet I subconsciously had a most uneasy feeling about it. I kept asking myself: "Are you really worthy to accept such an important call?" I was living the Word of Wisdom, I was a full tithe payer, I was faithful in all my Church activities, I was morally clean, and yet this uneasy feeling persisted.

I set about immediately to get my business and personal affairs in a condition where others could handle them while we were gone. While returning home from my office one afternoon, it really happened. I didn't hear a voice, but just as clearly as if a voice spoke to me something said: "You must go to your father's cousin and get things straightened out. You cannot go on this mission and teach the gospel of love when this terrible feeling exists between you."

I drove to his home, and with great fear and trepidation went up and rang the doorbell. There was no answer. After waiting a few minutes I went back to my car and said silently, "Lord, I made the attempt. I am sure this will be acceptable." But it wasn't. This uneasy feeling still persisted. I prayed earnestly about it.

The next day as I sat in a funeral service, my cousin came in and sat across the aisle from me. The Spirit moved me to ask him if I could see him at his home after the service. He agreed. This time I went with calmness and tranquillity in my soul because I had asked the Lord to prepare the way for me.

When I rang the doorbell he invited me into the living room and congratulated me on my mission call. We talked a few minutes about things in general, and then it happened. I looked at him with a feeling of love, which replaced all the old bitterness, and said: "I have come to ask foregiveness for anything I have ever said or done that has tended to divide us and our families."

At this point tears came into our eyes, and for a few minutes neither of us could say a word. This was one time when silence was more powerful than words. In a few minutes he said: "I wish I had come to you first." I replied: "The important thing is that it is done, not who initiated it."

At this moment we had a rich spiritual experience, which caused us to purge our lives and our souls of those things which had separated us, which has resulted in our having proper family relationships.

Now I could go on my mission and teach the true meaning of love, because for the first time in my life I had experienced its deepest dimension, and now I could honestly say that there wasn't a person in the world that I didn't love and appreciate. Since that day my life has never been the same, for it was then that I learned in a most positive way as I had never understood before the injunction of the Master to his disciples when he said: "A new commandment I give unto you, That ye love one another." (John 13:34.)

This same dimension of love is so beautifully portrayed by Leigh Hunt in the story of Abou Ben Adhem:

Abou Ben Adhem (may his tribe increase!)
Awoke one night from a deep dream of peace,
And saw within the moonlight in his room,
Making it rich and like a lily in bloom,
An angel writing in a book of gold;
Exceeding peace had made Ben Adhem bold,

And to the Presence in the room he said,
"What writest thou?" The vision raised its head,
And with a look made of all sweet accord,
Answered, "The names of those who love the Lord."
"And is mine one?" said Abou. "Nay, not so,"
Replied the angel. Abou spoke more low,
But cheerily still, and said, "I pray thee, then,
Write me as one that loves his fellowmen."
The angel wrote, and vanished. The next night
It came again with a great wakening light,
And showed the names whom love of God had blessed;
And, lo! Ben Adhem's name led all the rest!

Let us all strive to live worthy to have our names listed among those who love their fellowmen, and so prove our love for God.

Let us each covenant to seek God and live righteously by keeping his commandments and live in such a way that no one will ever be able to excuse himself because his parents, his adult neighbors, his teachers, or any with whom he might associate, through their actions had given him license or excuse to do anything to bring disastrous results, unhappiness, or failure. And let us so live to be a great influence for good and a light unto the world.

CHAPTER 6

Search for the Wanderers

As I speak to groups of Saints throughout the world, I often think and wonder about those out there who are not with us, who are not a part of the group because they think they are not wanted, understood, or loved.

There are in every ward and branch persons of all ages who, though they would deny it, are hungry for attention, for fellowship, for an active life in the Church.

Let us all—as leaders and as disciples of Christ—always remember and never forget that everyone is looking for happiness. Everyone wants to be happy. It is our great privilege and responsibility to show them the way to happiness and success. Often some little thing—some slight or misunderstanding—causes one to become inactive. There are those who are discouraged and inactive because they have felt neglected or have been offended; or they are guilty of some transgression of their own and, as a result, feel that they are outcasts or that there is no place for them, that they are not worthy or wanted. They feel that they are lost and cannot be forgiven. We must let them know and make them know that we love them, and we must help them to understand that the Lord loves them and that he will forgive them if they will truly repent.

Sometimes our youth wander because of the way they are treated, the way they are neglected. An important lesson can be learned by all of us in the parable of the Lost Sheep:

> Then drew near unto him [Jesus] all the publicans and sinners for to hear him.
>
> And the Pharisees and scribes murmured, saying, This man receiveth sinners, and eateth with them.
>
> And he spake this parable unto them, saying,
>
> What man of you, having an hundred sheep, if he lose one of them, doth not leave the ninety and nine in the wilderness, and go after that which is lost, until he find it?
>
> And when he hath found it, he layeth it on his shoulders, rejoicing.
>
> And when he cometh home, he calleth together his friends and neighbours, saying unto them, Rejoice with me; for I have found my sheep which was lost.
>
> I say unto you, that likewise joy shall be in heaven over one sinner that repenteth, more than over ninety and nine just persons, which need no repentance. (Luke 15:1-7.)

Every bishop, every stake president, every leader of any Church organization knows someone who needs attention, and you and we have the responsibility of going to find that lost sheep. If we had knowledge that some young man was lost right at this moment, that someone was drowning, we wouldn't hesitate one minute to do all in our power to save that one individual, to save the one who was lost, the one who was drowning, the one who was in need of our help. These young persons and these older persons who have strayed from the Church because of inactivity or for any reason need our help and need our attention just as much. They need our prayers and our consideration, and nothing will bring us greater joy and happiness than to see one come back into activity.

By saving one, we might save a family. We might even save a generation. By losing one, we may lose not only the individual but also a family and that person's posterity. The responsibility is great. Some of us seem to be very happy if we have from 40 to 70 percent attendance in our meetings. If we have 40 percent attendance, we have 60 percent who are not in attendance. And if we have 70 percent in attendance, we still have 30 percent who are not attending, and those are the ones who need our attention, and they need it badly.

I was greatly impressed as I attended a stake conference and called on a bishop to speak. As he spoke, tears came to his eyes, and it was difficult for him to speak when he said, "I want to acknowledge here tonight at this meeting my home teacher. I was an inactive senior Aaronic Priesthood holder, and this home teacher worked with me. I didn't want to see him at first; in fact, I refused, but he continued until I would let him come into my home and teach me. And here I am now, his bishop. I want to express to him my deep appreciation." Thank the Lord for such worthy men, who will not fail to do everything in their power to save those who are wandering.

When I was a stake president, we had a very able young man who had been trained in agriculture, and we needed an agricultural adviser on our welfare committee. He wasn't active in the Church. I knew that he wasn't keeping the Word of Wisdom, but I called and asked him to go to lunch with me one day; and as we sat and talked, I told him what I wanted of him. I said, "You are the best prepared, most able young man to do this job. We need you, and you need activity."

We talked for some time, and he said, "Well, President Tanner, you know that I don't keep the Word of Wisdom."

I said, "Well, you can, can't you?"

And he said, "President, that is a different approach. My bishop came to me last month and asked me if I would take a job in the ward. I told him that I wasn't keeping the Word of Wisdom. And he said, 'Well, then, we will get somebody else.' "

So I talked with him for a little while longer, and I said, "Listen, brother, you need activity in the Church, but we also need you—we really need *you*."

After we had talked a little while he said, "Do you mean that if I took a position like this I couldn't even have a cup of coffee?"

I said, "Yes, that is exactly what I mean. Any leader must be a leader, and you must be an example. If you are taken into a stake committee, we would expect you to live the gospel the way a man should live it."

He said, "Well, then, I shall have to think it over."

I said, "You think it over. But remember, you need activity, and we need you."

He said, "I will let you know."

He didn't call me the next day, nor the next day, nor the day after that. By the sixth day I thought, well, he doesn't want to admit that he can't keep the Word of Wisdom.

On the eighth day he called. He said, "President Tanner, do you still want me for that job?"

I said, "Yes, that is the reason I called you and talked to you about it the other day."

He said, "Then I will do it, and on your terms."

And he did it, and he did it on my terms. He was a single man, thirty-some years of age. He came into activity, and there was a young woman who was stake MIA president, a very fine young woman. He met her and became very well acquainted with her and fell in love with her and married her.

And then he became a bishop, and then a high councilor, and then a member of the stake presidency. You know, it has given me a great deal of satisfaction to know that that young man became active, and he now has children who are also active.

Regardless of where we are or who we are, we should realize that we have out there a boy or girl, a young man or woman, an older man or woman who is not active, and he or she wants to be active, if we can find a way to interest that person and let him know that he wants to be active.

I would like to challenge every leader in the Church to determine that he or she will begin actively to bring some young person or older person into activity. There is nothing more important in our whole lives than to save souls. We have programs and we have planning outlines for teachers, and we give them teacher development training and all those things to take care of those who are attending, but I fear too often we are forgetting and neglecting and ignoring those who are not always there, satisfied to say we had 50 percent or 60 percent in attendance.

I don't care at all for percentages or statistics, but I do care for the individual, that person who is outside. I appeal to every person in the Church, particularly those who hold office, to set about to do as the Lord has said: to find that lost sheep and bring him back into the fold, so that we will find joy with him when we meet our Heavenly Father.

And to our young people, there is no fun in being lost, and you can keep from being lost if you will keep the commandments of the Lord, listen to those who have been called by him to teach and lead you, and help others of your friends who may be having difficulty, that they may also be happy. This is the church and kingdom of God, and he has given us the responsibility of teaching and helping to save our fellowmen. May we do it in a way that will be acceptable to him, which will bring joy to us and help to prepare us for eternal life.

CHAPTER 7

"Judge Not, That Ye Be Not Judged"

The other day, as I overheard one neighbor criticizing another, I was reminded of these lines:

> Wouldn't this old world be better
> If the folks we meet would say:
> "I know something good about you,"
> And then treat us that way?

Then I thought of the words of one of our hymns:

> Let each man learn to know himself;
> To gain that knowledge let him labor,
> Improve those failings in himself
> Which he condemns so in his neighbor.
> How lenient our own faults we view,
> And conscience's voice adeptly smother;
> Yet, oh, how harshly we review
> The selfsame failings in another! . . .
> So first improve yourself today
> And then improve your friends tomorrow.
>
> —*Hymns,* no. 91

It seems common practice for people to talk about their friends and neighbors and to criticize their seeming peculiarities and weaknesses. In fact, it is so general that one would think that gossiping about and judging others was the thing to do. How often have we heard of young men who were criticized, judged, and ridiculed because of their peculiarities and yet who eventually became leaders in their different fields of endeavor.

Let me give you one or two examples of unjust criticism and judging without the facts.

There is a little story about Emma Ray McKay, the wife of President David O. McKay, when she began teaching school. As the principal introduced her to the class he pointed to a certain boy and said he was a troublemaker. She sensed the boy's embarrassment and feared he would live up to his reputation, so she wrote a note and slipped it to him as she passed his desk. It said, "Earl, I think the principal was mistaken about your being a bad boy. I trust you, and know that you are going to help me make this room the best in the school." Earl not only became a paragon of scholastic virtue but also one of the town's most important people.

Here is another example. One of our most respected community-minded citizens began to act as though his feelings had been hurt and to stay away from socials where, in the past, he had gone and taken a most active part. People started accusing him of being a sorehead, a poor sport, anti-social, etc., and even evaded him whenever possible. Later, a medical diagnosis showed he was suffering from a brain tumor which had been the cause of his lack of interest in activities that he had previously attended and even sponsored.

Let me give you another example or two of what I would call unrighteous judgment. First, a bishop who needs additional officers sees a member of his ward who, thought not active, seems to have ability, but he says to himself, "Oh, he wouldn't be interested. He wouldn't want to accept a position." So he does not approach him and the man remains inactive for years.

A new bishop is called to the ward, asks the man if he would be willing to accept a position, and finds that he is really ready and anxious to work.

Don't prejudge, but give the person an opportunity. Let him decide for himself to accept or decline.

On the other hand, we hear a man say to his family and to others, "I don't see why the bishop does this or that. You would think he would know better." Here he is judging the bishop without the facts, which, if known to him, would be full justification for the action taken. The man's judgment was not only unrighteous, but it had probably prejudiced his children and caused them to lose respect for the bishop and had weakened their faith.

These examples show how important it is that we do not judge, but encourage rather than denounce. Jesus Christ, some 2,000 years ago, realizing man's tendency to make unrighteous judgment, said:

Judge not, that ye be not judged.

For with what judgment ye judge, ye shall be judged: and with what measure ye mete, it shall be measured to you again.

And why beholdest thou the mote that is in thy brother's eye, but considerest not the beam that is in thine own eye?

Or how wilt thou say to thy brother, Let me pull out the mote out of thine eye; and, behold, a beam is in thine own eye?

Thou hypocrite, first cast out the beam out of thine own eye; and then shalt thou see clearly to cast out the mote out of thy brother's eye. (Matthew 7:1-5.)

It seems he is saying that unless we are without fault, we are not qualified to judge. By referring to Samuel's experience while choosing a king, we may get a better understanding of the fact that man is not qualified to judge. The Lord had rejected Saul as king of Israel and instructed the prophet Samuel to choose a new king. He told him to go to the house of Jesse, who had eight sons, and that while there the anointed one would pass before him and Samuel would know who was to be chosen. When the first son, Eliab, came before him, Samuel thought he was the chosen one, but the Lord refused him and then gave the prophet Samuel the key as to how to judge:

Look not on his countenance, or on the height of his stature;
because I have refused him: for the Lord seeth not as man seeth;
for man looketh on the outward appearance, but the Lord looketh
on the heart. (1 Samuel 16:7.)

Each of the seven sons then passed before Samuel and
was rejected. Then David, the youngest, was sent for and
was approved by the Lord.

The reason, therefore, that we cannot judge is obvious.
We cannot see what is in the heart. We do not know mo-
tives, although we impute motives to every action we see.
They may be pure while we think they are improper.

It is not possible to judge another fairly unless you
know his desires, his faith, and his goals. Because of a
different environment, unequal opportunity, and many
other things, people are not in the same position. One may
start at the top and the other at the bottom, and they may
meet as they are going in opposite directions. Someone
has said that it is not where you are but the direction in
which you are going that counts; not how close you are
to failure or success but which way you are headed. How
can we, with all our weaknesses and frailties, dare to
arrogate to ourselves the position of a judge? At best, man
can judge only what he sees; he cannot judge the heart or
the intention, or begin to judge the potential of his neighbor.

When we try to judge people, which we should not do,
we have a great tendency to look for and take pride in
finding weaknesses and faults, such as vanity, dishonesty,
immortality, and intrigue. As a result, we see only the
worst side of those being judged.

Our news media today also seem to be interested
mainly in controversial subjects or someone who is being
attacked; and regardless of the ninety-nine good things
one may do, it is the one weakness or error that alone is
emphasized and heralded to the world.

We are too prone to listen to, accept, and repeat such
adverse criticism, such maliciously spoken or printed

words, without stopping to realize the harm we may be doing to some noble person; and, as is done so often, we excuse and justify ourselves by saying, "Well, where there is so much smoke, there must be some fire," whereas in reality we are adding to the smoke, when the fire referred to may be only the fire of malice started by some envious person.

Sometimes even when our friends are accused of wrongdoing or gossip is started about them, we disloyally accept and repeat what we hear without knowing the facts. It is sad indeed that sometimes friendships are destroyed and enmity created on the basis of misinformation.

If there be one place in life where the attitude of the agnostic is acceptable, it is in this matter of judging. It is the courage to say, "I don't know. I am waiting for further evidence. I must hear both sides of the question."

Only by suspending judgment do we exhibit real charity. It is hard to understand why we are ready to condemn our neighbors and our friends on circumstantial evidence while we are all so determined to see that every criminal has a fair and open trial. Surely we can try to eliminate pride, passion, personal feeling, prejudice, and pettiness from our minds, and show charity to those around us.

Let us look for the good rather than try to discover any hidden evil. We can easily find fault in others if that is what we are looking for. Even in families, divorce has resulted and families have been broken up because the husband or wife was looking for and emphasized the faults rather than loving and extolling the virtues of the other.

Let us remember too that the further out of line or out of tune we ourselves are, the more we are inclined to look for error or weaknesses in others and to try to rationalize and justify our own faults rather than to try to improve ourselves. Almost invariably, we find that the greatest criticism of Church leaders and doctrine comes from those who are not doing their full duty, following the leaders, or living according to the teachings of the gospel.

An outstanding example of this can be found in the story of Cain and Abel. Cain neglected his own steward-ship and became so bitter over Abel's righteousness and favor in the eyes of the Lord that his insane jealousy caused him to murder his brother. How much better would his situation have been had he congratulated and honored his brother and set about to improve himself and correct his own failings.

Let us examine our own lives and actions, bring our-selves in tune with righteous principles, and never attack or spread misinformation about others.

Gossip is the worst form of judging. The tongue is the most dangerous, destructive, and deadly weapon avail-able to man. A vicious tongue can ruin the reputation and even the future of the one attacked. Insidious attacks against one's reputation, loathsome innuendoes, half-lies about an individual are as deadly as those insect parasites that kill the heart and life of a mighty oak. They are so stealthy and cowardly that one cannot guard against them. As someone has said, "It is easier to dodge an elephant than a microbe."

What a different world it would be if we would put into practice what we have heard so many times: ". . . whatsoever ye would that men should do to you, do ye even so to them: for this is the law and the prophets." (Matthew 7:12.) Instead, we are all so inclined to judge others by a standard different from the one by which we would wish or be willing to be judged.

When the woman accused of adultery was brought before Christ, he was indignant because of the accusers' injustice. They were wanting the woman to be judged on the basis of standards different from those by which they were willing to be judged and on a matter of which some were guilty.

He said: "He that is without sin among you, let him first cast a stone at her." Then, after stooping and writing in the sand, he looked up and said, ". . . where are those thine accusers?" (John 8:7, 10.)

If Jesus were to stand by and be asked to judge those whom we accuse and should say to us, "He that is without sin among you, let him first cast a stone at her," and then should stoop and write in the sand, how many of us would feel to steal away ashamed, convicted in our own conscience? How sound is his counsel!

If we could accept and practice the second great commandment, "Thou shalt love thy neighbour as thyself" (Matthew 22:39), and really learn to love our neighbors, there would be no vicious gossip or bearing false witness. In the Lord's prayer, we have these words: "And forgive us our debts, as we forgive our debtors," and then he says: "For if ye forgive men their trespasses, your heavenly Father will also forgive you: But if ye forgive not men their trespasses, neither will your Father forgive your trespasses." (Matthew 6:12, 14-15.)

Christ is our greatest example of forgiveness. To the woman brought before him accused of adultery, he said, "Neither do I condemn thee: go, and sin no more." (John 8:11.)

Then on the cross he prayed: "Father, forgive them; for they know not what they do." (Luke 23:34.)

Regardless of our ego, our pride, or our feeling of insecurity, our lives would be happier, we would be contributing more to social welfare and the happiness of others, if we would love one another, forgive one another, repent of our wrongdoings, and judge not.

It is true that we must have appointed judges to deal with the laws of the land and judges in the Church to deal with its members; and they are given the heavy duty and responsibility of judging, which they must not neglect, but they must give righteous judgment according to the law of the land and of the Church.

In an election year, there is much campaigning; we hear and argue the pros and cons of many questions; we have strong opposing views. Each must try to understand the questions and then stand firm by his convictions. But let us determine now that in the heat of the campaign we will never indulge in the vituperative talk of personalities that we so often hear. We must not rail against our brother and accuse him of lying and cheating or being dishonest or immoral.

Let us stand on principle—high principle. Also, it is most important that all of us, including our politicians, strive to live so that our actions will be above reproach and criticism.

We never gain anything or improve our own character by trying to tear down another. We have seen close friendships destroyed through words spoken and accusations made in the heat of a campaign. Tirades against men in office or against one's opponent tend to cause our youth and others to lose faith in the individual and others in government and often even our form of government itself.

As parents, we have the responsibility in our homes to guard against any of these things. Also, we must realize that every word and every act influences the thinking and attitude of the child. It is in the family that the child picks up the elementary lessons in getting along with people and the virtues of love, compassion, and concern. These lessons will have been well taught if parents can bring up their children without prejudicing them by precept or example against any other children on the grounds of color, race, religion, social status, or intellectual capacity, and if they teach them to love the Lord. I am so thankful that my parents, through their tolerance, were able to accomplish this with their children.

May I humbly say in all sincerity that I love the Lord

with all my heart and that I love my fellowmen. I hold no hard feelings of any kind toward any man, and I sincerely pray for forgiveness wherein I have offended anyone. I realize, as the Savior said, "Inasmuch as ye have done it unto one of the least of these my brethren, ye have done it unto me." (Matthew 25:40.)

To all the world, and especially to those who do not understand but who ridicule the teachings of The Church of Jesus Christ of Latter-day Saints, I wish to bear my witness and issue a challenge that you judge not until you know and understand those teachings which are contained in the restored gospel. We believe, with you, that God lives and that Jesus Christ is his Only, but truly, Begotten Son in the flesh, who came and gave his life and was resurrected so that all mankind might enjoy immortality and eternal life.

CHAPTER 8

"Woe Unto You...Hypocrites"

The other day I was talking to someone who said, "There goes a man in whom you can place full confidence. You always know where he stands. He never pretends, but is always sincere and just his best self."

That same day someone, referring to another man, said, "Isn't it too bad that you never know just where he stands? You are never sure you can depend on what he says. I think the Lord would have called him a hypocrite." I felt to agree with him.

In The Church of Jesus Christ of Latter-day Saints today we have approximately three million members, made up of all kinds of people, ranging from those who are fully dedicated and prepared to give all that they have in the service of the Lord and their fellowmen, to those who have not yet been fully converted and who do not see the importance of living the teachings of Jesus Christ or of being active and prepared to give service wherever possible.

If we are to enjoy the blessings of the Lord and the confidence of the people with whom we associate, we must be prepared to live the gospel and to be honestly and actively engaged in practicing and teaching its concepts, never pretending to be what we are not. The gospel of

Jesus Christ tells us how we should live in words found in ancient and modern-day scripture. For example:

We are told that "pure religion and undefiled before God and the Father is this, To visit the fatherless and widows in their affliction, and to keep himself unspotted from the world." (James 1:27.)

"I am the resurrection, and the life: he that believeth in me, though he were dead, yet shall he live: And whosoever liveth and believeth in me shall never die." (John 11:25-26.)

"Thou shalt love the Lord thy God with all thy heart, and with all thy soul, and with all thy mind.

"This is the first and great commandment.

"And the second is like unto it, Thou shalt love thy neighbour as thyself.

"On these two commandments hang all the law and the prophets." (Matthew 22:37-40.)

The Ten Commandments are given to us in very clear language, and they need no enlargement, and leave no question. The Sermon on the Mount leaves no doubt as to Christ's message to the human race and what our responsibilities are if we wish to enjoy his blessings and his Spirit to guide us. We also have our Articles of Faith, which outline the high code by which we should govern ourselves.

Jesus said: "Not every one that saith unto me, Lord, Lord, shall enter into the kingdom of heaven; but he that doeth the will of my Father which is in heaven." (Matthew 7:21.)

In these, the latter days, he said, "I, the Lord, am bound when ye do what I say; but when ye do not what I say, ye have no promise." (D&C 82:10.)

We are admonished to be true to the faith and warned against evil and hypocrisy. In fact, the Savior placed great emphasis on the evils of hypocrisy. He was very severe in his condemnation of those who professed one thing and practiced another. He said, "Woe unto you, scribes and

Pharisees, *hypocrites!* . . . Ye serpents, ye generation of vipers, how can ye escape the damnation of hell?" (Matthew 23:29, 33. Italics added.)

Woe, according to the dictionary, means miserable or sorrowful state, a condition of deep suffering, misfortune, affliction, grief. A *hypocrite* is one who pretends to have beliefs or principles that he does not have, or to be what he is not, especially a false assumption of an appearance of virtue or religion.

As recorded in the Gospels, the Savior refers to different examples of hypocrisy, and in each case he says, "Woe unto you, scribes and Pharisees, hypocrites!"

I should like to refer to these and other charges of hypocrisy. As I do so, we might well look at ourselves to see how these apply to us. As we look at the conditions in the world today, I am sure we will find that hypocrisy and the violation of the principles of righteousness and decency have brought our national and individual affairs to the sorry state in which they are now.

The Lord said:

. . . they bind heavy burdens . . . on men's shoulders; but they themselves will not move them with one of their fingers.

But all their works they do for to be seen of men. . . .

And love the uppermost rooms at feasts, and the chief seats in the synagogues.

. . . ye devour widows' houses, and for a pretence make long prayer: therefore ye shall receive the greater damnation.

. . . ye pay tithe of mint and anise and cummin, and have omitted the weightier matters of the law, judgment, mercy, and faith: these ought ye to have done, and not to leave the other undone.

Ye blind guides, which strain at a gnat, and swallow a camel.

. . . ye make clean the outside of the cup and of the platter, but within they are full of extortion and excess.

. . . ye are like unto whited sepulchres, which indeed appear beautiful outward, but are within full of dead men's bones, and of all uncleanness.

Even so ye also outwardly appear righteous unto men, but within ye are full of hypocrisy and iniquity.

. . . ye build the tombs of the prophets, and garnish the sepulchres of the righteous,

And say, If we had been in the days of our fathers, we would not have been partakers with them in the blood of the prophets. (Matthew 23:4-6, 14, 23-25, 27-30.)

We might well ask ourselves if such fallacies are present in our own alleged Christianity. In those days, as is so common today, they had brotherhoods in which the law was strictly kept, but they ignored those on the outside by regarding all others with contempt and condemnation, thereby avoiding the heresy of form but committing the heresy of the spirit.

How many of us are guilty of keeping the letter of the law and forgetting the spirit of the law in that we fail to show mercy and faith in our fellowmen? Do we place more stress on an external act to be seen of men than on a change of heart? The only way to cleanse ourselves inside is to be pure in heart by being humble and turning from our evil ways and by living the gospel of Jesus Christ to the best of our ability. We may be able to deceive men, but we cannot deceive God.

Is there danger that our whole civilization is like whitewashed tombs? We have marvelous machines, towering buildings, and thousands of signs of what we call progress; but within we have unrest, strife between men and nations, and unrelieved burden of the poor, and the dead men's bones of wholesale wars. Someone has said: "Still we try to safeguard ourselves by calcimining the tomb."

With all the crime, changing of population from rural to urban, loosened morals, pornographic movies and literature, etc., we must stand firm in the cause of right. How can persons for selfish reasons be hypocrites enough to urge the opening or widening of the liquor laws when they know that where consumption of liquor is greatly increased, there is a similar increase in multitudes of social problems?

How can a newspaper which records the highway accidents, the deaths, the health problems, and broken homes as a result of drinking advocate making liquor more easily available in order to attract more tourists and industry? The cost to communities and individuals far outweighs any benefits.

The American Council on Alcohol Problems passed a resolution which states: "While we share the concern of a majority of our citizens about the dangers in the use of marijuana, we are firmly convinced that alcohol remains the number one drug problem in America and that its damage to life, limb and the welfare of our people is vastly greater."

We must be equally concerned about the use of drugs that destroy lives and bring crushing misery, not only to users but to those around them. But hypocrisy in the lives of adults has a serious influence on our young people who are turning to this form of protest. What we are trying to say is that the kids are affected by the hypocrisy of those who accept the cocktail hour and other evil practices and yet get hysterical because the kids have found other ways to imitate their parents' behavior. The kids will pay attention only when the adults set the proper example.

As great as our responsibility is through legislation or other means to prevent our young citizens from falling prey to those intent on their becoming victims of these evil habits, we cannot minimize our responsibility to help rehabilitate those who have succumbed. How can we call ourselves Christians and say we love our neighbor—who is anyone in need of help—and fail to work with others who are endeavoring to set up facilities to assist alcoholics, drug-users, or parolees from our prisons? Yet there are those who would actually hamper such efforts because they object to having such facilities in their midst. These unfortunate people need our help. Surely we must be prepared to be the good Samaritan and help wherever possible.

How many of us keep the Word of Wisdom strictly, but are most intemperate in our prejudices and condemnations of others? Are there any of us who, as businessmen, are meticulously polite and most regular in church attendance and yet accept glaring inequities in the social structure, and who may be unfair or dishonest in dealing with our neighbor?

Are we truly interested in and concerned with the well-being of our neighbors? Do we visit the widows and fatherless, and feed, clothe, and comfort the poor and needy? The prophet Alma in his day "saw great inequality among the people, some lifting themselves up with their pride, despising others, turning their backs upon the needy and the naked and those who were hungry, and those who were athirst, and those who were sick and afflicted."

We read: "Now this was a great cause for lamentations among the people, while others were . . . succoring those who stood in need of their succor, such as imparting their substance to the poor and the needy, feeding the hungry. . . ." (Alma 4:12-13.)

Recent changes in their structure and program now enable our Relief Society sisters to devote more of their time and energy to the main purposes for which they were organized—namely, to look after the spiritual, mental, and moral welfare of the mothers and daughters in Zion. They should be teaching the gospel, preparing our women of all ages to be better homemakers, and giving compassionate service, yet there are still many who are sick or lonely or in need of comfort who are not reached. We *all* should be seeking for opportunities to give aid and comfort to the needy among us. We should not neglect this duty and opportunity in order to engage ourselves in seeking only after our own selfish worldly pleasures and material gain.

Too often we excuse ourselves from religious activity, which includes both showing love for our neighbors and regular church attendance, by comparing our activities with those of others, and by saying we are doing just as much as they, or we are no worse than they. Some say: "I don't go to church because I don't want to be a hypocrite, as he is. I can be religious without going to church. I can worship God on the lake or in the mountains, communing with nature."

Hear what the Lord has said:

And that thou mayest more fully keep thyself unspotted from the world, thou shalt go to the house of prayer and offer up thy sacraments upon my holy day;

For verily this is a day appointed unto you to rest from your labors, and to pay thy devotions unto the Most High;

Nevertheless thy vows shall be offered up in righteousness on all days and at all times. (D&C 59:9-11.)

We cannot choose which part of the gospel we think is true or which part we should live. We cannot compartmentalize our lives. As the Savior said: ". . . these ought ye to have done, and not to leave the other undone." (Matthew 23:23.) We must be Christians in very deed, and by our lives show our love for the Lord, our God, and show love for and be interested in one another. We, you and I, must put our personal houses in order. We must not be hypocrites.

Harry Emerson Fosdick observed that there are two kinds of hypocrisy: when we try to appear better than we are, and when we let ourselves appear worse than we are. We have been speaking of the kind of hypocrisy where people pretend to be more or better than they are. Too often, however, we see members of the Church who in their hearts know and believe, but through fear of public opinion fail to stand up and be counted. This kind of hypocrisy is as serious as the other; it makes it difficult for others to respect us, and often adversely affects or influences the lives of other members of the Church who expect us to stand by our commitments to the Church and not hesitate to manifest our faith.

Only when we are seriously striving to live the teachings of Christ can we make any real spiritual progress. We must not fear, wherever we are, to live up to our convictions and to the standards of the Church. People, though they may criticize and ridicule, expect us to do so, and they respect us if we do. Living high standards cannot offend conscientious, fair-minded people.

Not long ago I was talking to a father and mother and their little boy who were converts of not many months. During our conversation the father said they had become inactive and were not attending church, and I asked them why. He explained that the missionaries were such fine examples of good and clean-living, righteous people; but when they came to the ward they found so many people who were not living what the Church teaches, or what they professed to be, and as a result they became discouraged and lost faith in the Church. I think this gives us two very important lessons:

First, it is our responsibility to live so that we will influence the lives of people for good and that we will never cause doubt in their minds because of hypocrisy in our own lives.

The other lesson is that we should always guard against letting hypocrisy in the lives of others influence our lives or cause us to doubt and fail to live according to the teachings of the gospel.

It is most important that we as members of the Church stand firmly and unitedly in the cause of truth and righteousness. We have declared to the world that we have the gospel of Christ, that we are going to stand against vice. Shall we stand firm, or shall we waver and be driven by the wind and tossed? Shall we forsake the cause of righteousness in order to please men, because we desire to give lip service rather than heart service, or because of some political power that is brought to bear upon us?

We must not be like those to whom John referred when

he said: "Nevertheless among the chief rulers also many believed on him; but because of the Pharisees they did not confess him, . . . For they loved the praise of men more than the praise of God." (John 12:42-43.)

Imagine the great influence the Church, with its approximately three million members, could have upon the world if each of us would be what we profess to be; if everyone were a real, truly dedicated Christian, living every day and not pretending; if we were honest, true, chaste, benevolent, virtuous, doing good to all men, and always seeking for things virtuous, lovely, or of good report and praiseworthy.

Let us listen to the prophets and live by their words. Let us not be guilty, as were the scribes and Pharisees of old, of increasing the agony of our Savior by rejecting him and his teachings, which he gave to us, together with his life, that we might have happiness here and eternal life hereafter. Let us not find ourselves in the condition which he describes as he concludes his chastisement of the hypocrites:

"Behold, your house is left unto you desolate. For I say unto you, Ye shall not see me henceforth, till ye shall say, Blessed is he that cometh in the name of the Lord." (Matthew 23:38-39.)

CHAPTER 9

The Brotherhood of Man

Brotherhood Week each year provides a wonderful opportunity to promote civic cooperation and mutual understanding among men of goodwill of all religions and ethnic groups. Our ideas should be to build one united nation, under God, indivisible, with liberty and justice for all.

It is not an "interfaith" movement. It does not aim at any sort of amalgamation of religious bodies or a least common denominator of doctrine. It does not engage in common worship. It seeks in all its work to guard against the dangers of religious indifferentism. Catholics, Protestants, Jews—all of God's children—should, without compromise of conscience or of their distinctive and important religious differences, work closely together to build better relationships among men of all religions, races, and nationalities for a "united nation" that will be an example to all the world.

In 1966 President Lyndon Johnson said, regarding Brotherhood Week:

An unstinting dedication to freedom, tolerance, and individual dignity gave us our mighty nation. United and determined we must stand ready to preserve our legacy. Americans of all races, creeds, and walks of life must join hands to meet the problems which threaten to corrode the very core of our nation's life. Beginning with the family and local community, we must together seek to extend to every American the human compassion and liberty of opportunity which have been the hallmark of America's greatness.

President Hugh B. Brown, representing the Church, has made a very significant statement:

During recent months, both in Salt Lake City and across the nation, considerable interest has been expressed in the position of The Church of Jesus Christ of Latter-day Saints on the matter of civil rights. We would like it to be known that there is in this church no doctrine, belief, or practice that is intended to deny the enjoyment of full civil rights by any person regardless of race, color, or creed.

We say again, as we have said many times before, that we believe that all men are the children of the same God and that it is a moral evil for any person or group of persons to deny any human being the right of gainful enmployment, to full educational opportunity, and to every privilege of citizenship, just as it is a moral evil to deny him the right to worship according to the dictates of his own conscience.

We have consistently and persistently upheld the Constitution of the United States, and as far as we are concerned this means upholding the constitutional rights of every citizen of the United States.

We call upon all men everywhere, both within and outside the Church, to commit themselves to the establishment of full civil equality for all of God's children. Anything less than this defeats our high ideal of the brotherhood of man.

The United States has been doing much in the past few years in trying to make available to all citizens full rights of citizenship. The United States of America is made up of people from all nations, all of whom may become citizens of this great democarcy. They should be treated as citizens, and they should act as such. I like the words of Emma Lazarus inscribed on the Statue of Liberty in New York Harbor:

Give me your tired, your poor,
Your huddled masses yearning to breathe free,
The wretched refuse of your teeming shore.

Send these, the homeless, tempest-tossed, to me:
I lift my lamp beside the golden door.

Brotherhood means giving to others the rights and respect you want for yourself. It is desirable that every one of us pause and evaluate our own personal attitudes and rededicate ourselves to making brotherhood a reality in every way.

As members of a family we should be bound together and loyal to one another. In that family we should be taught respect for the feelings of one another and for the feelings and ideals and beliefs of people in other families. What a great strength to the community, the state, and the nation if we would all act as brothers.

Never before in the history of the United States has there been more need for people to be united and to develop a feeling of brotherhood. As this is done, and only as it is done, can we enjoy real peace and freedom and harmony, and until this is done we cannot extend this feeling to the rest of the world. As President Franklin D. Roosevelt so wisely said: "If civilization is to survive, we must cultivate the science of human relationships, the ability of all people, of all kinds, to live together in the same world at peace."

In this regard, I like the words of Ella Wheeler Wilcox:

God, what a world, if men in street and mart
Felt that same kinship of the human heart
Which makes them, in the face of fire and flood,
Rise to the meaning of true brotherhood.

Then, in the words of Conrad Hilton:

Until we open our hearts and minds to the thoughts of all peoples, wherever they may be; until we realize that folks aren't queer because they eat different food and speak different tongues; until we are prepared to agree that the aspirations of others are as important to them as ours are to us, we cannot hope to live in a truly peaceful world. (Reader's Digest, February 1966.)

If we are to enjoy true brotherhood, what we need most in this rapidly changing, materialistic world is a belief in God as its Creator and as our Father, in whose image we are made. We are free to serve God and keep his commandments or to be ruled by a dictator. Lip service is not sufficient. We are really God-fearing people only as we keep his commandments. We are Christians only as we accept Christ as the Savior of the world and as we govern our lives by the plan of life and salvation that he gave us. We are truly brothers only as we love one another and recognize our brothers as the children of God.

Dr. Marcus Bach gives us the following message:

I believe that we understand a person best when we understand what he believes. I think we all have a code to live by . . . most people have a spiritual code by which they live. . . .

But the point I wish to make is that when we think of religion in America we dare not think only of the churches; we must think in terms of the spiritual quest of every person, because everyone is religious by nature. Everyone is looking for a way of life. He wants to come to terms with God. . . .

Weatherhead said, "Truth is really not truth until it has been validated by an intuitive experience. In this way, you see, religion is very much like love. You cannot always reduce it to logical premises."

. . . If the student is oriented in the Christian faith, he will say, "Give me a religion with the Christ in it, but not the dogmatic, theological, abstruse Christ, but rather One who lives and walks with men, who understands my life and helps me better to understand His. Give me most of all a religion which has words to live by, techniques, affirmations, and which consists of a fellowship of people who are living the life, so that by my association with them I may realize better what I, too, may become."

. . . True religion is what we do with life. The philosopher Kant said that it is accepting all of our duties as divine commandments. William James described religion as the manner of man's total reaction upon life.

Someone has expressed it this way:

"Your task, to build a better world," God said. I answered, "How? The world is such a large vast place, so complicated now!

And I so small and useless am, there's nothing I can do." But
God in all his wisdom said, "Just build a better you."

Dr. Bach continues:

. . . This is the kind of thing I am talking about. The personal
involvement in the spiritual experience is the crying need of our
time. It is all right for us to applaud others like a Mellon or a
Schweitzer for what they are doing, but what about our careers?
What about us? *Let us add to this ingredient of the mystical ex-*
perience our own personal dedication. (From "Facing the Challenge
of the Changing Times," Boy Scouts of America, pp. 22-31.)

In religion and among churches there should be the
greatest brotherhood. The Lord, speaking to Moses, said:
". . . thou shalt love thy neighbour as thyself. . . . the
stranger that dwelleth with you shall be unto you as one
born among you, and thou shalt love him as thyself. . . ."
(Leviticus 19:18, 34.)

Our feelings toward one another must be those of
brotherly love. Religion should cement and strengthen and
never weaken this feeling. It is most important that we
respect and honor the religious beliefs and feelings of
our neighbor.

Poet Patience Strong gives us this message in her
poem, "The Vision":

Our eyes have seen a vision of a new and greater world
In which all nations live at peace, their tattered banners furled;
Where all men work, and find fulfillment in the common good,
And spiritually men are banded in a brotherhood.
War, with its vaunting tyranny, has had its bloody day,
Now let cold reason lift her voice! We know a better way
To shape this formless stuff of dreams into reality
And graft a greater glory on our empire's history,
That future generations may remember us and say:
"These people saw a vision in their dark and troubled day.
Though tyrants raged across the earth with savage hate and lust,
With bleeding hands they built a shining world out of the dust."
Thus may we be remembered—not by might on land or sea,
But by the service we have rendered to humanity.

Because I believe that Christ is born and is really the begotten Son of God in the flesh, and others do not, is no cause for ill feelings, hate, or lack of brotherhood. Because I believe, as a Mormon, or you as a Catholic, you as a Protestant, or you as a Jew, we should not shun or criticize or have ill feeling, but should respect each other in his views, realizing that everyone's belief in God makes him a better man, a better citizen, to the extent that he follows God's teachings—particularly, as the Savior said, "Love one another, as I have loved you."

CHAPTER 10

Our Concern for the Lamanite

The growing years are precious times in the lives of our Lamanite youth. It is encouraging to hear the testimonies and experiences of those who have participated in the Indian Placement Program, and I underline the goals and objectives of this program: to make possible educational, spiritual, social, and cultural opportunities.

I was raised near the Blood Indian Reservation and got very well acquainted with the Indians. My father used to hire as many as twenty at a time to come and help us with our harvesting. They loved my father and we learned to think a great deal of them. Probably more because of that than anything else, I have been interested in this program.

The First Presidency approved this program back in 1954, and I assure you that it is approved by the Church, by the First Presidency, and has the blessings of our President today.

We as members of the Church have a heavy responsibility. Why? Because we have the Book of Mormon—the only people in the world who have been given this book and who know what it is and understand it and its message. It is a record of the people of Nephi and also the Lamanites, written to the Lamanites to show unto this

remnant of the house of Israel what great things the Lord
had done for their fathers, that they may know of the covenants of the Lord and the promises in store for them.

The gospel must play an important part in the lives
of these Indian students who are brought into our Latter-
day Saint homes. This program offers a great privilege
to further the work of the Lord. I don't know where there
is a greater privilege than to build the kingdom of God.
Those who hear and accept the gospel in their lives are
enriched.

In Second Nephi we read:

> And now, I would prophesy somewhat more concerning the
> Jews and the Gentiles. For after the book of which I have spoken
> shall come forth, and be written unto the Gentiles, and sealed up
> again unto the Lord, there shall be many which shall believe the
> words which are written; and they shall carry them forth unto the
> remnant of our seed. (2 Nephi 30:3.)

This is a prophecy, a direction, a responsibility that
is placed upon us without any reservations.

> And then shall the remnant of our seed know concerning us,
> how that we came out from Jerusalem, and that they are descen-
> dants of the Jews.
> And the gospel of Jesus Christ shall be declared among them;
> wherefore, they shall be restored unto the knowledge of their
> fathers, and also to the knowledge of Jesus Christ, which was had
> among their fathers.
> . . . and their scales of darkness shall begin to fall from their
> eyes; and many generations shall not pass away among them, save
> they shall be a white and delightsome people. (2 Nephi 30:4-6.)

This is the promise, if we do our part and take the
message to our Lamanite brethren. We have the greater
responsibility, the privilege, of bringing this chosen people,
this remnant of the house of Israel, unto the understanding
of the gospel.

Now, it is the responsibility of the stake presidents and
the bishops and branch presidents to see that this program

works, because it is a program of the Church. And when the Prophet says this is the thing for us to do, we can't go wrong by doing it. It is the responsibility of our priesthood leaders to choose homes of active Latter-day Saints, preferably with children, and to work closely with the assigned caseworkers.

I was very fortunate sometime ago to go with Brother Delbert L. Stapley to visit with members of the Crow Creek Indian Council. A number of them were there who had come to learn more about how they could apply the gospel and make it a part of their lives on the Indian reservation. They were the chiefs or leaders of the different tribes, and we sat and discussed things. They asked questions; we asked questions. They answered questions; we answered questions. And I was thrilled to hear three or four of these leaders say that they thought it was the best program that they had ever heard about any place in the world and how much they appreciated our missionaries in their reservation.

The son of one of these chiefs had attended Brigham Young University, and his father said, "He's a different boy from what he was when he left."

Then we asked if this boy could speak for a few minutes. He said (I don't remember the exact words, but this is the essence): "You men [meaning those Indian leaders] here today seem to be interested entirely in material things. You can't enjoy these things as you should until you accept the spiritual things that the Church of Jesus Christ offers you."

Then one of these chiefs said to me, "How can we take this miracle and get it to our people and get them to adopt this program?"

My answer was, "You accept it and live it, and take it to your people."

We were thrilled not long after to hear that the Church program has been accepted by this man; they have taken the program into their tribe and have reported that they are making good success.

This is a program where many members of the Church and their families in the stakes and wards and branches can be serving the Lord and doing missionary work. Surely every family in this church that is able should be happy to accept an Indian student and make him a part of the family, realizing that they are doing the work of the Lord. We are the people who have been chosen to do it because the Book of Mormon has been given to us, with the challenge, the assignment, the responsibility, and the great blessings that will come to every one of us if we will accept it and carry it out.

Adapted from a talk given at a special meeting concerning the Church's Indian Student Placement Program.

IV

Seek to Exercise Free Agency

VI

CHAPTER 11

"Thou Mayest Choose for Thyself"

One of God's greatest gifts to man is freedom of choice.

At an early period in the journey through life, man finds himself at a crossroad where he must choose one of two great highways—the right, leading to progress and happiness; and the wrong, leading to retardation and sorrow. There exists this eternal law that each human soul, through the choices he makes, will shape his own destiny. Our success or failure, peace or discontent, happiness or misery, depends on the choices we make each day.

According to the scriptures, the first and most important question pertaining to the individual was that of freedom of choice. Before the world was, and in a great council in heaven, God the Father presented his plan to organize and people the earth.

He explained that his spirit children would go to earth, gain bodies of flesh and blood, be tried and tested in all things to see if they would keep all of his commandments, and prepare to come back to his eternal presence.

Lucifer, a son of the morning, came forth with his plan to redeem all mankind by force, that not one soul would be lost, for which he wanted the honor. Then Christ presented his plan, which was to follow the will of the Father and allow all men to choose for themselves, and the glory would go to the Father. Christ's plan was accepted, and all who come to dwell upon the earth in bodies of flesh and blood elected in that great council to follow Jesus Christ.

Satan rebelled and influenced a third of the hosts of heaven to follow him.

At that time, Satan, with his followers, committed himself to destroy our free agency and the cause of righteousness. While Satan is determined to destroy us, the Savior says: ". . . this is my work and my glory—to bring to pass the immortality and eternal life of man." (Moses 1:39.)

He gave his life so that all mankind might enjoy immortality; and through his gospel and the teachings of the prophets, both ancient and modern, we are given a clear understanding of the purpose of life and how to distinguish right from wrong, with promises of salvation and exaltation to all who keep the commandments. But remember that Satan has committed himself to destroy mankind and is continually at work to accomplish this one thing. The scriptures tell us:

Satan stirreth them up, that he may lead their souls to destruction.

And thus he has laid a cunning plan, thinking to destroy the work of God; . . .

And . . . he . . . leadeth them along until he draggeth their souls down to hell; . . .

And thus he goeth up and down, to and fro in the earth, seeking to destroy the souls of men. (D&C 10:22-23, 26-27.)

The reality of Satan and the power and influence he wields have been evident since that first temptation in the Garden of Eden. He influenced Cain to slay his brother Abel, which resulted in great suffering and sorrow. The Book of Mormon is replete with examples of the destruction of individuals and groups who refused to follow the teachings of the Lord and instead succumbed to the influence of Satan.

Now, in the Bible we have the story of the great flood,

when, because of the wickedness of the people, none but Noah and his family were spared. We know what happened to the great cities of Sodom and Gomorrah because the people chose to follow Satan. In secular history we read of the fall of the Roman Empire; and accounts are too numerous to mention of the destruction of other civilizations, cities, and individuals who chose to turn away from the Lord.

In a recent challenging speech, which was titled "Who Is Tampering with the Soul of America?" Jenkin Lloyd Jones said the pathway of history is littered with the bones of dead states and fallen empires. He points out that Rome did not fall because its walls were low, but because Rome itself was low. The sensuality, orgies, and gradually weakened fibre of a once self-disciplined people brought Rome down. (Speech delivered to the American Society of Newspaper Editors.)

With all of these examples, what more or greater evidence do we need to convince us that when we choose evil rather than good, we lose our freedom and become the slaves of those who would destroy us and deprive us of the blessings attendant upon righteousness? As we make our choices each day, we must keep in mind that as we sow, so shall we reap. We cannot sow seeds of iniquity and reap a harvest of blessings. Let me relate a story to illustrate.

A certain man, well up on the ladder of success, had great prospects for a very bright future. Then one day at a businessmen's luncheon he decided that social drinking would make him more popular and successful. He soon began looking forward to the cocktail hours, and then found they didn't come often enough. Finally he became an alcoholic, lost his job, his wife, and his friends. Because of the wrong choice at a moment of decision, he had lost everything he once so hopefully and diligently set out to accomplish.

On the other hand, we have the examples of Joseph,

who was sold into Egypt; of Moses, who led the Israelites from bondage; of Daniel, through whom the Lord gave marvelous prophecies and predictions and of whom it was said, as he was taken from the lion's den: ". . . no manner of hurt was found upon him, because he believed in his God." (Dan. 6:23.) They, with many others, had the courage to say no to temptation and to choose the right, and thereby save themselves and their people from destruction.

Self-discipline is essential in helping us make proper choices. It is much easier to drift than to row, to slide downhill than to climb up. Satan is constantly at work to drag us down by placing temptations in our way in the form of alcohol, tobacco, drugs, pornography, deceit, dishonesty, and flattery, always waiting to catch us in our misdeeds.

How can we combat the evil that surrounds us and which is so prevalent in the world today? Satan is trying harder than ever before to claim souls for his own domain. We must and we can thwart him, but only by choosing to follow the teachings of Jesus Christ and making our influence an active and positive force. As leaders, as parents, as teachers, and as neighbors, all good people everywhere who are striving for liberty and freedom, peace, success, happiness, and for eternal life with our Father in heaven must by example and precept be actively engaged in fighting against those forces which are threatening us and endangering our well-being and that of our children.

Don't let us be fooled or misled by the claim extant in the world today that restraints and conventions are damaging to the psyche of a child. In promoting a permissive and unrestricted society, they would have a child undisciplined for misbehavior. This is a false premise, and we are better advised to heed the counsel of the Lord when he said:

And again, inasmuch as parents have children in Zion, or in any of her stakes which are organized, that teach them not to understand the doctrine of repentance, faith in Christ the Son of the living God, and of baptism and the gift of the Holy Ghost by the laying on of the hands, when eight years old, the sin be upon the heads of the parents.

And they shall also teach their children to pray, and to walk uprightly before the Lord. (D&C 68:25, 28.)

Children do not learn by themselves how to distinguish right from wrong. Parents have to determine the child's readiness to assume responsibility and his capacity to make sound decisions, to evaluate alternatives, and the results of doing so. While we are teaching them, we have the responsibility to discipline them and to see that they do what is right. If a child is besmudged with dirt, we do not let him wait until he grows up to decide whether or not he will bathe. We do not let him wait to decide whether or not he will take his medicine when sick, or go to school or to church. By example, persuasion, and love we see that he does what we know is best for him. We cannot over-emphasize the importance of example. The late J. Edgar Hoover said that if fathers and mothers would *take* their children to Sunday School and church regularly, they could strike a felling blow against the forces that contribute to juvenile delinquency.

Parents also should teach their children early in life the glorious concept and fact that they are spirit children of God, and choosing to follow the teachings of Jesus Christ is the only way to enjoy success and happiness here and eternal life hereafter. They must be taught that Satan is real and that he will use all agencies at his disposal to tempt them to do wrong, to lead them astray, make them his captives, and keep them from the supreme happiness and exaltation they could otherwise enjoy.

To meet the serious issues facing us in our respective communities today, we must be examples of virtue and righteousness ourselves and choose today to take our stand on the moral issues which threaten us. We do not want our civilization to decay and fall because we failed to keep it

on a high spiritual plane and allowed it to sink to the level
where the animal instincts and passions dominate.

Let me refer again to Jenkin Lloyd Jones. He said
that we are suffering from a collapse of moral standards
and the blunting of our capacity for righteous indignation.
Then, referring to our Puritan ancestors, he said: "For all
their exaggerated attention to sin, their philosophy rested
on a great granite rock. Man was the master of his soul.
You didn't *have* to be *bad*. You *could* and *should* be *better*.
And if you wanted to escape the eternal fires, you'd well
better be."

Then concerning our present-day entertainment he
said:

> Can anyone deny that movies are dirtier than ever? But they
> don't call it dirt. They call it "realism." Why do we let them fool
> us? Why do we nod owlishly when they tell us that filth is merely
> a daring art form, that licentiousness is really social comment? Isn't
> it plain that the financially-harassed movie industry is putting gobs
> of sex in the darkened drive-ins in an effort to lure curious teenagers
> away? . . . Last week the screen industry solemnly announced that
> henceforth perversion and homosexuality would no longer be barred
> from the screen provided the subjects were handled with "delicacy
> and taste." What nonsense!
>
> We are drowning our youngsters in violence, cynicism, and
> sadism piped into the living room and even the nursery. The
> grandchildren of the kids who use to weep because The Little
> Match Girl froze to death now feel cheated if she isn't slugged,
> raped, and thrown into a Bessemer converter. . . .
>
> The quick-buck boys have apparently convinced our bum-
> fuzzled judges that there is no difference between a peep show and
> a moral lecture.
>
> . . . We have reached the point where we should re-examine
> the debilitating philosophy of permissiveness. Let this not be con-
> fused with the philosophy of liberty. . . .
>
> It's time we hit the sawdust trail. It's time we revived the idea
> that there is such a thing as sin—just plain old willful sin. It is
> time we brought self-discipline back into style.

It is also time we realized that these are all Satan's
ways of destroying mankind. Now, what must we do? If

there is pornography or obscenity in bookstores, on television or radio, or in places of entertainment, if there are those who would make more easily available to the young and inexperienced alcohol and its attendant evils, including drunken driving, highway fatalities, broken homes, and if we are threatened with the passage of laws which violate the commandments of God, it is our duty and responsibility as individuals to speak out, to organize, and to protect ourselves and our community against such encroachments. We have seen how people react to the high price of food. It is far more important that we react effectively against the immorality and evil in our communities which threaten the morals and the very lives of our children. As President Richard M. Nixon has said, the only way to attack crime in America is the way crime attacks the people—without pity.

People who argue that they have constitutional rights and want to use what they call their free agency to accomplish unrighteous ends abuse the idea of free agency and deprive others of *their* constitutional rights. While many of our problems are caused by those who are deliberately trying to further their own selfish and devilish interests, there is also a vocal, misled minority which is responsible for other problems as they exist in our country and in our communities. We must be equally vocal and firm in our efforts to maintain the quality of our surroundings, where we can enjoy family solidarity, which is the strength of any nation. We must take a firm stand against the concerted efforts in many areas to destroy the family unit.

As we contemplate these devastating conditions rampant in the world today—the wars, death, suffering, poverty, and disease—and while many question why God permits such troublous conditions to plague us, let us remember that man himself is responsible. Even though the innocent suffer with the wicked in many instances, all the

strife and contention and wickedness abroad in the land
today is because man has chosen to follow Satan instead of
accepting and living according to the teachings of Jesus
Christ. From the beginning we have been told that there
must be opposition in all things in order that we might
progress according to God's plan for us. Again we turn to
the scriptures:

For it must needs be, that there is an opposition in all things.
If not so, . . . righteousness could not be brought to pass, neither
wickedness, neither holiness nor misery, neither good nor bad. . . .
Wherefore, the Lord God gave unto man that he should act
for himself. Wherefore, man could not act for himself save it should
be that he was enticed by the one or the other.
Wherefore, men are free according to the flesh; and all things
are given them which are expedient unto man. And they are free
to choose liberty and eternal life, through the great mediation of
all men, or to choose captivity and death, according to the captivity
and power of the devil; for he seeketh that all men might be
miserable like unto himself. (2 Nephi 2:11, 16, 27.)

Men are not created to be miserable, for "men are that
they might have joy." (2 Nephi 2:25.) To assist us and guide
us in our choices, to counteract the forces of Satan, and to
give us the joy and happiness for which we are all seeking,
God has seen fit through his Son Jesus Christ to reestablish
upon the earth in these, the latter days, his church and
kingdom, with the restored gospel in its fullness. He has
reestablished the priesthood, which is the power to act in
God's name, with a prophet through whom God speaks to
direct us. I join with thousands of others in bearing witness
to all the world that the gospel alone offers the only true
way to happiness and peace which passeth understanding,
and eternal life to all who will accept it and *keep the
commandments.*

Yes, every day of our lives we are determining by our
choices whether we shall reap good or evil, whether
salvation or destruction, whether eternal life with our
Father or the utter despair at being cast out from his

presence. Each day we choose whether or not we believe in God the Eternal Father and in his Son Jesus Christ, and whether or not we will accept their teachings and *keep the commandments.*

We choose whether or not we will accept President Harold B. Lee as a prophet of God, listen to his voice, and follow him, in the sure knowledge that he is the mouthpiece of the Lord and the leader of God's children on the earth today. We choose whether or not we are prepared to accept and live by the Articles of Faith and be honest, true, chaste, benevolent, virtuous, honorable and upright in our dealings with our fellowmen, showing our love for them by being good neighbors. As we choose to seek first the kingdom of God and his righteousness, we can know that all other things for our good will be added unto us.

We cannot go astray if we listen to the prophet's voice and follow him, and as we do so we will be led in the path of truth and righteousness and enjoy the love, respect, and confidence of our fellowmen, and eventually enjoy eternal life with our Father in heaven. Or we may refuse and lose all these great blessings.

"Nevertheless, thou mayest choose for thyself."

CHAPTER 12

"Choose You This Day Whom Ye Will Serve"

How many of us realize what a great privilege, opportunity, and blessing it is for us to live in a free country where we have our free agency; where we have the right to choose our lives and what we'll be; and where we have the knowledge that if we set about in all earnestness to achieve our goals, we shall have an opportunity to succeed? As one of our ancient prophets has said, "For behold, this is a land which is choice above all other lands . . . and whatsoever nation shall possess it shall be free from bondage, and from captivity, and from all other nations under heaven, if they will but serve the God of the land, who is Jesus Christ. . . ." (Ether 2:10-12.) Any nation whose people will serve God and keep his commandments will likewise be free.

Shortly before he died, Joshua, a great Israelite leader, made this memorable statement: "Choose you this day whom ye will serve; . . . but as for me and my house, we will serve the Lord." (Joshua 24:15.)

The word *choose* implies that we have the freedom, right, and privilege to choose; man is the only creature that can think and reason, know right from wrong, and choose his course. *You* means that it is up to you and to me—to all of us—to make our own choices and to take full responsibility for them and for the consequences that will follow. *This day* means that now, today, is the time to choose, to determine our course, not tomorrow, for there is no tomorrow—only today—and if there were a tomorrow, it might be too late. *Whom* means whom or what God we will serve. And *serve* is not a passive acceptance of lip service, but full acceptance of all that the word implies.

Life is made up of choices: what to eat, what to wear, what to do, where to go, etc. We either choose the right or we reject it. The choices we make determine the extent of our future success and happiness and also the contribution we are able to make to the world.

Our first great choice was made in the council of heaven in the spirit world, where all of us were present. It was in this council that Satan, the son of morning, came forward with a plan whereby he would come to earth and force all mankind to be saved and bring them back to God. By accepting his plan, man would have lost his free agency; therefore, Satan's plan was rejected. He and a third of the hosts of heaven who followed him rebelled and were cast out.

When Satan's plan was rejected, Jesus Christ came forth with his plan and said that he would teach the plan of life and salvation that would make it possible for man to come back into the presence of God, but would let men choose for themselves. We who are here today have come to earth because we chose to follow his plan. It was this choice that makes it possible for us through our mortal existence to enjoy our free agency—God's greatest gift to man.

Free agency is the prime purpose of man's mortal existence, for it affords him the opportunity to choose between good and evil, virtue and vice, life and death. Imagine our state of existence if we should lose the right

to choose. Today, however, we are being threatened with
the loss of this most precious gift. In fact, as a result of
their lack of appreciation and understanding of the value
of free agency, many people in countries that are dominated by dictators have practically lost their freedom. At
all costs, we must maintain our free agency—the right to
choose.

When Adam and Eve were placed in the Garden of
Eden they were told not to partake of the forbidden fruit;
but God said, ". . . nevertheless, thou mayest choose for
thyself." (Moses 3:17.) He pointed out the consequences
of their actions and left them to choose for themselves. All
down through the ages as recorded in the ecclesiastical
and secular histories of the world, men have made their
choices and have received the blessings or suffered the
consequences of their actions.

Sir Winston Churchill once said, "I have seen many
things happen, but the fact remains that human life is presented to us as a simple choice between right and wrong."
One of our ancient prophets said, ". . . men are, that they
might have joy." (2 Nephi 2:25.) And the Lord said, "For
behold, this is my work and my glory—to bring to pass the
immortality and eternal life of man." (Moses 1:39.) He
also said, ". . . seek ye first the kingdom of God, and his
righteousness; and all these things shall be added unto
you" (Matthew 6:33), with a further promise that "I, the
Lord, am bound when ye do what I say; but when ye do
not what I say, ye have no promise" (D&C 82:10).

In all of these admonitions we are free to choose and
take the consequences. Abraham Lincoln made his position
clear when he said, "God rules this world and I am a full
believer that He knows what he wants men to do—that
which pleases Him. It is never well for that man who heeds
it not. Without that assistance from that Divine Being I
cannot succeed, and with it I cannot fail."

My purpose is not to tell anyone how to choose or

what he should do; but I am convinced that it is most important that we decide at an early age just what we want out of life; what we want to accomplish; what we want to be; the kind of community in which we want to live; the kind of parents we want to be and the kind of families we want to have; and whether or not we want to serve God and keep his commandments. No one else can make our decisions for us, nor would anyone want to make them; that is our own responsibility. The power of choice is with each one of us, and the roads are clearly marked: one that offers an unhappy existence, and the other life abundant.

My close association with young people throughout the years has convinced me that with very few exceptions, they all really want to enjoy life, to accomplish something worthwhile, and to be recognized and respected. However, we are sometimes faced with the question, "Why do we choose to go against basic principles of truth, sometimes deliberately?" It is not because a person wants the result that is sure to follow; it may be that he is trying to be popular for the time being. Some will do almost anything, even to the breaking of laws, to get attention. To compromise, of course, only leads to regret and sorrow. Choose the right, stand by your standards, and let the consequence follow. No one has ever regretted having followed the teachings of Christ. Those who refuse to follow always come to the day of repentance or sorrow.

Again, I wish to emphasize that we do have our free agency to choose what we will do, and the choice is fairly and squarely before us as to whether we accept God as the Creator of the world and accept the principles of the gospel as laid down by Jesus Christ, or whether we choose to keep the commandments of men who profess to be Christians.

With this freedom and responsibility, man needs a purpose and a cause or an aim toward which to work. It is only natural that we would like to choose that which will bring us the greatest joy and success and satisfaction as we go through life and that which will lead us to eternal life. Paul Edmond has said, "The whole theory of the universe is pointed unerringly to one individual, namely, you." The whole world was made for you and me to dwell on. We are God's children and his most important creation. And as Goethe has said, "The whole purpose of the world seems to be to provide a physical basis for the growth of the spirit."

Let us remember that God created man in his own image; that he "so loved the world, that he gave his only begotten Son, that whosoever believeth in him should not perish, but have everlasting life" (John 3:16); that through the atonement of Jesus Christ all mankind may be saved; and that through obedience to the laws and ordinances of the gospel all may enjoy eternal life and exaltation. As Milton so wisely said, "The end of all learning is to know God, and out of that learning to love and imitate him."

Let us consider briefly what one of our modern-day prophets has said:

I believe in God's law. I believe that it is his right to rule in the world. I believe that no man has or should have any valid objection in his mind to the government of God, and the rule of Jesus Christ, in the earth. Let us suppose, for a moment, that Christ were here and that he was bearing rule in the world. Who would come under his condemnation? Who would be subject to his chastening word? Who would be in disharmony or unfellowship with God? Would the righteous man? Would the virtuous man? The pure and virtuous woman? The pure and honest in heart? The upright? The straightforward? Those who do the will of heaven? Would they be in rebellion to Christ's rule, if he were to come here to rule? No. They would welcome the rule and reign of Jesus Christ in the earth. They would welcome his law and acknowledge his sovereignty, they would hasten to rally to his standard and to uphold the purpose and the perfection of his laws and of his righteousness. Who would, then, be recreant to the rule of Christ? The whoremonger, the adulterer, the liar, the sorcerer, he who bears false witness against his neighbor, he who seeks to take advantage of his brother, and who would overcome and destroy him for his own worldly gain or profit; the murderer, the despiser of that which is good, the unbeliever in the eternities that lie before us, the atheist, perhaps, although I think that he would not be so far from Christ as some who profess to be teachers of his doctrines and advocates of his laws. It would be the rebellious, the wicked, those who would oppress their neighbors and enslave them if they could. Such as these would be the people who would not welcome the reign of Christ. (Joseph F. Smith, *Gospel Doctrine*, Deseret Book Co., 1971, p. 54.)

When the world was created, God blessed man and commanded him to replenish the earth and subdue it, and gave him dominion over every living thing that lives upon the earth. It is important that we take our places in the world, that we contribute wherever we can to the welfare of man and to the building up of our communities, and the improving of conditions therein, that we prepare ourselves to make the greatest contribution possible. It is also essential to remember that when men put forth all their efforts acquiring temporal goods and possessions and power and positions, they are seeking things of secondary value or importance. The choosing of those things which will ensure success of the soul is our most important responsibility and privilege and will bring lasting joy to all. To gain success of the soul, one must apply the principles of the gospel and accept the challenge which is his. Let us remember that religious life does more than anything else to strengthen an individual, and that man is the only creature that has been given the ability to think, reason, and choose between right and wrong. There can be no fullness of life where there is slavery, and as we break the laws of God, as we become addicted to bad habits and become subject to our appetites and passions, we become the most abject slaves. *We remain free only as we choose the right.*

If we choose to serve the Lord, let us do so with all our might, mind, and strength. Let us be not ashamed of the gospel of Christ or make apologies for following him.

By choosing to keep the laws and commandments of God, which include the laws of nature and the laws of the land, and by striving to improve the conditions of our fellowmen, we make our right of choice more secure. Also, the more we choose to serve others, realizing that "even as you have done it unto one of the least of these my brethren, you have done it unto me," the happier we will be and the greater progress we will make. Our mental attitude and the extent to which we have disciplined and are prepared to discipline ourselves will determine the quality of service we give. The old saying, "The service we give is the rent we pay for the privilege of living in this old world" is true. The greater and better the service we give, the better world we will have to live in. One never needs to try to improve himself or his position at the cost of others. To be of true service to our fellowmen, which includes our children, we appraise that which has been passed on to us as our heritage and then go forth with courage, stamina, faith, and determination to maintain and improve it. We must not take things for granted.

The greatest achievement in life is not the acquisition of money, position, or power. In my opinion, it is to come to the end of one's day having been true and loyal to his ideals. I can think of no achievement greater than that.

Anyone can take the easy road and succumb to temptation, even the animal. Character is developed by overcoming.

Life here and hereafter is one continual existence, premortal to postmortal, without a break in this endless chain. As we go from one stage to another, we must realize that all we can take with us is ourselves—that is, our intelligence, character, and experience. We must realize, however, that we are the children of God, and with that spark of divinity in us, our possibilities are unlimited. We should never be persuaded to deprive our minds or to debauch our bodies or sell our freedom for temporary gain, or sell our heritage for a mess of pottage.

All I am suggesting is that we should ask ourselves these questions: Why am I here? What are my problems? What do I want to accomplish? Do I wish to be successful in my life? What kind of parent do I want my children to have? Do I wish to find the greatest joy—the joy of the soul?

Each one of us is the architect of his own fate. If we determine to follow the teachings of God, we have first to make up our minds to that end and then discipline ourselves, realizing that the laws of nature and the commandments of God are not always convenient. They do not bend themselves to our convenience. We are all happier and better off when we adapt ourselves to the commandments.

As we make our choices wisely, God will give us clear vision, strong wills, courageous hearts. And, having chosen wisely, may we, with heads erect, have open countenances indicating that we have wronged no one; and even though the tasks of life may become heavy, and sorrow may weigh upon us, may the light of Christ's life beckon us on still undismayed. May we all choose wisely whom we will serve—and may that choice be to serve the Lord.

CHAPTER 13

Reverence for Law

Every citizen should be sincerely concerned with his country's efforts to advance freedom and individual opportunity, to curb lawlessness, and to achieve equal justice for all.

We are most fortunate to be able to live in a land which is choice above all other lands. There is no other place where the people enjoy such high standards of living, where they can choose their lives and what they will be, worship according to the dictates of their own conscience, and go and come as they choose. It is a land that is governed by law, not by force.

We as a people, then, have greater responsibility than people any place else in the world to obey, honor, and sustain the law. I like the Church declaration of belief regarding governments and laws:

We believe that governments were instituted of God for the benefit of man; and that he holds men accountable for their acts in relation to them, both in making laws and administering them, for the good and safety of society.

We believe that no government can exist in peace, except such laws are framed and held inviolate as will secure to each individual the free exercise of conscience, the right and control of property, and the protection of life.

We believe that all men are bound to sustain and uphold the respective governments in which they reside, while protected in their inherent and inalienable rights by the laws of such governments; and that sedition and rebellion are unbecoming every citizen thus protected, and should be punished accordingly; and that all governments have a right to enact such laws as in their own judgments are best calculated to secure the public interest; at the same time, however, holding sacred the freedom of conscience.

We believe that every man should be honored in his station, rulers and magistrates as such, being placed for the protection of the innocent and the punishment of the guilty; and that to the laws all men owe respect and deference, as without them peace and harmony would be supplanted by anarchy and terror; human laws being instituted for the express purpose of regulating our interests as individuals and nations, between man and man; and divine laws given of heaven, prescribing rules on spiritual concerns, for faith and worship, both to be answered by man to his Maker.

We believe that the commission of crime should be punished according to the nature of the offense; that murder, treason, robbery, theft, and the breach of the general peace, in all respects, should be punished according to their criminality and their tendency to evil among men, by the laws of that government in which the offense is committed; and for the public peace and tranquility all men should step forward and use their ability in bringing offenders against good laws to punishment. (D&C 134:1-2, 5-6, 8.)

Laws are not made alone to curb the evil doer or as a negative restraint, nor as a static drag on the efforts of free men, but to protect the rights and liberties of every citizen. We must not be blind to the basic knowledge of law because of some of the restraints that specific laws place on our activities.

As John C. Cornelius said, "Laws are the rules by which the game of life is played."

In fact, it is law that brings order into the affairs of men and that enables them to plan for the future, to accumulate possessions, to develop the arts, to pursue knowledge, and to enjoy life among their fellows. Without it, free society could not be held together.

There is no reason nor justification for men to disregard the law and try to take it into their own hands. As

Abraham Lincoln once said: "Bad laws, if they exist, should be repealed as soon as possible; still, while they continue in force, they should be religiously observed."

Christ himself, while here upon the earth, was one of our greatest examples of a law-abiding citizen. When he was asked by those who were trying to discredit him, "What thinkest thou? Is it lawful to give tribute unto Caesar, or not?" his answer was, "Render . . . unto Caesar the things which are Caesar's; and unto God the things that are God's." (Matthew 22:17, 21.)

And even when he was being tried for his life, he maintained a submissive demeanor toward the chief priests and council who were plotting his death. When he stood before Caiaphas he remained silent and made no reply to the questions asked until the high priest said, "I adjure thee by the living God, that thou tell us whether thou be the Christ, the Son of God." (Matthew 26:63.) When the high priest spoke thus with official authority, the Savior gave an immediate answer, thus acknowledging the office of the high priest, however unworthy the man.

Someone wisely said, "To us law is the bedrock of our basic ideals: democracy, freedom, justice. However, from day to day most of us take the law for granted. We forget about it until we need it or break it, but law looks over our shoulders constantly, seldom intruding on us, so much a part of our lives that it has become more of a guide than a restriction, more protection than threat of punishment."

Here in the United States, and in most democratic countries, everyone has the right—

1. to a good education,
2. to live where he pleases,
3. to choose his vocation,
4. to own property,
5. to a secret ballot,
6. to start his own business,
7. to a fair and speedy trial if accused of crime, and

8. to worship according to the dictates of his own conscience.

These rights, privileges, and blessings are just not available to those who live in communist countries. It is a great privilege to live in a country where all people, regardless of race, religion, or national origin, can live together in peace and prosperity; where we have established a form of law by free men for the good of all; where all men enjoy the inalienable right to be free and self-governed in a country that has given independence to its former possessions, and that is spending billions of dollars sharing its resources and sacrificing manpower to help other countries enjoy government by law and not by force.

The greatness of our Constitution and government by law is attested by the fact that the United States today, despite its comparative youth, is one of the great powers and has one of the oldest governments in existence. Our democratic way of life where free men make the laws has contributed greatly to the stability of the country, the civil rights of man, a keen sense of justice, and a large measure of social progress.

Our present way of life, however, is being threatened on all sides, and we have only one great security. As one citizen has said:

We may think that our Constitution or our statutes are our security. They are nothing but words on a piece of paper. We may feel that our government is our security. None of these has any force whatever unless the citizens have a sound and uncorrupted public opinion which will give life to our Constitution, vitality to our statutes, and to make our government machinery efficient. . . .

We must never allow ourselves to be deluded by men using cunning devices such as monetary discouragement or temporary panic or a fit of enthusiasm for an individual who would cause us to follow him and trust him with powers which would take away our liberties and enable him to subvert our institutions.

Thus a continuation and strengthening of respect for the laws of the land and the manner in which justice is administered becomes for each loyal American citizen a matter of survival, to say nothing of the legal and moral obligations involved. From day to day it is the responsibility of every citizen to strengthen his own and his neighbor's collective respect for law and order. This is a small price to pay for liberty and the other blessings that Americans enjoy.

One must never forget that vigilance is the price of liberty. We often ask the question, Why are Americans prepared to take these things for granted, and fail to accept their responsibility?

One thing that makes it difficult for Americans to become aware of the need of dedication to the law and its maintenance is because we are just too comfortable and well taken care of. John W. Gardner, government and business leader, said:

> The men who founded this nation knew that in a world largely hostile to the idea of freedom, a free society would have to prove that it is capable of, and worthy of, survival. The requirement is unchanged today. Free societies must prove their ability to make good on their promises and to keep alive their cherished values. And they must prove their vigor, their capacity to practice the disciplined virtues. Above all, they must prove their capacity to achieve excellence.
>
> The free society is still the exceptional society, and the world is still full of people who believe that men need masters. The survival of the idea for which this nation stands is not inevitable. It may survive if enough Americans care enough.
>
> It would be easier to grasp that truth if we weren't so blessedly comfortable. Part of our problem is how to stay awake on a full stomach. Since the beginning of time most humans have had to work hard either because subsistence demanded it or because their taskmasters required it. Now we don't have to work very hard to stay alive; and free people have no taskmasters. With such release from outward pressures, free men may make the fatal mistake of thinking that no effort is required of them.
>
> Nothing could be more dangerous to our future. Free men must be quick to understand the kinds of effort that are required to keep their society vital and strong. If they have the wisdom to demand much of themselves, their society will flourish. But a free society that refuses to exert itself will not last long. And freedom alone won't save it.

We should all pay strict heed to the words of Abraham Lincoln, wherein he said:

Let reverence for the law be breathed by every American mother to the lisping babe that prattles on her lap; let it be taught in schools, in seminaries and in colleges; let it be written in primers, spelling books and almanacs; let it be preached from the pulpit, proclaimed in legislative halls and enforced in courts of justice. And, in short, let it become the political religion of the nation; and let the old and the young, the rich and the poor, the grave and the gay of all sexes and tongues and colors and conditions sacrifice unceasingly upon its altars.

And let us never forget that we adults can break no law with impunity without our children losing respect for the law. Everything we prize so highly and enjoy most depends on honoring, obeying, and sustaining the law. The juvenile delinquent is in trouble because he has not learned the importance of abiding by the law or has not learned to adjust his conduct to the standards of the community of which he is a part. Some causes of the delinquent's troubles are:

1. Disregard for law in the home.
2. Lack of discipline in the home.
3. Example of adults.
4. Expressed sympathy for criminals and criticism of police.
5. Failure to accept Christ as the Savior of the world.
6. Failure to keep the laws of God.

The only solution to these problems is for adults to honor the laws of God and the laws of the land, and to cultivate in our youth an understanding of and respect for the rules of civilized living that make an orderly society possible. A voluntary acceptance of the law is the civilized substitute for riots, chaos, and terror.

Though we hear much of the juvenile delinquent, I have every confidence in our youth, and I often wish that I could live long enough to see how much better they administer public affairs than they are being administered today. However, they need guidance, example, courage, and discipline.

I think a "Modern American Fable" by Al McIntosh illustrates well this point:

One day, when Junior was fourteen, he noticed his father grinning all over when he came home from the office. "Got pinched for speeding," he admitted, "but got Jake down at the City Hall to fix the ticket for me."

When Junior was fifteen, he was with his mother in the family car when she backed into a tree. The damage would easily exceed $100. "We'll say that someone rammed us when we were parked downtown," his mother said. "Then we'll collect insurance for it, because that's what insurance companies are really for."

When Junior was sixteen, he listened to grandfather reminisce about "the good old days of rationing," when he made thousands of dollars black-marketing cars.

That same night Uncle John was bragging that on a good share of his business he sent no bills and took no checks—just cash. "Why be a sucker and let them punks in Washington get it all?" he said.

When Junior was seventeen, he listened one night to his lawyer uncle bragging about how cute he'd been in getting his client off scot-free in a court case. "It took a little high-class arm twisting on one of the witnesses," he bragged, "and by the time he got to court, we had it made. Even if you know they're guilty, you never want to plead them guilty, because you can't make any money at that," said the uncle.

When Junior was eighteen, his family pulled every possible string to get him a paying scholarship at a coveted Ivy League school. They even storied about the family income, to make it seem that Junior needed financial aid. He didn't make the grade there, but by a stroke of good luck he wangled an appointment to a service academy.

Junior was having it a bit tough scholastically. An upperclassman sold him the answers to the calculus examinations. Junior was caught and expelled.

On his return home his mother went into paroxysms of hysterical weeping over the disgrace. "How could you have done this to us?" she sobbed. "This isn't the way we raised you!"

"Unbelieveable," said the father. "I can't understand it." (First published in *Western Voice*, Englewood, Colorado.)

We as citizens, each and every one of us, including our youth, have a heavy responsibility to obey and enforce the law. Imagine what our country would be today without law! No traffic regulations, no marriage laws, no property rights, no police protection, no courts of justice.

Yet we find all too many people rushing to beat an amber light, speeding on the highways, driving while intoxicated, ignoring marriage vows, carrying on illegal demonstrations and rioting, collecting undeserved employment insurance, and breaking the law in many other ways.

In a recent case a sixteen-year-old boy obtained alcohol from a liquor store and, under its influence, stole a truck and crashed into a parked taxi, causing severe injuries to the driver. Since the regulations at that time forbade the sale of liquor to those under twenty-one, the government employee who sold the liquor broke the law and contributed to juvenile delinquency.

Just the other day a drunken driver ran a red light and crashed into another car, killing two people, ruining two cars, and injuring other passengers. What a tremendous loss to him and to the families of those who lost their lives, and what a great loss and lasting sorrow because of his ignoring the law! We have cases every day where people are suffering because of disobedience to law.

We have learned that in abiding by the law, individuals can live together in peace as families; families as communities or municipalities; municipalities in the states; states in the Union—all of which have been good for mankind, giving them greater opportunities, greater security, and greater protection.

One of the most important and urgent challenges to everyone today is to establish peace in the world. This can be done by international law if mankind will set its mind to it. These things, however, can be achieved only by dedicated men who are interested in liberty and justice for mankind, using all of their vision, wisdom, talent, and vitality to attain these goals.

As Judge Learned Hand said:

Liberty lies in the hearts of men and women; when it dies there, no constitution, no law, no court can save it. No constitution, no law, no court can ever do much to help it. . . . The spirit of liberty is the spirit which seeks to understand the minds of other men and women. The spirit of liberty is the spirit which weighs their interests alongside its own without bias. The spirit of liberty remembers that not even a sparrow falls to earth unheeded. The spirit of liberty is the spirit of Him who, near two thousand years ago, taught mankind that lesson it has never learned, but has never quite forgotten: that there may be a kingdom where the least shall be heard and considered side by side with the greatest.

We have long espoused freedom and justice for man as the promise of the world. We must now espouse the rule of law as the one and only way to achieve and maintain peace, freedom, and justice among and within nations. Freedom, liberty, and peace can be fully enjoyed only as the laws of the land and the laws of God are honored and obeyed. Therefore, let us adopt the slogan: "As for me and my house, we will honor, obey, and sustain the law, and use our best influence to encourage others to do the same, and to enforce it."

Let us remember too, and never forget, that if we keep the laws of God, the greatest of all law givers, we will automatically keep the laws of the land, and that the laws of God, if kept, will ensure peace, security, and happiness here on this earth, and lead us to immortality and eternal life.

CHAPTER 14

Our Civic Responsibilities

The question is often asked, How can good Church members honor and sustain the law of the land in the different countries in which they live? We all know that governments of the different countries vary greatly. The answer is given to us in the fifth verse of section 134 of the Doctrine and Covenants:

We believe that all men are bound to sustain and uphold the respective governments in which they reside, while protected in their inherent and inalienable rights by the laws of such governments; and that sedition and rebellion are unbecoming every citizen thus protected, and should be punished accordingly; and that all governments have a right to enact such laws as in their own judgments are best calculated to secure the public interest; at the same time, however, holding sacred the freedom of conscience.

A member of the Church can honor and sustain the law and make the greatest contribution to his country and to the welfare of mankind by (1) obeying strictly all the laws of the land; (2) teaching his children, by precept and by example, to honor and sustain the law and those in authority, in the home, in the community, and in the Church; (3) using his best influence to improve the law by all legal means at his disposal; (4) striving to elect good, honorable men to office and actively supporting them; (5) being prepared to accept office and serve diligently in the best interests of the community and country; and (6) observing and keeping the laws of God.

The Attorney General of the State of Utah, Vernon B. Romney, made a significant statement some time ago: "No secular endeavor gives a person more opportunity to do good on behalf of his fellowmen than does the field of government and politics." To this I would add public service. Then he added, "Nevertheless, no other field can be more misused by crooks, grafters, and charlatans unconcerned about the welfare of their fellow citizens."

In recent decades we have seen great centralizing of government authority and power, and this is something that each citizen must guard against if we are to continue to enjoy the democratic form of government which has made it possible for America to progress beyond any other country. Those in government are responsible for trying to administer affairs in the best interest of the people whom they represent, and never doing for the people what they are capable of doing for themselves.

This country was founded on the cornerstone of individual liberty and personal responsibility. You cannot have one without the other. Realizing this, our constitutional fathers set up a government dedicated to the proposition that we as individuals are to provide for our own welfare and not be dominated by or dependent upon government. President Grover Cleveland, who vetoed a bill that was to give to the farmers certain seeds, said, "Though the people should support the government, the government should not support the people." And let us not forget the words of Thomas Jefferson, author of the Declaration of Independence, who said, "That government governs best which governs least."

We are most fortunate to enjoy the blessings and privileges of a democratic form of government. When I became a citizen of the United States some years ago, I made this statement:

> I am determined to join with all law-abiding citizens, to dedicate myself to this nation's ideals of equality and justice under law, and to our responsibility as free men. The Constitution, together with the Bill of Rights, is meant to insure for each of us the rights to which people everywhere are entitled. It is to these principles and the principles of democracy and belief in God that the United States has become the most powerful, prosperous and freest country in all the world.

Every American citizen should be sincerely concerned with the nation's efforts to advance freedom, individual opportunity, curb lawlessness, and achieve equal justice. It is a land that is governed by law, not force. The law of the land is a set of rules established by free people. Those who enter government as civil or public administrators or as representatives of the people have the responsibility to uphold our form of government and see that it works.

Our national birthright is a country where all people, regardless of race, religion, or national origin, can live together in peace and prosperity, and it is the responsibility of those administering the law and the citizens together to do all in their power to see that this birthright is maintained.

The Lord has declared that the Constitution of the United States was established "by the hands of wise men whom I raised up unto this very purpose." Article Five of the Constitution provides a way whereby it can be amended. Pursuant to that Article, there have been twenty-six amendments, the last of which was ratified on June 30, 1971, and lowered the voting age to eighteen years. This amending clause provided for needed flexibility in the Constitution, and the stringent conditions for amending it give assurance that the Constitution will not be changed for frivolous reasons. Consequently, changes adopted in the prescribed way are as much a part of the Constitution as the original document. In fact, one of the most important parts of the Constitution, the Bill of Rights, became part of it by the amending process.

One of the heavy responsibilities of those who administer public affairs is to participate fully in community enterprises and also to help the people to understand the importance and blessing of our democratic form of government by example and precept.

Those who have gone before are responsible for what America is. And each of us today has a great responsibility to determine what America is going to become. Our challenge is to continue to study changing conditions in the world and to be prepared to meet these exciting challenges and concern ourselves seriously with these conditions so as to be able to do our part to help in solving them. We should always remember that while these many changes are taking place and much progress is being made, none of the fundamentals have altered, nor will they alter. The laws of nature, although not fully understood, have not changed, nor have the laws of God.

In order for those in public life to serve their fellow citizens as they should, it is important that they recognize and help develop the religious and moral nature of American society. Though we are living in a materialistic society, we must realize that material things, though important, will not in themselves bring happiness to the owner.

To enjoy life to the full, one cannot neglect the spiritual side. We must acknowledge God as the giver of all things, as the Creator of the earth and the universe, and as the Father of our spirits, and realize that he has given a plan of life that will lead us to salvation.

A question often asked is: How can we compete in a materialistic world and still remain active in the Church and live according to the teachings of the gospel?

My answer is, and always has been, "Seek ye first the kingdom of God, and his righteousness; and all these things [meaning everything for your good] shall be added unto you." (Matthew 6:33)

There is no doubt that if a man loses himself in service—whether he be in government, a civil engineer, a teacher, doctor, lawyer, or in any other profession or trade—and will go forward with the idea of giving the best possible service, being honest, true, chaste, benevolent, and virtuous, he will be loved and respected and admired by all.

While in government service I prayed continually for guidance and that I would never do anything that would embarrass the Church in any way. And I can assure you that I received guidance on different occasions. "Counsel with the Lord in all thy doings, and he will direct thee for good. . . ." (Alma 37:37.)

President Joseph F. Smith said:

It is nonetheless our patriotic duty to guard our nation whenever and wherever we can against those changeable and revolutionary tendencies which are destructive of a nation's weal and permanence.

No man can be a good Latter-day Saint and not be true to the best interests and general welfare of his country. The allegiance claimed from the members of the Church does not prevent a member from being a loyal citizen to the nation. . . . A good Latter-day Saint is a good citizen in every way. I desire to say to the young men of our community, be exemplary Latter-day Saints and let nothing deter you from aspiring to the greatest position which our nation has to offer. Having secured a place, let your virtue, your integrity, your honesty, your ability, your religious teachings that have been implanted in your heart at the knees of your devoted . . . mother, so shine before men that they may see your good works and glorify your Father which is in Heaven.

Every person builds his own personality and then in turn his personality determines almost every other situation in his life. We may employ our personalities in the search for power and pleasure, or war or peace, or in our quest to inherit eternal life and happiness. One must determine whether he will use his personal qualities in the pursuit of his own glory or in the making of money, or in serving his fellowmen, or in some other field. One of the amazing wonders of the world is to see the potential power that one's personality has. One may print what you say as a sermon or as a discourse on any subject, and it is easy to put down on paper a man's theme, his paragraphs, his words, his objectives, and his illustrations. But even after all this you still don't have the man, nor can you write his personality.

As one assumes or accepts public service, he must be prepared to discipline himself and keep himself above reproach. I had the good fortune of working very closely with the Premier of Alberta, who is an excellent example of the miracle of personality. This was the Honorable E. C. Manning. He was born and raised on a farm in a rural area of Saskatchewan in a very humble home. In fact, he worked on the farm with his overalls being held together by a nail. However, he had high ideals. He became interested in religion and his fellowmen. He set out to learn all he could about the Bible and how to improve conditions in the country.

He worked and studied and prepared until the public became aware of the kind of person he was. He was elected to the Alberta Legislature when he was only twenty-seven years old and appointed to the Cabinet the same year as the youngest minister ever to hold a cabinet position in the British Empire. He later became leader of the political party and Premier of the Province. He was a man of great integrity. People from all political parties respected and trusted him to the extent they crossed party lines and voted for him. As a result, his party remained in power for thirty-five years with him as Premier until he voluntarily resigned. Even while he was Premier, with all the heavy responsibilities of his position, he preached from the Bible every Sunday over radio throughout Canada. He was 100 percent trustworthy and sincere, with no hypocrisy of any kind. When he resigned as Premier of the Province, the Federal Government, of a different political party, showed its confidence in him by appointing him as Senator of Canada. This is an honorary lifetime position.

It is not what you have or what you control, but it is what you are that determines the kind of service you will give and the influence you have and the real success you will achieve. So often men in office are not strong enough to live by their standards, but are influenced through selfishness, pride, and self-aggrandizement. I know of men who, when they assumed office, were very highly regarded, but through socializing, social drinking, etc., have thrown away their bright future and have actually ruined and lost all they might have had.

We who know that we are spirit children of God should realize more than any other that our potential is unlimited and that it is impossible for us to estimate the great influence an individual can have on the lives of others and even on government. A poem appropriate to this theme says:

Trust in thine own untried capacity
As thou wouldst trust in God himself.
Thy soul is but an emanation from the whole;
Thou dost not dream what forces lie in thee—
Vast, unfathomed as the grandest sea.

No man can place a limit on thy strength;
Such triumph as no mortal ever dreamed may yet be thine
If thou wilt but believe in thy Creator and thyself.
At length some feet shall stand on heights now unattained;
Why not thine own? Press on—achieve, achieve!

And as William Shakespeare so aptly said, "To thine own self be true, and it must follow, as the night the day, thou canst not then be false to any man."

CHAPTER 15

The Blessings of Obedience

We are all concerned about conditions in the world today, and are searching for answers to the many problems that are affecting our personal lives, our communities, and countries throughout the world. Though it is true that the trend in the world today is toward lawlessness, rioting, and rebellion, we are sick and tired of having it played up so much both in conversation and in news media. We, with a positive approach, need to center our efforts on living and teaching the gospel, thereby eliminating the cause and improving conditions. Every man, including the rebellious, who is honest with himself must admit that what he is ultimately seeking is happiness and a better way of life.

Recently I was talking to a young man who said, in effect, "I am fed up and tired of being told, 'You *have* to do this,' or 'You *have* to do that.' I want to be free to decide for myself what I want to do."

My response was: "You *are* free to choose *exactly* what you want to do, as long as it does not restrict or impose on the rights or liberties of others, but you must be responsible for your acts and prepared to take the consequences."

I explained that the Lord's greatest gift to mortal man is threefold: first, the right to immortality and eternal life; second, the plan by which he can gain it; third, his free agency to choose what he will do. The Lord gave us the plan which will bring us the greatest joy and happiness on this earth and which will prepare us for eternal life. All we have to do to enjoy this is to obey the law and keep his commandments.

I suggested to this young man that he consider with me the physical or natural laws, which are fixed and immutable, and which apply to all, regardless of their station or learning or intention. If a person, whether knowingly, ignorantly, intentionally, or accidentally, touches a hot stove or a bare high-voltage wire, he will be burned to the extent of the exposure. If for any reason he steps in front of a rapidly moving vehicle, even to save another life, he will be injured and possibly killed. Numerous examples could be given to show that we are subject to these laws regardless of who we are or what our intentions might be. We cannot change the laws of nature.

As we understand the natural laws and respect them, we can apply them to our good. If we violate law, we suffer; and if we obey it, we are blessed. How fortunate we are to know that we can depend on these natural laws; that the sun will rise at a certain time every morning; that electricity, though we don't know exactly what it is, will respond always under the same conditions; that the sun will be eclipsed by the moon at a certain time on a certain day in a certain year, all because the laws of nature never vary. Imagine an engineer, doctor, or scientist in any field not being able to depend on the laws of nature, or disregarding them. Man can never ignore the natural laws affecting his operations and be successful. In fact, to ignore them could be disastrous.

All the laws of God and the laws of nature and the laws of the land are made for the benefit of man, for his comfort, enjoyment, safety, and well-being; and it is up to the individual to learn these laws and to determine whether or not he will enjoy these benefits by obeying the law and by keeping the commandments. Laws do exist for our benefit, and to be successful and happy, we must obey the laws and regulations pertaining to our activities; and these laws will function either to our joy and well-being or to our detriment and sorrow, according to our actions.

To accomplish man's great flights to the moon, every law of nature affecting this endeavor has to be kept in the most minute detail. The law of physics, the law of chemistry, the law of gravity, and every other law pertaining to the flights have to be understood and applied by those who are concerned and engaged in the preparations. They do not think of these laws as being restrictions or impediments to them in any way, but rather as a means by which they may carry out their program; and they are determined to learn all they can about the laws on which their success is dependent, and to obey or apply them so they might be successful in their mission.

This is so true in life. To be a musician, to be an athlete, to get a degree, to accomplish anything worthwhile, we must set our goals, determine what we want to do and wish to accomplish, and set about to find out which laws if obeyed will make this possible, and then discipline ourselves in order to accomplish it. When we do this, we are on our way to success, while those who continually fight the laws and refuse to obey, and who complain about things that are required, become frustrated, begin to rebel and fail to accomplish.

As someone has said, you do not break the law, but actually break yourself by refusing to respect it as it applies to your condition. The law applies, and our actions determine the result. Too often we are not prepared to discipline ourselves and do that which is necessary to accomplish the things we desire most.

If all people were to recognize law as a benefit to man and then honor and obey it, it would contribute greatly to our health, well-being, and happiness. Laws are essential. Imagine a city, community, state, or country without law and regulations. To the extent we disregard, disobey, or flout the law, we are losing our freedom, depriving others of theirs, and leading to anarchy. If a bad law exists, then the people should take proper legal measures through their governing bodies to improve or change the law, but while it is law, it should be obeyed.

In life generally we have to determine the kind of life or environment of which we want to be a part. We still have in the human race today people in the jungles who practice cannibalism, where the animal instincts in man rule, and where the laws of the jungle apply. If that is the kind of life we wish, it is available to us. Part of the purpose of our existence, however, is to rise above these animal instincts and to teach the highest plane of human behavior in our social relations.

In order that we may accomplish this, God, our Father, and his Son, Jesus Christ, have given us laws which, if applied in our lives, will improve our social conditions and our relationships to one another. Yes, if all of us would obey these laws, we would have none of the disturbing conditions so prevalent today, and our young people would have no reason, need, nor desire to demonstrate against a society that today does not practice what it preaches.

Let us refer to some of the Ten Commandments, which are as applicable today as they were in the time of Moses, and which later were taught by Christ. If everyone would obey the commandments, "Thou shalt not steal, kill, covet, commit adultery, or bear false witness," we could leave our homes or properties unattended, walk down the street any place at any time, or feel secure in our homes, without fear of thieves or robbers, or that someone might be trying to take our lives.

Imagine too the joy of living in a community in which there were no covetousness, backbiting, or adultery; where everyone was living according to the law. In addition to the peaceful and happy existence we would lead, and the strength and help we could be to one another, just think of the money we would save on law enforcement and the effects of crime, all of which money could be diverted to fighting poverty, or improving health and educational facilities, and for other worthwhile purposes. We cannot begin to number the temporal blessings we would receive from obedience to these commandments.

Another commandment that is so important in the lives of all of us in the Lord's law of health, which is called the Word of Wisdom, and which should be taught in every home by example and by precept. In this Word of Wisdom we are warned against the use of tobacco and alcohol and other things that are harmful to the body. I am sure we can include the use of drugs.

Though this law of health was given to us by the Lord over a hundred years ago, it was generally ignored until scientists and experience proved beyond doubt that these things are not only harmful to the body, but are a menace to society. Many *still* ignore and defy this law, and are prepared to take the risks. The use of these things results in broken homes, diseased and broken bodies and spirits, destruction of property, misery, and death on the highway, and many other tragedies too numerous to mention, all of which are now causing society, lawmakers, law enforcement officers, and all of us serious concern.

In just one evening I gleaned the following information from reading the newspaper:

One-car fatal accidents double this year.

Twenty-six percent of all fatal accidents occurred after the driver had been drinking.

A well-known television personality died of lung cancer at age 45. He had publicly stated he would rather smoke and take a chance than be a "fat neurotic." He quit when he learned he had cancer.

A hotel fire caused by a cigarette claimed 14 lives, and a burning cigarette in another building caused ten thousand dollars worth of damage.

Marijuana harm is very real, and drugs put blinders on youth.

We owe it to ourselves, to our youth, to the future of our country, to restrict and if possible do away entirely with the use of these devilish and deleterious things that are causing so much tragedy in the world today.

Let me refer to another very important commandment, which is: "Remember the sabbath day, to keep it holy. Six days shalt thou labour, and do all thy work: But the seventh day is the sabbath of the Lord thy God: in it thou shalt not do any work." (Exodus 20:8-10.)

And the Lord has told us: "And that thou mayest more fully keep thyself unspotted from the world, thou shalt go to the house of prayer and offer up thy sacraments upon my holy day." (D&C 59:9.)

In spite of what so many say to the contrary, this is a law of God, a religious and therefore a moral law. If observed it will bring many blessings not otherwise enjoyed; and, like any other law, if not obeyed it will bring condemnation to the soul.

Keeping the Sabbath day holy gives us an opportunity to learn and understand the teachings of the gospel through worship and study, and to learn to know God, which is essential to our eternal destiny.

The Lord has said: "And this is life eternal, that they might know thee the only true God, and Jesus Christ, whom thou hast sent." (John 17:3.)

Surely for one day in seven we can and need to turn our thoughts to our Maker and feed our spiritual selves, to learn obedience to God, and to teach reverence and obedience to our children. One of the greatest lessons we can learn in life is that "man shall not live by bread alone, but by every word that proceedeth out of the mouth of God." (Matthew 4:4.)

Someone has wisely said: "Woe unto those who consider the laws of God only as forces of convenience, to be ignored or employed at will. Woe unto those individuals, classes and nations that believe in the might of their wealth, in the strength of their armor, in the invincibility of their positions."

No culture can last, no nation or union of nations can survive if they ignore God's laws. The Lord has admonished:

". . . seek ye first the kingdom of God, and his righteousness; and all these things shall be added unto you" (Matthew 6:33), meaning everything that is for our good.

We cannot keep the Sabbath day holy, nor enjoy the blessings thereof, by seeking to satisfy our material wants and pleasures. It is truthfully said that "material things have no power to raise the sunken spirit. The wealth of the world cannot heal a broken heart, and the wisdom of the universities cannot turn into righteousness a wayward soul."

As important as it is that we attend the house of prayer and keep the Sabbath day holy, teaching spirituality cannot be left to the churches alone. Parents have the first and great and important responsibility to teach the laws of God in the home. The Lord has told us:

And again, inasmuch as parents have children in Zion, or in any of her stakes which are organized, that teach them not to understand the doctrine of repentance, faith in Christ the Son of the living God, and of baptism and the gift of the Holy Ghost by the laying on of the hands, when eight years old, the sin be upon the heads of the parents.

And they shall also teach their children to pray, and to walk uprightly before the Lord. (D&C 68:25, 28.)

This means to keep his commandments—to love, honor, and obey him. Parents, if we are to teach our children to obey and keep the commandments and walk uprightly before God, we must be their living example. We cannot break any law with impunity and expect our children to honor and obey us or the law. We cannot question the teachings and commandments of the Lord without causing great doubts in the minds of our children as to why they should keep the commandments. We cannot be hypocrites. We cannot teach or profess a belief in one thing and live another, and expect our children to honor their parents.

Children who are taught obedience, to honor and obey the law, to have faith in God, and to keep his commandments, will, as they grow up, honor their parents and be a credit to them; and they will be able to meet and solve their problems, find greater success and joy in life, and contribute greatly to the solution of the problems now causing the world such great concern. It is up to the parents to see to it that their children are prepared through obedience to law for the positions of leadership they will occupy in the future, where their responsibility will be to bring peace and righteousness to the world.

Surely if we love the Lord we will keep his commandments, and if we will love our fellowmen we will enjoy utopia here on earth. As the Lord further has promised: ". . . he who doeth the works of righteousness shall receive his reward, even peace in this world, and eternal life in the world to come." (D&C 59:23.)

I bear witness that as we accept God as our Father, and his Son, Jesus Christ, as the Savior of the world, and keep the commandments, we will have greater joy here on the earth and eternal life in the world to come.

V

Seek to Know and Keep the Commandments of God

Chapter 16

"The Heavens Are Open"

What do we as Latter-day Saints believe, and particularly, what sets us apart from the rest of the world? On March 1, 1842, in the publication *Times and Seasons* in Nauvoo, Illinois, were outlined thirteen fundamental statements proclaiming concisely the standard principles, ordinances, and doctrines of the Church. These statements were written by the Prophet Joseph Smith in response to a request from John Wentworth, editor of the Chicago *Democrat*. They have come to be known as the Articles of Faith. Perhaps we can gain a better understanding of what does set us apart from the rest of the world by examining three of these important articles.

The first article states: *"We believe in God, the Eternal Father, and in His son, Jesus Christ, and in the Holy Ghost."*

The God we believe in is a living God with body, parts, and passions, in whose image we were made, who is the Father of the spirits of all mankind, and under whose direction the world was created and all things therein. He is a loving Father who is interested in us and our welfare and stands ready to answer our call if we will but go to him.

We believe that Jesus Christ is literally the Son of God, the Only Begotten in the flesh; that he was born of mortal mother; that he dwelt among men; that he gave man the plan of life and salvation; that he was crucified, and that he had power over death and willingly gave his life and was literally resurrected so that man might be saved and resurrected from the dead and enjoy eternal life.

"For since by man came death, by man came also the resurrection of the dead. For as in Adam all die, even so in Christ shall *all* be made alive." (1 Corinthians 15:21-22. Italics added.)

The third Article of Faith states: *"We believe that through the Atonement of Christ, all mankind may be saved, by obedience to the laws and ordinances of the Gospel."*

Belief in Christ is not sufficient, but obedience to his laws is essential to salvation and exaltation, for, as recorded in Matthew 7:21, Christ himself said: "Not every one that saith unto me, Lord, Lord, shall enter into the kingdom of heaven; but he that doeth the will of my Father which is in heaven."

And again, "Jesus answered, Verily, verily, I say unto thee, Except a man be born of water and of the Spirit, he cannot enter into the kingdom of God." (John 3:5.)

And then, as recorded in Revelation: "And I saw the dead, small and great, stand before God; . . . And they were judged every man according to their works." (Revelation 20:12-13.)

Also, we believe the Bible and the Book of Mormon to be the word of God, and we believe that they contain records of revelations God gave directly to his prophets in the different dispensations of the gospel. In fact, as stated in our ninth Article of Faith: *"We believe all that God has revealed, all that He does now reveal, and we believe that He will yet reveal many great and important things pertaining to the Kingdom of God."*

It is this belief more than any other that sets us apart from the rest of the world. Protestant churches, as we all know, were formed at the beginning of, and during the period of, the Reformation and resulted from the fact that many people were dissatisfied with the teachings and practices of the dominant church, which they claimed had transgressed the laws, changed the ordinances, and broken the everlasting covenant, and therefore had apostatized.

The Protestant churches, therefore, were established by men who were courageous enough to take a stand and risk their lives, and some of them even gave their lives, in an endeavor to correct the malpractices with which we are all so well-acquainted.

I have not the inclination to go into any details about the malpractices or the Reformation. I do say, however, that these Protestant churches were formed and organized by men who were dissatisfied with and protested against these malpractices. Though they were good men with high ideals and the best of intent, they did not claim any divine revelation or direct authority from God to organize their different sects. In fact, they claimed that there were no such things as visions or revelations in these days: that all such things had ceased with the apostles, and that there would *never* be any more of them. On the other hand, Joseph Smith, the founder of The Church of Jesus Christ of Latter-day Saints, claimed that he was called by revelation and given divine authority direct from God and Jesus Christ and had received the keys of the priesthood under the hands of Peter, James, and John.

Throughout the history of mankind, from Adam down to the present time, God has revealed his will to his chosen prophets; for, as Amos the prophet taught: "Surely the Lord God will do nothing, but he revealeth his secret unto his servants the prophets." (Amos 3:7.)

As we look back over the history of God's dealings with his people and read the revelations that he gave to his prophets to guide and direct them and prepare them for the future, we cannot help marveling at the continued interest he has shown in his people and the patience he has shown and the care that he has taken to see that they were continually directed in the paths of truth and righteousness, if they would but listen to his holy prophet through whom he was speaking.

The Bible testifies that revelation began with Adam and Eve, who heard the voice of the Lord God while walking in the garden. (Genesis 3:8.) God revealed to Adam his origin, the purpose of mortality, his future destiny, and the requirements for exaltation. He also gave direction in solving the special problems of his dispensation. Though the gospel plan has remained the same from the beginning, important truths have been abandoned and forgotten, and therefore it has been necessary from time to time for God to raise up prophets to restore the gospel truths, to testify to the people, and to instruct them in righteousness. Also, each dispensation faced different problems, and therefore continuous revelation was necessary to cope with them.

I have always been impressed with the way Moses was protected and preserved by the Lord, who had chosen him and through direct revelation prepared and directed him day by day as to what he should do and how he should prepare to lead the children of Israel out of bondage and out of Egypt; how the Lord personally instructed Moses how to deal with Pharaoh, and how, through God's commands, plagues were imposed and withdrawn by the Lord; how the Lord protected the people as they crossed the Red Sea; and how he continued to lead and guide and direct them as long as they were prepared to listen to the prophet and follow his instruction.

It was Moses to whom the Lord, by direct revelation, gave the Ten Commandments as a set of rules by which the people should govern their lives. These remain today as much the word of the Lord as at any other time and apply equally to the people in these, the latter days. Yet, while he was receiving these commandments directly from the Lord, the people, whom he had led out of bondage and whom the Lord had taught through him, turned away from the true God and began to worship idols.

The Bible is replete in both the Old and New Testaments with records of revelations given by God to his chosen prophets. God has always stood ready to lead and direct his people if they would but listen to his word.

As recorded in the Book of Mormon, Lehi was warned that Jerusalem would be destroyed, and he was advised to take his family and leave. As he listened to the voice of the Lord and followed his instructions, he and his family were led out of the city to safety and into the new world, later to be known as America, while they who remained were destroyed or taken into captivity.

While the prophets in the old land were receiving revelations from God, the people of Lehi on this, the American continent, were not left without guidance. Prophets were raised up through whom God spoke and directed his people in all their doings as they would listen. He revealed to them also, 600 years before Christ's coming, that he would come, that he was the Savior of the world, that he would be persecuted and crucified, and that he would be resurrected.

This was foretold clearly by Lehi, Nephi, Alma, and others, including Samuel, to whom it had been revealed the exact time that Jesus Christ would be born. They were told of the signs which would be shown at the time of Christ's birth and crucifixion. Every word that had been revealed to them regarding these events was fulfilled. Following his crucifixion Christ appeared personally to the people on the American continent, and he taught them the truths of the gospel.

Many of the revelations recorded in the Old and New Testaments, as well as in the Book of Mormon, refer most clearly to these, the latter days. Some of these are not generally understood by the world and can only be understood through revelations that were received by the Prophet

Joseph Smith. One example of these is that of John the Revelator who, when looking into the future, said:

And I saw another angel fly in the midst of heaven, having the everlasting gospel to preach unto them that dwell on the earth, and to every nation, and kindred, and tongue, and people,

Saying with a loud voice, Fear God, and give glory to him; for the hour of his judgment is come: and worship him that made heaven, and earth, and the sea, and the fountains of waters. (Revelation 14:6-7.)

This revelation was fulfilled and clearly understood when the Angel Moroni did fly in the midst of heaven and appeared to Joseph Smith and told him of the plates which contained the gospel in its fullness. Joseph said that as the Angel Moroni appeared to him, he called him by name and told him that "there was a book deposited, written upon gold plates, giving an account of the former inhabitants of this continent, and the source from whence they sprang. He also said that the fulness of the everlasting Gospel was contained in it, as delivered by the Savior to the ancient inhabitants." (Joseph Smith 2:34.)

Thus we know that the angel, as predicted or prophesied by John the Revelator, has flown; that this great and glorious gospel has been restored in its fullness by the Lord through the Prophet Joseph Smith to be preached to every nation, kindred, tongue, and people.

Another revelation recorded in the Old Testament that refers to these, the latter days, and has reference to the Book of Mormon is that received by Ezekiel wherein he says:

The word of the Lord came again unto me, saying:

Moreover, thou son of man, take thee one stick, and write upon it, For Judah, and for the children of Israel his companions: then take another stick, and write upon it, For Joseph, the stick of Ephraim, and for all the house of Israel his companions:

And join them one to another into one stick; and they shall become one in thine hand. (Ezekiel 37:15-17.)

As I read this, I went to the *Interpreter's Bible*, which is written in twelve volumes and is a commentary on all of the Old and New Testaments. This commentary was prepared by thirty-six consulting editors with over one hundred recognized, capable contributors, and deals with all quotations from the Bible, taking them verse by verse and explaining their meaning and application. When I came to Ezekiel, 37th chapter, verses 15 through 17, no feasible explanation was given, but conjectures only were made. This is no reflection on the editors or contributors to this great commentary, as they knew of no way to get the meaning.

Here again, by direct revelation, and by direct revelation only, do we understand clearly what Ezekiel meant. Here, the stick of Judah as referred to is the Bible, and the stick of Ephraim, which is written for Joseph and all the house of Israel his companions, is the Book of Mormon. Through the power of God and by direct revelation, this Book of Mormon, which contains the gospel in its fullness, was translated, and it, with the Bible, became "one in thine hand." How clear and simple the words of Ezekiel become if we will but listen to the prophet's voice!

Then again, Malachi records a revelation which refers to these, the latter days, wherein the Lord said: "For, behold, the day cometh, that shall burn as an oven; and all the proud, yea, and all that do wickedly, shall be stubble." (Malachi 4:1.)

And then he said:

> Behold, I will send you Elijah the prophet before the coming of the great and dreadful day of the Lord:
> And he shall turn the heart of the fathers to the children, and the heart of the children to their fathers, lest I come and smite the earth with a curse. (Malachi 4:5-6.)

Again I went to the *Interpreter's Bible* to see what they had to say about this passage, and though it had been in the Jewish scriptures for centuries, they did not understand it, and therefore were unable to explain its meaning.

I do not mention this to belittle in any way this very complete and thought-provoking commentary, but to point out that the full meaning and impact of this prophecy and promise could in no wise be understood until Elijah himself actually appeared to Joseph Smith and Oliver Cowdery in 1836.

Joseph records four revelations that he and Oliver Cowdery received in the Kirtland Temple. First, the Lord Jesus Christ himself appeared and talked to them; then Moses, and then Elias appeared and revealed certain things unto them. And then Joseph said:

> After this vision had closed, another great and glorious vision burst upon us; for Elijah the prophet, who was taken to heaven without tasting death, stood before us, and said:
> Behold, the time has fully come, which was spoken of by the mouth of Malachi—testifying that he [Elijah] should be sent, before the great and dreadful day of the Lord come—
> To turn the hearts of the fathers to the children, and the children to the fathers, lest the whole earth be smitten with a curse—
> Therefore, *the keys of this dispensation are committed into your hands;* and by this ye may know that the great and dreadful day of the Lord is near, even at the doors. (D&C 110:13-16. Italics added.)

How enlightening, encouraging, and consoling it is to be able to read this revelation and know that Elijah has actually appeared!

The prophecies contained in these revelations have all been fulfilled and point up clearly the need of direct revelation in these, the latter days, for the guidance of the people, that they might know the will of the Lord.

Without modern revelation the world would be left in complete darkness regarding, first, the Book of Mormon, which is a new witness for Christ and contains the gospel in its fullness; second, the purpose and importance of temple work; third, vicarious work for the dead; and many other things pertaining to the kingdom of God.

It is my testimony to you that God truly lives and that Jesus is the Christ, the Savior of the world, who gave his life for you and me; that the priesthood of God has been restored; that the church of Jesus Christ has been re-established in these the latter days with the same organization that existed in the primitive church, all by direct revelation; that by direct revelation and the power of God we have the Book of Mormon, which contains the gospel in its fullness; that the heavens are as open today as they were in the days of Moses, Abraham, Peter, James, and John, and Paul; and that God still answers the prayers of the righteous and still reveals his mind and will through his ordained prophets.

From the very time that the young boy Joseph, at the age of fourteen, went into the grove to ask God which church he should join, until today, he and those who have followed him as presidents of this church have been led by revelation in all things pertaining to the kingdom of God.

May we all hold fast to the iron rod, which is the word of God, and listen to the prophet's voice and serve God and keep his commandments.

CHAPTER 17

The Gospel Our Bulwark

It is trite but true to say that never before in the history of the world have we or our young people been faced with more evil, serious problems, and challenges than we are today. Wherever we go, and regardless of whatever news media we pick up or listen to, or whatever company we may be in, we hear discussed and have forced upon our minds the importance of such questions as divorce and family disintegration, new morality, new freedom, new security, the "God is dead" theory, war and strife, murders, riots, burglaries, and all kinds of crime and deception.

It is most important that we be acquainted with the evils of the day and realize how insidious they are and accept our responsibility to guard against them. We should realize that the new morality is nothing more than the old immorality, that the new freedom is nothing more than disrespect for law and the rights of others and will lead to anarchy. The new security gives one the idea that the world owes him a living; it destroys individual initiative and infringes on his liberty and freedom.

I am convinced that the only way to guard successfully against these evils is to accept the gospel of Jesus Christ, which offers not only a better way of life but the solution to these and all other problems facing us today. In fact, we would have no more war or strife or any of the evils that I have enumerated if the world would accept God as the Creator of the world and Jesus Christ as its Savior.

We as leaders and as members of the Church have a heavy responsibility to help our youth to know and understand that the Bible and the Book of Mormon, which were written on opposite sides of the world, are records of God's dealings with his people on these two hemispheres. They are not fairy tales, but testimonies of many righteous men whose integrity cannot be questioned. These testimonies have been handed down to us by the prophets from Adam to the present day.

These records show that in every dispensation those who accepted the word of God and kept his commandments prospered and were happy, successful, and blessed, while those who denied God and Jesus Christ and refused to accept the gospel have suffered heartaches, defeat, Godless dictatorship, and general anarchy.

We all know the story of Moses and the Israelites. We know that when they followed the instructions of God and kept his commandments, they were blessed and preserved from their enemies, and how quickly they were left to the buffeting of Satan when they turned away from and ignored God and his teachings.

Another story with which we are all familiar is that of David and Goliath, how Goliath, that powerful leader of the Philistines, was slain by David with his sling. We should remind our youth of the words of these two men that show why David was successful and Goliath slain. David kept the commandments of God and had complete faith in his power. Listen to the boastful words of Goliath and to David's humble but confident response.

And the Philistine said to David, Come to me, and I will give thy flesh unto the fowls of the air, and to the beasts of the field.

Then said David to the Philistine, Thou comest to me with a sword, and with a spear, and with a shield: but I come to thee in the name of the Lord of hosts, the God of the armies of Israel, whom thou hast defied.

This day will the Lord deliver thee into mine hand. . . . (1 Samuel 17:44-46.)

As a result, Goliath and the Philistines were defeated and the Israelites were saved by the power of God. The scriptures are replete with records of individuals and nations who succeeded or failed as a result of their faithfulness or disobedience.

Also, we should appreciate and help our young people to understand that the greatest leaders of recorded history, and of today, in industry and government, have always believed in God.

George Washington, in his first inaugural address, said: "It would be peculiarly improper to omit in this official act, my fervent supplication to the Almighty Being who rules over the universe. . . ." And in his famous farewell address he said, "Of all the dispositions and habits which lead to political prosperity, religion and morality are indispensable supports."

Abraham Lincoln, in that oft-repeated statement, said: "Without the assistance of that Divine Being, . . . I cannot succeed. With that assistance I cannot fail. . . ."

Christopher Columbus also had great faith in God. This famous explorer, in his report to the king and queen of Spain, wrote near the end of his letter, "And the eternal God, Our Lord, gives to all who walk in his way victory over things which appear impossible, and this [voyage] was notably one."

He concluded this letter with the suggestion that "all Christendom ought to feel joyful and make great celebrations and give solemn thanks" for the privilege of bringing Christ's message to the people of these new-found lands. Because of his faith and courage he was able to withstand the mutinies and succeed in his mission. (Wendell J. Ashton, in *The Instructor*, October 1966.)

One of our great industrialists, John D. Rockefeller, Jr., included in his creed under the heading "I Believe":

I believe in an all-wise and all-loving God, . . . and that the individual's highest fulfillment, greatest happiness, and widest usefulness are to be found in living in harmony with his will.

I believe that love is the greatest thing in the world; that it alone can overcome hate; that right can and will triumph over might.

Many who argue that Christianity has failed excuse themselves for their actions by saying that men who profess God and Jesus Christ are hypocrites and do not live the teachings that they profess. Too often men waste their time questioning even the existence of God instead of accepting his teachings and enjoying his blessings.

It is something like those who try to prove that Shakespeare never lived, that he was not the author of the Shakespearian plays, some of the choicest of all literature. While they waste their time arguing, others are enjoying the beauty and philosophy of his works.

Christ's teachings, which are so important to our happiness, security, and exaltation, may be summed up in the Ten Commandments, the Sermon on the Mount, Christ's answer to the lawyer as to which is the great commandment in the law, and the Articles of Faith as given by Joseph Smith.

No one will argue that the keeping of the Ten Commandments would not make for a better and happier individual or contribute to a happy and spiritual home, a better community, and a better world in which to live. You are familiar with the old Chinese proverb that says:

If there is righteousness in the heart there will be beauty in the character;

If there is beauty in the character there will be harmony in the home;

If there is harmony in the home there will be order in the nation;

If there is order in the nation there will be peace in the world.

In fact, the Ten Commandments leave us with the impressive message that we are free either to serve God and keep his commandments or to be ruled by tyrants.

Homes are broken, individuals are confused and lost, and prisons are full of men who do not believe in God and who fail to love their neighbors. And many argue that we cannot be honest and compete, that we cannot love our fellowmen as ourselves without their taking advantage of us, and that we cannot apply the principles of the gospel in dealing with other nations.

There are those, too, who claim that the gospel is old-fashioned; that men through scientific development are becoming more and more self-sufficient and need not rely on God. Others argue that the gospel is too restrictive, that it takes away our liberty, and that we cannot enjoy the advantages of a broad education, accept scientific truths, and participate in worthwhile community activities.

This is just not true. We know that the Lord has given us the earth and all things therein for our use and for our benefit. We have been told to subdue the earth. As members of the Church we are encouraged to gain an education, to learn what we can, to prepare ourselves to take our places in the world, and to contribute all we can to the good and welfare of mankind.

We know that great strides have been made in science and in subduing the earth. We know that mankind is enjoying conveniences, comforts, and blessings far greater than at any other time in the history of the world. However, we must also realize that no scientist or group of scientists or philosophers has ever, through scientific research, been able to find out or give us an understanding of the relationship of God to man or where we came from, why we are here, or even when the spirit enters the body or what happens to it when we die.

Elder James E. Talmage, in his book *The Articles of Faith*, emphasizes the importance of gaining an education, and we know that it is extremely important. He says that in the short span of mortal existence it is impossible for a man to explore with thoroughness any considerable part of the vast realm of knowledge. It therefore becomes necessary for him to determine which field of knowledge will be of greatest worth to him in his chosen field of endeavor and then to learn everything he can about it. However, he emphasizes the importance of everyone gaining theological knowledge, for a personal knowledge of God is essential to the salvation of every human soul. Therefore, its importance cannot be overestimated.

This theological knowledge has been given to us by revelation down through the ages from Adam to our present-day prophet. However, from the history of mankind we learn that as man and the world prosper they have a tendency to forget God and to depend on their own knowledge and strength. As a result, millions of men and women are disturbed and confused, and many of them are committing suicide. They need something positive.

Let me emphasize again that those who have contributed most to the world are men who have had a belief in God and have tried to govern their lives accordingly. How much happier is an individual who can go to bed knowing that he has been honest with his fellowmen, that he is morally clean, that he is at peace with God, his Creator.

How much happier are those who live in a community made up of God-fearing people!

In my experience as a bishop, a stake president, and a General Authority, I have never had anyone who understands the gospel and who has an abiding faith in God come to me with serious personal problems.

J. Edgar Hoover, in his analysis of "The Problems of the Day," said:

The basic cause of the present situation is that so many of our young people have no real sense of moral responsibility which comes from an infinite knowledge of God's teachings. The tragic lack of God and prayer in their lives weakens our homes and our nation's welfare.

Then he emphasized that either faith in God must triumph in the United States or we will be dominated by criminals and Communists.

Let us go forward with a positive attitude. Be not ashamed. Be not influenced by those who ridicule and those who question and those who deny God. Let us not be among those who believe but do not have the courage and the strength to live according to the teachings of the gospel. As recorded in John: "Nevertheless among the chief rulers also many believed on him; but because of the Pharisees they did not confess him, lest they should be put out of the synagogue: *For they loved the praise of men more than the praise of God.*" (John 12:42-43. Italics added.)

Let us enjoy the good things in life. Let us enjoy the gospel and its teachings. Let us not waste our time looking for things to criticize in the gospel or in our neighbors. We must look at ourselves and repent and improve. And let us remember that there is nothing else quite so sure as that we will one day leave this frail existence. Let us set about to prepare ourselves for that day, for "the day cometh that all shall rise from the dead and stand before God, and be judged according to their works." (Alma 11:41.)

If we are to stop the onslaught of immorality, divorce and family disintegration, lawlessness, strife, riots, burglaries, murders, crime, and deception, we must not ask what are *they* doing about it. We must ask and answer the question, "What am *I* doing?" Let us examine ourselves, acknowledge our faults, and repent where we should.

We must begin by having righteousness in our own hearts, by disciplining ourselves, by having love and harmony in our homes, and by truly loving our neighbors. Let us have the wisdom, courage, and determination to say with Joshua: ". . . choose you this day whom ye will serve; . . . but as for me and my house, we will serve the Lord." (Joshua 24:15.)

I pray that each and every one of us will realize how important it is that we have family prayer in our home, that we have family home evening, that we keep the Sabbath day holy, and that we dedicate ourselves to overcoming evil and keeping his commandments.

Let us realize that "this is life eternal, that they might know thee the only true God, and Jesus Christ, whom thou hast sent" (John 17:3), and set about to learn to know God.

CHAPTER 18

"Where Art Thou?"

I should like to discuss the significance of God's first question to Adam, "Where art thou?"—a direct and searching question which applies to every one of us today.

To do this intelligently we need to understand the purpose for man's existence here upon the earth, and why God posed this question to Adam, who represents all mankind. In the council in heaven before the world was, the Gods decided to create an earth on which man would dwell, and God said:

> . . . we will prove them herewith, to see if they will do all things whatsoever the Lord their God shall command them;
>
> And they who keep their first estate shall be added upon; and they who keep not their first estate shall not have glory in the same kingdom with those who keep their first estate; and they who keep their second estate shall have glory added upon their heads for ever and ever. (Abraham 3:25-26.)
>
> And I, God, created man in mine own image, in the image of mine Only Begotten created I him; male and female created I them.
>
> And I, God, blessed them, and said unto them: Be fruitful, and multiply, and replenish the earth, and subdue it, and have dominion over the fish of the sea, and over the fowl of the air, and over every living thing that moveth upon the earth. (Moses 2:27-28.)

And I, the Lord God, planted a garden eastward in Eden, and there I put the man whom I had formed. . . . to dress it, and to keep it.

And . . . commanded the man, saying: Of every tree of the garden thou mayest freely eat,

But of the tree of the knowledge of good and evil, thou shalt not eat of it, nevertheless, thou mayest choose for thyself, for it is given unto thee; but, remember that I forbid it. . . . (Moses 3:8, 15-17.)

It is evident therefore that the earth was made as a dwelling place for man, and all things therein were given to him for his use, for his good, and for his enjoyment; but God has pointed out to us, as to Adam, that if we are to enjoy life to the full there are things we must do and things which we must not do. In other words, we are given everything for our benefit and blessing, but we must remember that there are a few "forbidden fruits" which will deprive us of full enjoyment and bring sorrow and regret to us if we partake.

At the council in heaven, two plans were presented for man's salvation. Christ's plan was approved and he was chosen as the Savior of the world, and Satan's plan was rejected and he rebelled. The record states:

Wherefore, because that Satan rebelled against me, and sought to destroy the agency of man, which I, the Lord God, had given him, and also, that I should give unto him mine own power; by the power of mine Only Begotten, I caused that he should be cast down;

And he became Satan, yea, even the devil, the father of all lies, to deceive and to blind men, and to lead them captive at his will, even as many as would not hearken unto my voice. (Moses 4:3-4.)

In the Doctrine and Covenants we read:

Satan stirreth them up, that he may lead their souls to destruction.

And thus he has laid a cunning plan, thinking to destroy the work of God; . . .

Yea, he saith unto them: Deceive and lie in wait to catch, that ye may destroy; . . . And thus he flattereth them, and telleth them that it is no sin to lie. . . .

And thus he . . . leadeth them along until he draggeth their souls down to hell; . . .

And thus he goeth up and down, to and fro in the earth, seeking to destroy the souls of men. (D&C 10:22-23, 25-27.)

Immediately after God left Adam and Eve in the garden, telling them to partake freely of the fruit of all the trees except one, of which they were commanded not to partake, Satan began his nefarious plan for their destruction. Following Satan's successful attempt, God returned to the garden, and because they were ashamed Adam and Eve were hiding from him, so he called: "Where art thou?" —a question which can and does apply to every one of us individually and collectively, and one which we might well be asking ourselves as it applies to our relationship to God and our fellowmen.

Adam replied:

. . . I heard thy voice in the garden, and I was afraid, because I was naked; and I hid myself.

And he said, Who told thee that thou wast naked? Hast thou eaten of the tree, whereof I commanded thee that thou shouldest not eat?

Adam, as we all are inclined to do, tried to blame someone else, and replied:

. . . The woman whom thou gavest to be with me, she gave me of the tree, and I did eat.

And Eve said:

. . . The serpent [meaning Satan] beguiled me, and I did eat. (Genesis 3:9-13.)

Conditions surrounding Adam and Eve, and those surrounding us today, point up clearly the influence of Satan and the frailties of man, the temptations and problems that he has to meet in life, and how the Lord has prepared a way for him to overcome.

When God said "Where art thou?" he knew where Adam was. With his omniscience he knew what had taken place, but he was calling Adam to consider the seriousness of his actions and to report to him. But Adam had hidden himself because he was ashamed.

We are all like Adam in that when we partake of "forbidden fruits" or do the things we are commanded not to do, we are ashamed, and we draw away from the Church and from God and hide ourselves, and if we continue in sin, the Spirit of God withdraws from us. There is no happiness in disobedience or sin. We have all learned from our childhood that we are happier when we are doing right.

Sometimes we do not understand why it is necessary for us to keep the commandments and do certain things to receive certain blessings, except that the Lord commanded it. We cannot explain why we should be baptized or have the laying on of hands or other ordinances. Some even question the teachings of God. But if by faith we obey his commandments, we will receive the promised blessings. Jesus said that unless we become as little children, who have such great faith, we cannot enter the kingdom of heaven. We must learn to have explicit faith.

Then, too, we must understand the importance of obedience. The prophet Samuel taught that "to obey is better than sacrifice, and to hearken than the fat of rams." (1 Samuel 15:22.) The scriptures give us many examples of obedience by faith alone. After Adam and Eve were driven out of the Garden of Eden, the Lord—

gave unto them commandments, that they should worship the Lord their God, and should offer the firstlings of their flocks, for an offering unto the Lord. And Adam was obedient unto the commandments of the Lord.

And after many days an angel of the Lord appeared unto Adam, saying: Why dost thou offer sacrifices unto the Lord? And Adam said unto him: I know not, save the Lord commanded me.

And then the angel spake, saying: This thing is a similitude

of the sacrifice of the Only Begotten of the Father, which is full
of grace and truth. (Moses 5:5-7.)

When Nephi was recording the history of his people,
he explained that he had received a commandment to make
two sets of records — one for an account of the ministry
of his people, and the other for an account of the reign
of the kings and the wars and contentions of his people.
Then he said:

> Wherefore, the Lord hath commanded me to make these plates
> for a wise purpose in him, which purpose I know not.
> But the Lord knoweth all things from the beginning; where-
> fore, he prepareth a way to accomplish all his works among the
> children of men. . . . (1 Nephi 9:5-6.)

This, as we now know, proved to be of great importance at the time of the translation of these records. If
we will only have the faith to keep the commandments,
whether we fully understand them or not, we will be
blessed, and just as surely, we will reap the results of disobedience.

I remember so well that when I was just a young
man, to be obedient to the teachings of the Church I re-
frained from the use of tea, coffee, liquor, and tobacco. At
that time the world did not understand, and scientists had
not proven, that the use of these things was detrimental
to the body and not good for man. Today they have proven
that these things are harmful and that we should not partake of them; and yet in spite of this knowledge there
are many in the world today who are suffering ill health,
much unhappiness, and even death as a result of partaking
of these "forbidden fruits."

In fact, most of the contention, strife, and unhappiness
in the world are caused by our refusing to accept and
live the commandments of the Lord. As was pointed out
before, we are here to prove ourselves, and no matter
how busy we are, or how successful, we must realize that
death will come to us and is not far away. We might well

ask ourselves: What am I doing to prepare for death and eternal life? Where am I when it comes to the performance of my duty to God and to my fellowmen?

Our duty lies in studying the word of God, developing our faith in him, supporting our faith by our actions, and in the heavy responsibility of teaching our families their duty. Again we might ask: Where am I when it comes to teaching my family, by example as well as by precept, to walk uprightly before the Lord, to be honest and honorable in all their dealings, including the payment of tithes and offerings to the Lord? Are we keeping the Sabbath day holy, or do we compromise in certain respects? Are we observing the Word of Wisdom strictly, or do we tamper with any of these "forbidden fruits"? Am I aware of the increasing availability of illegal drugs, and warning my children of the dangers involved? What am I doing in my community to clear up problems pertaining to drug addiction, alcoholism, sexual promiscuity and disease, which are more prevalent than most parents realize? In your own community these are threatening the children of every home.

Where am I when it comes to loyalty to my country? Am I teaching my family to be loyal citizens? Am I teaching them that in order to enjoy the good things in life they must accept responsibility as citizens and contribute to making theirs a better community? Is my home an example of love and harmony and peace? Am I holding regular home evenings so as to be close to my family? Are we having family prayer regularly in order that we may report to the Lord "where we are" and ask for his help and guidance?

I was impressed the other day when I read an article on the family. The author said that juvenile crimes of the times do not reflect on the great body of the young people involved as much as they reflect on the manner in which the adult population is discharging its responsibility. This observation was voiced recently by the Chief Justice of the Supreme Court in Ontario, Canada. The group that is causing most of the trouble, he contends, is the product of the undisciplined homes and irresponsible parents.

We must realize that it is our duty and privilege to be good neighbors, especially to those who have no families, and to visit the sick, the poor, and the needy. The Lord has said that the second great commandment is to love our neighbors as ourselves. Are my family and I qualifying in this respect? Are we interested in their welfare and ready to help wherever possible? We read in James that "pure religion and undefiled before God and the Father is this, To visit the fatherless and widows in their affliction." (James 1:27.)

We are aware that there has always been a conflict between right and wrong, righteousness and evil, good and bad. We must prepare ourselves to meet these conflicts and teach our children and help others to choose the right and make the decisions that will keep them from yielding to temptation. Someone asked me the other day why we have all these temptations, and why the Lord has given us the desires such as appetites and passions, and why we have to be tempted and tested.

One reason is to help us develop and grow through the schooling we receive in the experiences we encounter in mortal life. Brigham Young said: "I am happy . . . for the privilege of having temptations." (*Journal of Discourses*, vol. 3, p. 195.) Temptations are necessary for our advancement and our development. "When temptations come to you, be humble and prayerful, and determined that you will overcome, and you will receive a deliverance and continue faithful, having the promise of receiving blessings." (*JD*, vol. 16, p. 164.)

All of these temptations—these appetites and passions —are for our good and enjoyment if we will but let wisdom's voice control. Temptations come to all, but long before we are faced with them, we and our children must have determined what our course will be. It is too late if we wait until the moment of temptation before making our decision. If we have been taught and determined always to choose the right and resist evil, we will have the strength to overcome.

We must remember that Satan is always on the job, determined to destroy the work of the Lord and to destroy mankind, and as soon as we deviate from the path of righteousness, we are in great danger of being destroyed. The scriptures and history give us many examples of men in high places who, when they turned from and despised the teachings of the Lord, or in any way deviated from the path of righteousness, suffered much sorrow, loss of position, loss of friends and even family.

Conditions in the world today cause us to reflect on the prophecy made by Paul to Timothy, wherein he said:

This know also, that in the last days perilous times shall come.

For men shall be lovers of their own selves, covetous, boasters, proud, blasphemers, disobedient to parents, unthankful, unholy,

Without natural affection, truce breakers, false accusers, incontinent, fierce, despisers of those that are good,

Traitors, heady, highminded, lovers of pleasures more than lovers of God;

Hav'ng a form of godliness, but denying the power thereof: from such turn away. (2 Timothy 3:1-5.)

This causes us to ask: Where are we individually on each of these counts? Where are we as a nation and as the world? Are conditions in this great country and in the whole world comparable to the conditions that caused the downfall of Sodom and Gomorrah and Rome and other civilizations that have fallen because of moral decadence? How far have we moved, and how rapidly are we moving away from God and his teachings? Again, where are we and what will be our destiny if we as individuals and as a country and the world refuse to repent and turn to God, and quit hiding ourselves from him?

How fortunate we are to have the gospel of Jesus Christ as a guide, and the promise that if we will serve God we will be saved from destruction and, in fact, enjoy life to the full here and eternal life hereafter. Christ's whole mission was to make it possible for us to enjoy immortality and eternal life, and he gave us the plan by which we can accomplish this.

If every family in the Church were to live the principles of the gospel, the influence for good in the world would be tremendous. And if every family in the world would accept and live the teachings of Jesus Christ, we would have none of the prevalent ills, and all would be living together in love and peace. Such a thought staggers the imagination!

However, in the Book of Mormon we read of such a condition:

> And it came to pass . . . the people were all converted unto the Lord, upon all the face of the land . . . and there were no contentions and disputations among them, and every man did deal justly one with another . . . because of the love of God which did dwell in the hearts of the people.
>
> And there were no envyings, nor strifes, nor tumults, nor whoredoms, nor lyings, nor murders, nor any manner of lasciviousness; and surely there could not be a happier people among all the people who had been created by the hand of God. (4 Nephi 2, 15-16.)

As individuals, families, communities, leaders, and governments, we must turn to God, acknowledge him as the Creator of the world and the universe, and as Father of us all, and seek his guidance and keep his commandments. No one can state too plainly or emphasize too strongly this eternal truth that only through the atonement of Christ can mankind be saved. Because of his atoning sacrifice all men will be raised in immortality and live forever as resurrected beings, but only those who believe and obey his laws will enjoy exaltation and eternal life.

I humbly pray that we may have the wisdom, knowledge, desire, courage, and strength to overcome and repent. I make a special appeal to our youth that they will always keep themselves clean and pure, and never be guilty of doing anything that will bring sorrow to them and their families and make them feel to hide from the Lord because they are ashamed.

I appeal to each member of the Church to ask himself: Where am I? Am I ashamed so that I want to hide, or am I where I should be, doing what I should be doing, and preparing to meet God? Let each of us determine to humble ourselves and repent, and prove ourselves worthy of the great promise that those who keep their second estate shall have glory added upon their heads forever and ever.

CHAPTER 19

The Power of Prayer

I have great faith in prayer, and I believe that "more things are wrought by prayer than this world dreams of." (Alfred, Lord Tennyson, *Morte d'Arthur.*) I constantly pray that those who doubt might be helped to see and understand that God is our Father, that we are his spirit children, that he is really there and has said, "Ask, and it shall be given you; seek, and ye shall find; knock, and it shall be opened unto you: For every one that asketh receiveth; and he that seeketh findeth; and to him that knocketh it shall be opened." (Matthew 7:7-8.)

I often wonder if we really realize the power of prayer, if we appreciate what a great blessing it is to be able to call on our Father in heaven in humble prayer, knowing that he is interested in us and that he wants us to succeed.

As the late Elder Richard L. Evans so beautifully said:

Our Father in heaven is not an umpire who is trying to count us out. He is not a competitor who is trying to outsmart us. He is not a prosecutor who is trying to convict us. He is a loving Father who wants our happiness and eternal progress and who will help us all he can if we will but give him in our lives an opportunity to do so with obedience and humility, and faith and patience.

To pray effectively, and to feel that one can be heard and have his prayers answered, one must believe that he is praying to a God who can hear and answer, one who is interested in his children and their well-being. The first record we have of anyone praying to the Lord is that recorded by Moses in these words:

And Adam and Eve, his wife, called upon the name of the Lord, and they heard the voice of the Lord from the way toward the Garden of Eden, speaking unto them, and they saw him not; . . .
And Adam and Eve, his wife, ceased not to call upon God. . . . (Moses 5:4, 16.)

Great and influential men have always prayed for divine guidance. Even this great nation was founded on prayer. U.S. Senator Strom Thurmond of South Carolina reminded us of this when he said:

The Mayflower Compact, written in November of 1620, begins with a prayer, "In the name of God," and goes on to state: "We . . . having undertaken, for the glory of God, . . . do by these presents solemnly and mutually in the presence of God, and of one another, covenant and combine ourselves together into a civil body politic."

Thus our nation began founded on prayer. The kneeling figure of George Washington through that bitter winter in Valley Forge is a part of this country that should never be forgotten. . . .

The Constitutional Convention in June of 1787 had been meeting for weeks without agreement, when Benjamin Franklin rose to his feet and addressed George Washington:

"Mr. President: The small progress we have made after four or five weeks close attention and continual reasonings with each other . . . is a melancholy proof of the imperfection of the human understanding. . . . We have gone back to ancient history for models of government that now no longer exist. And we have viewed modern states . . . but find none of their constitutions suitable to our circumstances. . . . How has it happened, Sir, that we have not, hitherto, once thought of humbly applying to the Father of Light to illuminate our understandings?

"In the beginning of the contest with Britain, when we were sensible of danger, we had daily prayers in this room for divine protection.

"Our prayers, Sir, were heard; and they were generously answered. . . .

"I, therefore, beg leave to move:—

"That henceforth, prayers imploring the assistance of Heaven and its blessings on our deliberations be held in this assembly every morning before we proceed to business." ("A Priceless Asset," *Spotlight*, May 1966.)

This was done, and now we enjoy the fruits of their labors in answer to prayer. Prayer has never been outmoded in this great country. Abraham Lincoln, who prayed to the Lord continually for guidance, said:

It is the duty of nations as well as of men to own their dependence upon the overruling power of God, to confess their sins and transgressions in humble sorrow . . . and to recognize the sublime truth that those nations only are blessed whose God is the Lord.

President Dwight D. Eisenhower, at the time of his inauguration, petitioned the Lord:

Give us, we pray, the power to discern clearly right from wrong, and to allow all our works and actions to be governed thereby, and by the laws of this land . . . so that all may work for the good of our beloved country, and for thy glory. Amen.

Samuel F. B. Morse, inventor of the telegraph, said that whenever he could not see his way clearly, he knelt down and prayed for light and understanding.

We have that sweet and simple prayer recorded by astronaut Gordon Cooper while orbiting the earth:

Father, thank you, especially for letting me fly this flight. Thank you for the privilege of being able to be in this position, to be up in this wondrous place, seeing all these many startling, wonderful things that you have created.

I join with Senator Thurmond in his appeal to "our people to pray more, to examine the religious heritage of our country, and to see the benefit of seeking God's blessings. Prayer is the only way in which the finite can communicate with the infinite; . . . in which the visible may be in touch with the invisible. You may easily see, if you but examine the history of our Nation, that prayer and communication with God is the very cornerstone of our society. If you allow it to be abandoned now, you will be casting away the greatest asset this Nation, or any other nation, has ever known."

All of the prophets, from Adam to our present prophet, have prayed unceasingly for guidance, and even the Savior prayed continually to God the Eternal Father. We read, regarding the Savior: "And it came to pass in those days, that he went out into a mountain to pray, and continued all night in prayer to God." (Luke 6:12.)

The Lord has admonished all of us to pray, and through the prophet James has given us this promise:

> If any of you lack wisdom, let him ask of God, that giveth to all men liberally, and upbraideth not; and it shall be given him.
> But let him ask in faith, nothing wavering. For he that wavereth is like a wave of the sea driven with the wind and tossed. (James 1:5-6.)

This promise is given to every one of us—high and low, rich and poor. It is universal, unrestricted to you and to me and to our neighbors. He has told us that we must believe and have faith in God. We should know that the Lord stands ready to help his children if they will put themselves in tune through prayer and by keeping his commandments. In fact, the Lord has said: "I, the Lord, am bound when ye do what I say; but when ye do not what I say, ye have no promise." (D&C 82:10.)

We must be prepared to recognize God as the Creator of the world, and that he, through his Son Jesus Christ and his prophets, has given us in simple language man's relationship to God, information regarding our premortal existence, the purpose of our mission here on earth, and the fact that our postmortal existence, or our life after death, is real, and that what we do here will condition us for the world to come.

We must not be misled by the doctrines of men. All the studies of science and philosophy will never answer

the question: "What is man and why is he here?" But it
is answered clearly and simply in the gospel of Jesus Christ,
and we are instructed: "If any of you lack wisdom, let
him ask of God. . . ."

Let us be prepared to do this and not be as those
to whom the Savior referred, when he said:

> . . . well did Esaias prophesy of you, saying,
> This people draweth nigh unto me with their mouth, and
> honoureth me with their lips; but their heart is far from me.
> But in vain they do worship me, teaching for doctrines the
> commandments of men. (Matthew 15:7-9.)

Yes, it is important, and the Lord emphasizes that we
must humble ourselves and accept the teachings of Jesus
Christ and keep his commandments if we would expect
him to hear and answer our prayers. We should all be
prepared to say truthfully, as Paul did, in speaking to the
Romans, "For I am not ashamed of the gospel of Christ:
for it is the power of God unto salvation to every one that
believeth. . . ." (Romans 1:16.)

It is difficult to understand why some cannot believe,
or find it very hard to believe that God can hear and answer
our prayers, and yet they believe that astronauts can leave
the earth and travel in outer space at thousands of miles
per hour and still be directed from home base; that they
can keep in touch with home base and receive instructions
and be led in their activities and then be brought back
to a safe landing here upon the earth.

How can we question God's ability to hear and answer
our prayers and direct us in all things if we will but keep
in tune with him and at the same time have no doubt that
marvelous machines and men can be sent out from the
earth to the moon and there be directed by mere man
here upon the earth?

We are as astronauts, sent out by God to fill our missions here upon the earth. He wants us to succeed. He
stands ready to answer our prayers and assures us a safe

landing as we return if we will but keep in touch with him through prayer and do as we are bid.

As we pray, however, are we prepared to ask the Lord to bless us as we answer his call or acknowledge and serve him?

Are we prepared to ask the Lord to forgive us as we forgive one another?

We may well stop and analyze our own situation. Do we wait until we are in trouble and then run to the Lord? As we pray, do we give orders to the Lord by saying, "Bless this," and "Bless that," "Give us this," and "Give us that," "Do this," and "Do that"?

Or do we pray that we might be led to do that which is right, or be blessed with those things which are for our best good? We should always pray for the desire and strength and determination to do the will of our Heavenly Father, and always stand ready to do his bidding.

Men pray for different reasons. Many are driven to their knees out of fear, and then only do they pray. Others go to the Lord when in dire need of immediate direction for which they know of no other place to go. Nations are called by their governments in case of a national tragedy, drought, or plague, famine or war, to call upon God for his blessings, for his protection, and for his direction. Some people ask to be healed, others to be strengthened. They ask for the blessings of the Lord to attend their families, their loved ones, and themselves in all their righteous endeavors. This, I am sure, is all good in the sight of the Lord.

It is most important, however, that we take time to express our gratitude to our Father in heaven for the many blessings we receive. I was deeply touched one day following our family prayer when one of our little daughters said, "Daddy, I don't think we ought to ask for more blessings. The Lord has been very good to us, but I do think we should ask him to help us to be worthy of the blessings we receive." Since then we have tried more diligently to express our gratitude to our Father in heaven and pray for guidance that we might be worthy of that which he has given us.

As we express our appreciation for our many blessings, we become more conscious of what the Lord has done for us, and thereby we become more appreciative. We all know what it means to hear or receive an expression of gratitude for anything we might have done. Our forefathers set aside a day of thanksgiving. I fear that some of us even forget that day.

I wonder if we are sometimes guilty of not expressing to the Lord our gratitude, even as the lepers who were healed. We all remember so well the story of Jesus healing the ten lepers, who cried:

> . . . have mercy on us.
> And one of them, when he saw that he was healed, turned back, and with a loud voice glorified God,
> And fell down on his face at his feet, giving him thanks: and he was a Samaritan.
> And Jesus answering said, Were there not ten cleansed? but where are the nine?
> There are not found that returned to give glory to God, save this stranger. (Luke 17:13, 15-18.)

And as Mark Antony said when referring to Caesar, who recognized his friend Brutus among his assassins:

> This was the most unkindest cut of all;
> For when the noble Caesar saw him stab,
> Ingratitude, more strong than traitors' arms,
> Quite vanquished him: then burst his mighty heart. . . .
> (William Shakespeare, *Julius Caesar*, Act 3, sc. 2.)

I am sure that the Lord expects us to express our gratitude for our many blessings as we ask for his continued blessings, and to ask forgiveness for our failings and the desire and strength to do right.

When we pray, it is important that we set about to do all in our power to make it possible for the Lord to answer our prayers. As my father said to me when I was just a boy, "My son, if you want your prayers to be answered, you must get on your feet and do your part."

I often think how much more effective it would be, when the country's president calls upon his people to set aside a day of prayer, if we were all living righteous lives and were prepared to acknowledge God as our Creator and keep his commandments. It seems that many have lost belief in God entirely, and others question his ability to answer our prayers. Others have faith and confidence in their own learning and in their own strength and power.

The Lord has instructed parents to teach their children to have faith in Christ, the Son of the living God, and to pray and to walk uprightly before the Lord. There is no doubt that our children, if they are taught to pray to a living God in whom they have faith, can more easily walk uprightly before the Lord.

I shall never be able to express fully my appreciation to my parents for teaching me to pray secretly and to participate with them in family prayer. My mother taught me at her knee. She made me feel and know that I was talking to the Lord, to our Maker, our Father in heaven, and that he was conscious of my acts and my wishes and my needs. I was taught that I should express my sincere thanks, ask for forgiveness, and ask for strength to do the right. This has always been a great strength to me throughout my life, and today I pray even more diligently than I ever did before that the Lord will guide and direct me in my activities, that whatever I do will be acceptable to him.

As I think back to when we used to kneel as a family in prayer every morning and every evening, I realize what it meant to us as children to hear our father call upon the Lord and actually talk to him, expressing his gratitude and asking for the blessings of the Lord on his crops and flocks and all of our undertakings. It always gave us greater strength to meet temptation when we remembered that we would be reporting to the Lord at night.

Family prayer in any home will draw the family closer together and result in better feelings between father and mother, between parents and children, and between one child and another. If children pray for their parents, it makes them more appreciative of their parents, and as they pray for one another, they feel closer to one another and part of each other, especially as they realize that they are talking to their Father in heaven while on their knees in family or secret prayer. Then is when we forget our differences and think of the best in others, and pray for their well-being and for strength to overcome our own weaknesses. There is no doubt that we are better people when we try to tune in to the spirit of our Father in heaven so that we might communicate with him and express our desire to do his will as we pray for his blessings.

The Lord has admonished us to "pray always, lest you enter into temptation and lose your reward. Be faithful unto the end, and lo, I am with you. These words are not of man nor of men, but of me, even Jesus Christ, your Redeemer, by the will of the Father." (D&C 31:12-13.)

I have often asked myself and tried to answer the question, Why do some people refuse to pray? Is it because they feel they have not the time?

I remember very well a father coming to me one day regarding his oldest son, with whom he was having some difficulty. The boy was a good boy, but he was getting out of hand. I asked the father if they had regular family prayers in their home. He answered, "Well, no, but sometimes. You know, we are too busy and we go to work at different times, and therefore it is most difficult for our family to get together for family prayer."

I asked, "If you knew that your boy was sick nigh unto death, would you be able to get your family together each night and morning for a week to pray that his life might be spared?"

"Why, of course,"'he said.

I tried then to explain to him that there are other ways of losing a boy than by death. I also explained that where families pray together, they usually stay together, and their ideals are higher, they feel more secure, and they have a greater love for one another.

Next, do they feel too independent, too smart, and think they can go it alone? Or are they ashamed to call upon God? Do they think it shows a weakness? Or do they not believe in or have faith in God? Or is it that they do not appreciate their many blessings? Or do they not feel worthy?

If one does not feel worthy, he should acknowledge his weaknesses, express regret, repent, covenant to do right, and ask for guidance.

Is it because some do not know how to pray? If that is true, I suggest that you go to your Heavenly Father in secret. Pour out your heart to him. Pray regularly so that you can feel at home and comfortable while communicating with him. All one needs to do is express his feelings, which the Lord understands. He has invited all of us to call on him regularly and has promised that he will hear our supplication.

The ancient prophet Moroni, referring to the Book of Mormon, said:

And when ye shall receive these things, I would exhort you that ye would ask God, the Eternal Father, in the name of Christ, if these things are not true; and if ye shall ask with a sincere heart, with real intent, having faith in Christ, he will manifest the truth of it unto you, by the power of the Holy Ghost.

And by the power of the Holy Ghost ye may know the truth of all things. (Moroni 10:4-5.)

This promise applies to all of us if we will but repent and go to the Lord, knowing that he can hear and will hear and answer our prayers. We should all realize that we are God's children and that he is still as interested in us as he ever was. He still answers the prayers of the righteous and those who diligently seek him.

Chapter 20

The Plan of Life and Salvation

The passing of loved ones always causes us to stop and ponder such questions as: Who am I? Why am I here? When I die, will I live again? Where am I going? How can I best prepare myself?

I am sure that thousands and thousands have said, "If I knew the answers to these questions, I would know better how to govern my life." It is impossible for any of us, including philosophers, astrologers, astronomers, and scientists in any field, with our finite minds, to answer these questions without referring to the word of God as contained in the scriptures.

We mortals have never experienced death and the resurrection, nor do we remember our preexistence. Therefore, it is not commonly believed or understood that we had a premortal existence, that we are the spirit children of God, the Eternal Father, and that when we have finished our life here upon the earth we will enjoy a literal resurrection and may continue on in eternal progression. In fact, many who question this say that if someone would return from the dead as a witness of these things, they would believe. This is not necessarily so.

Let us remember the parable of the rich man who prayed that Lazarus be sent from the dead to his father's house to testify to his brethren, saying that if one went to them from the dead, they would repent. Abraham said unto him: "If they hear not Moses and the prophets, neither will they be persuaded, though one rose from the the dead." (Luke 16:31.)

How fortunate we are that the Lord God, from the time of Adam down through the ages to the present time, has given us the answers to these very important questions and we have them recorded in Holy Writ. Yes, God has seen fit to talk to his people through his chosen prophets, and those who have heard and believed and followed have been blessed.

It is sad but true that many, many people are not acquainted with the words of the prophets, and many refuse to believe, and others scoff and ridicule the teachings of the Savior. It is extremely sad that many, through their own learning and their sensuous knowledge, become self-satisfied and think that they are sufficient unto themselves and need not heed the word of God; and often, because they have not heard, seen, touched, or talked to God, they deny even his very existence and use their influence to dissuade others.

But all of this ignorance, derision, scoffing, and ridicule does not destroy truth, which finally will triumph. We must learn to live by faith and believe in the words of the Lord, especially in those things which we mortals do not and cannot fully comprehend. Probably the greatest evidence to the fact that God speaks to his prophets is the fulfillment of the prophecies made by them. Many of these prophecies and their fulfillment are a matter of historical and scriptural record.

As I was pondering the questions to which I have referred, and their answers, I turned to the scriptures and read again this significant and most important statement: "And this is life eternal, that they might know thee the

only true God, and Jesus Christ, whom thou hast sent."
(John 17:3.)

Many ask, "How can a man know God and Jesus
Christ, whom he has sent" The answer must be clear that
it is through prayer and faith and study of the words of
God as given through his prophets and by Jesus Christ.
Let us refer to some revelations received and prophecies
made by both ancient and modern prophets that tell us
about God and our relationship to him, and that will help
us to know and understand the purpose of our mission
here on earth.

Probably the very earliest scriptural account we have
of man and his relationship to God, and which shows beyond doubt that we had a premortal existence in the spirit
world with God, is the record of the council in heaven as
revealed to Moses and Abraham:

> Now the Lord had shown unto me, Abraham, the intelligences
> that were organized before the world was; . . .
> And God . . . stood in the midst of them, and he said: These
> I will make my rulers; for he stood among those that were spirits,
> . . . and he said unto me: Abraham, thou art one of them; thou
> wast chosen before thou wast born.
> And there stood one among them that was like unto God, and
> he said unto those who were with him: We will go down, for
> there is space there, and we will take of these materials, and we
> will make an earth whereon these may dwell;
> And we will prove them herewith, to see if they will do all
> things whatsoever the Lord their God shall command them;
> And they who keep their first estate shall be added upon;
> and they who keep not their first estate shall not have glory in the
> same kingdom with those who keep their first estate; and they
> who keep their second estate shall have glory added upon their
> heads for ever and ever. (Abraham 3:22-26.)

And the Lord told Moses:

> And I, God, said unto mine Only Begotten, which was with me
> from the beginning: Let us make man in our image, after our like-
> ness; and it was so. . . .

And I, God, created man in mine own image, in the image of mine Only Begotten created I him; male and female created I them. (Moses 2:26-27.)

God told Moses that Christ was chosen as the Savior of the world and that Satan rebelled, and God said:

Wherefore, because that Satan rebelled against me, and sought to destroy the agency of man, which I, the Lord God, had given him, and also, that I should give unto him mine own power; . . . I caused that he should be cast down;

And he became Satan, yea, even the devil, the father of all lies, to deceive and to blind men, and to lead them captive at his will, even as many as would not hearken unto my voice. (Moses 4:3-4.)

As spirit children of God, we were all present at that council and voted to sustain Jesus Christ as the Savior of the world. In Paul's Epistle to the Hebrews, in Ecclesiastes, in Jeremiah, and in many other accounts in both the Old and the New Testaments, as well as in modern scripture, we have further evidence that we are the spirit children of God and dwelt with him in the spirit world.

There is also further indisputable evidence that Jesus was with God before he came here. Just before his crucifixion, he went into Gethsemane, and in his agony he prayed unto the Father in these words:

Father, the hour is come; . . .

I have glorified thee on the earth: I have finished the work which thou gavest me to do.

And now, O Father, glorify thou me with thine own self with the glory which I had with thee before the world was. (John 17:1, 4-5.)

How comforting and encouraging it is for us to know that "God so loved the world, that he gave his only begotten Son, that whosoever believeth in him should not perish, but have everlasting life." (John 3:16.)

The coming of the Savior was foretold to Adam right after he and Eve were driven out of the Garden of Eden.

They were told by the Lord to offer sacrifice, and they were obedient. After many days an angel of the Lord appeared unto Adam and explained:

This thing is a similitude of the sacrifice of the Only Begotten of the Father, which is full of grace and truth.

Wherefore, thou shalt do all that thou doest in the name of the Son, and thou shalt repent and call upon God in the name of the Son forevermore. (Moses 5:7-8.)

Then we have the writings of many Old Testament prophets as well as American prophets, as recorded in the Book of Mormon, who foretold of the birth, teachings, persecution, crucifixion, and resurrection of the Savior. We all know that these prophecies have been fulfilled.

It is most reassuring to know that the prophets in different climes and in different dispensations were in complete harmony, and that their prophecies have been fulfilled to the letter. And always they gave us this assurance, as did Nephi, that "all those who shall believe on his name shall be saved in the kingdom of God." (2 Nephi 25:13.)

Though we should need no further evidence of the Savior's divinity and of the importance of his mission as it pertains to us, let us recall the strong and stirring testimony of Paul, who was a great persecutor of the saints. He records that as he was going to Damascus to bring saints unto Jerusalem to be punished, "suddenly there shone from heaven a great light round about me. And I fell unto the ground, and heard a voice saying unto me, Saul, Saul, why persecutest thou me?"

When he asked who was speaking, the voice said, "I am Jesus of Nazareth, whom thou persecutest."

Then Saul said, "What shall I do, Lord? And the Lord said unto me, Arise, and go into Damascus; and there it shall be told thee of all things which are appointed for thee to do." (Acts 22:6-10.)

You will remember that he was blinded by the glory of the light, so he had to be led to Damascus and to Ananias, who said, "Brother Saul, receive thy sight" (Acts 22:13), and he could see. From that time Saul, who was also called Paul, became one of the most valiant and strong of the Christian preachers and defenders. Then we find him falsely accused and forced to defend himself before the governor and other officials, and finally before King Agrippa. Think of his boldness and courage as he stood in chains before the king and recounted the story of his conversion, after which he said:

Whereupon, O king Agrippa, I was not disobedient unto the heavenly vision:

But shewed first unto them of Damascus, and at Jerusalem, and throughout all the coasts of Judaea, and then to the Gentiles, that they should repent and turn to God, and do works meet for repentance.

For these causes the Jews caught me in the temple, and went about to kill me.

Having therefore obtained help of God, I continue unto this day, witnessing both to small and great, saying none other things than those which the prophets and Moses did say should come:

That Christ should suffer, and that he should be the first that should rise from the dead, and should shew light unto the people, and to the Gentiles.

And as he thus spake for himself, Festus said with a loud voice, Paul, thou art beside thyself; much learning doth make thee mad.

But he said, I am not mad, most noble Festus; but speak forth the words of truth and soberness.

For the king knoweth of these things, before whom also I speak freely: for I am persuaded that none of these things are hidden from him; for this thing was not done in a corner.

King Agrippa, believest thou the prophets? I know that thou believest.

Then Agrippa said unto Paul, Almost thou persuadest me to be a Christian.

And Paul said, I would to God, that not only thou, but also all that hear me this day, were both almost, and altogether such as I am, except these bonds. (Acts 26:19-29.)

The strength of his deep conviction had been previously manifest when he said to his friends who were trying to protect him and persuade him not to go to Jerusalem: "What mean ye to weep and to break mine heart? for I am ready not to be bound only, but also to die at Jerusalem for the name of the Lord Jesus." (Acts 21:13.)

I would that we, as Paul, could all feel and show our deep love and devotion to Jesus Christ, who, because of his great love for us, was prepared to suffer and give his life to redeem us from the grave. All through the scriptures we have the words of the prophets bearing witness that Jesus Christ is the Son of God and that he came and gave his life for us. He also gave us the Ten Commandments, the Sermon on the Mount, and the whole plan of life and salvation—the blueprint of life—which if lived will not only bring joy to us here on earth but will prepare us for immortality and eternal life, where we can dwell with God the Father and his Son Jesus Christ and our loved ones who have gone there before us.

Our Heavenly Father, knowing our weaknesses and our need for constant direction, sends us prophets to continually teach us and keep us reminded of this plan of life and salvation. Our salvation, and that of our loved ones, depends on our listening to and heeding the words of the prophets, realizing that we must believe all that God has revealed, all that he does now reveal, and that he will yet reveal many great and important things pertaining to the kingdom of God.

To those who question these things, I should like to emphasize this one fact: Everything that was taught by the prophets and by Jesus Christ himself, as recorded in Holy Writ, is for the benefit of mankind, and if accepted and lived will make better individuals, better communities, a better world where we can live in love and peace with one another.

Man by his own formula has failed to accomplish these things. He has no effective plan, and any failure is not because the gospel has failed, but because man has failed to live its teachings. To those who doubt or question, but have no answers, and who look for hope out of the midst of their despair, I urge that they accept the word of God the Eternal Father and believe in the gospel, which is uplifting and beautiful and will bring peace and contentment to their souls. How much better to hope than to despair, and the words of hope and everlasting life with the Father and the Son are to be found in the gospel of Jesus Christ.

It is important to understand that we are here to prove ourselves, to prepare ourselves to go back into the presence of our Heavenly Father; and the choices we make will determine our future happiness. Hear the words of the American prophet Lehi to his sons, which message has been given repeatedly to the children of men through the ages:

> Wherefore, men are free according to the flesh; and all things are given them which are expedient unto man. And they are free to choose liberty and eternal life, through the great mediation of all men, or to choose captivity and death, according to the captivity and power of the devil; for he seeketh that all men might be miserable like unto himself.
>
> And now, my sons, I would that ye should look to the great Mediator, and hearken unto his great commandments; and be faithful unto his words, and choose eternal life, according to the will of his Holy Spirit;
>
> And not choose eternal death, according to the will of the flesh and the evil which is therein, which giveth the spirit of the devil power to captivate, to bring you down to hell, that he may reign over you in his own kingdom. (2 Nephi 2:27-29.)

Jacob, Lehi's son, taught, "Therefore, cheer up your hearts, and remember that ye are free to act for yourselves —to choose the way of everlasting death or the way of eternal life." (2 Nephi 10:23.)

To summarize, we read from Ecclesiates 12:13: "Let us hear the conclusion of the whole matter: Fear God, and keep his commandments: for this is the whole duty of man."

CHAPTER 21

Privileged Priesthood Holders

I am always thrilled and inspired when I meet with the priesthood of The Church of Jesus Christ of Latter-day Saints, which is the priesthood of God. I often feel to ask the question: Do you really believe and appreciate the fact that the priesthood is the power of God, delegated to you to act in his name in the things which you are directed to do when you are ordained to the priesthood you hold and the office therein?

If we did nothing more than answer that question and renew our determination to keep the covenants we make when we are ordained to the priesthood and let our lives be lives of example to our children, to one another, and to the world, our gathering would be very, very profitable indeed.

The priesthood is the power by which all things were created and the power by which God has revealed all truth and done all things connected with the restoration of his gospel. For us as individuals it is the power of God that has been delegated to us to act in his name in the office which we hold. And it is a great privilege, a great blessing, and a great responsibility to have that priesthood bestowed upon us.

Sometimes our young men feel they should have the priesthood when they reach the respective ages for ordination as deacons, teachers, and priests, regardless of their situation as to their activity or how they are living. They should realize what a great privilege it is to hold that priesthood. When a person receives it, he takes upon himself a very heavy responsibility.

I should like to read just a few words to you, taken from the Doctrine and Covenants:

> Behold, there are many called, but few are chosen. And why are they not chosen?
> Because their hearts are set so much upon the things of this world, and aspire to the honors of men, that they do not learn this one lesson—
> That the rights of the priesthood are inseparably connected with the powers of heaven, and that the powers of heaven cannot be controlled nor handled only upon the principles of righteousness.
> That they may be conferred upon us, it is true; but when we undertake to cover our sins, or to gratify our pride, our vain ambition, or to exercise control or dominion or compulsion upon the souls of the children of men, in any degree of unrighteousness, behold, the heavens withdraw themselves; the Spirit of the Lord is grieved; and when it is withdrawn, Amen to the priesthood or the authority of that man.
> Behold, ere he is aware, he is left unto himself, to kick against the pricks, to persecute the saints, and to fight against God. (D&C 121:34-38.)

I interpret that as referring to those who fail to magnify their priesthood, or who use it as it should not be used. I know of many cases where a man has gradually failed to magnify his priesthood and moved away from activity in the Church. As a result, a man who has been very active loses his testimony and the Spirit of the Lord withdraws from him, and he begins to criticize those in authority, and to persecute the saints, apostatize, and fight against God.

We also find these words of the Lord in the Doctrine and Covenants: "The Holy Ghost shall be thy constant

companion, and thy scepter an unchanging scepter of righteousness and truth; and thy dominion shall be an everlasting dominion, and without compulsory means it shall
flow unto thee forever and ever" (D&C 121:46)—that is,
if we magnify our priesthood.

I am sure all of you have read the oath and covenant
of the priesthood, and have heard it many times. To me
it is very important.

> For whoso is faithful unto the obtaining these two priest-
> hoods of which I have spoken, and the magnifying their calling,
> are sanctified by the Spirit unto the renewing of their bodies.
> They become the sons of Moses and of Aaron and the seed
> of Abraham, and the church and kingdom, and the elect of God.
> And also all they who receive this priesthood receive me,
> saith the Lord;
> For he that receiveth my servants receiveth me;
> And he that receiveth me receiveth my Father;
> And he that receiveth my Father receiveth my Father's king-
> dom; therefore all that my Father hath shall be given unto him.
> (D&C 84:33-38.)

I should like to emphasize that these blessings are
promised to those who magnify their priesthood every day
in every way.

> And this is according to the oath and covenant which be-
> longeth to the priesthood.
> Therefore, all those who receive the priesthood, receive this
> oath and covenant of my Father, which he cannot break, neither
> can it be moved.
> But whoso breaketh this covenant after he hath received it,
> and altogether turneth therefrom, shall not have forgiveness of
> sins. . . . (D&C 84:39-41.)

The Lord says here that he cannot break his covenant,
but if we break ours, there is no promise.

> Wherefore, now let every man learn his duty, and to act in
> the office in which he is appointed, in all diligence.
> He that is slothful shall not be counted worthy to stand, and
> he that learns not his duty and shows himself not approved shall
> not be counted worthy to stand. Even so. Amen. (D&C 107:99-100.)

Therefore, blessed are ye if ye continue in my goodness, a light unto the Gentiles, and through this priesthood, a savior unto my people Israel. The Lord hath said it. (D&C 86:11.)

We are living in a troubled world, and the world has reason to and every right to expect some leadership somewhere to give direction and understanding of where to go and what to do. People need to understand that there is a purpose in life and what that purpose is, and they have every reason to look to the priesthood of God, which is what our brethren have.

You cannot realize and appreciate the influence the priesthood in this church could have on the whole world if every man would magnify his priesthood. Brethren, the priesthood, if magnified, is a stabilizing influence and strength. It should be. Every wife and mother has a perfect right and responsibility to look to her husband who holds the priesthood for guidance, for strength, and for direction. And he has the responsibility of magnifying his priesthood so he might be able to give this direction, this security, this strength that is needed in the home. And he can do this. If he will magnify his priesthood, he will be magnified by the Lord in the eyes of his family, and his influence will be felt for good.

Boys, we have a responsibility to our sisters. Every sister should look to a brother who holds the priesthood, whether he is twelve years of age or older, and she has a right to expect in him a living example of what the priesthood should be, and to look to him for strength and counsel and direction and to feel safe with him. Every sweetheart should be able to depend entirely on a young man holding the priesthood who is going out with her. She should be able to feel he would do anything, even to the giving of his life, to protect her womanhood and her virtue, and would never think of depriving her of it, if he is magnifying his priesthood; and he will not be tempted if he is thinking of the priesthood that he holds and the responsibility that he has.

How important it is to live to enjoy the Spirit and blessings of the Lord, and the respect and confidence of parents, friends, and church leaders, and the Lord himself, particularly so you can look them in the face with a clear conscience, and also yourself in the mirror, and know that you have been living as you should.

The Lord, speaking of Satan when he was cast out, said:

> And he became Satan, yea, even the devil, the father of all lies, to deceive and to blind men, and to lead them captive at his will, even as many as would not hearken unto my voice. (Moses 4:4.)

He tries to tempt every one of us, every one from a deacon to Christ himself. You remember how he tried to tempt Christ. He chooses emissaries, those who follow him and those who are too weak to do what is right. These emissaries will try to point out the weaknesses in an individual, in the leaders of the Church, in the organizations, and every place they can find any weakness at any time, and they will be saying, "Don't be a coward; don't be a sissy; come on."

I should like to say to all our young men that not one young man who is living according to the teachings of the gospel and honoring his priesthood would ever say that to you.

Thank the Lord that he was strong enough to say to Satan, "Get thee behind me, Satan," and I hope we can all do the same, as we honor our priesthood. Those who succumb to temptation are always defeated and miserable, unless they repent.

Former Vice President Spiro Agnew, when he visited with the First Presidency of the Church, said that one thing that appealed to him about our youth, as he was on the BYU campus, is that they are well self-disciplined; and they seemed to be doing their own thing, which was doing what they should be doing, and were happy in doing it.

I would like our young men to know that those who are frustrated, who are complaining, who are not living as they should, are not happy. There is no happiness in wrong-doing. They have their problems, and they are not trying to accomplish. Of course I feel sorry for them because they do not know as you know that all of us are spirit children of God. They do not know that God really lives, that Jesus is the Christ; that through his birth, death, and resurrection we may all be resurrected; and that this life is not the end but just the beginning of eternal life.

May we all appreciate this and do our best wherever we are to live worthy of it so that we can look into the mirror and see ourselves and say, "Thank the Lord I was strong enough to overcome, to resist." To you who have weakened in any way, who have taken a cigarette, or anything of the kind, just quit it now and be happy. You will be happy. The Lord will bless you. People will respect you, and you will be successful, and you will be doing your duty in helping to bring about the immortality and eternal life of man.

CHAPTER 22

The Word of Wisdom

When I was a boy and heard people talk about the Word of Wisdom, all I thought of was that this was a religious requirement. In fact, we were told a good many times: A cup of coffee won't hurt you; a cup of tea won't hurt you; one cigarette won't hurt you; a drink won't hurt you; it's getting the habit that will bother you. And we kids used to think that the Church was prudish and odd for trying to get us to do things that made us look funny in the sight of the boys with whom we associated who were not members of the Church.

I should like to say just a few words about the breaking of the Word of Wisdom and what it means to us, the danger of tampering with things that the Lord has told us not to tamper with, both as it affects our bodies and as it affects our ability to resist if we get on the wrong side of the line.

This has been said about Satan, as we read in the Doctrine and Covenants:

Satan stirreth them up, that he may lead their souls to destruction.

And thus he has laid a cunning plan, thinking to destroy the work of God; but I will require this at their hands, and it shall, turn to their shame and condemnation in the day of judgment.

Yea, he stirreth up their hearts to anger against this work.

Yea, he saith unto them: Deceive and lie in wait to catch, that ye may destroy; behold, this is no harm. And thus he flattereth them, and telleth them that it is no sin to lie that they may catch a man in a lie, that they may destroy him.

And thus he flattereth them, and leadeth them along until he draggeth their souls down to hell; and thus he causeth them to catch themselves in their own snare.

And thus he goeth up and down, to and fro in the earth, seeking to destroy the souls of men. (D&C 10:22-27.)

There is no doubt but that Satan is out, going up and down, here and there, trying in every way he can to destroy us. It is interesting that over 130 years ago a prophet of God said, ". . . tobacco . . . is not good for man." (D&C 89:8.) Now scientists all over the world say that tobacco is not good for man. You have heard it talked about a good deal, but I would like to appeal to all our youth to realize what a great danger is involved in partaking of tobacco and alcohol and these other things that are advised against.

Dr. William H. Stewart has said that the so-called "next-guy theory"—that it can happen to someone else but not to me—is the psychology that is preventing anti-cigarette campaigns from making more headway. The fallacy of this kind of reasoning is illustrated in the story of a Honolulu reporter, who said, "It just can't happen to me; I'm safe." But this Hawaiian newsman, Mark Waters, spoke from the grave to readers of the Honolulu *Star Bulletin*. Waters died of lung cancer at the age of fifty-six on the day the *Star Bulletin* ran his last story. It was a by-line account of a forty-two-year rendezvous with his killer.

The story was written in the hospital five days before his death. Waters read proof on the story and made final corrections the day before he succumbed, observing that it might help someone else.

He told how he started smoking at fourteen, stealing cigarettes from his father's pack, and how he continued at the rate of two packs a day, even after suffering a stroke and contracting bronchitis. Doctors discovered cancer in his left lung. A lobe was removed. Waters gained ten pounds after the September operation and felt fine. Four months later pain returned. The doctor removed fluid from his chest cavity but had to tell him that he had little time to live.

"Not a soul I've preached to has stopped smoking," he wrote from his hospital bed, "not a single, solitary soul.

"It's one of those things. You always think, it'll happen to others, but never to me. When you get lung cancer, God help you."

Like the rest of his story, Waters' conclusion was terse.

"I'm short of breath. I can't take five steps without having to sit.

"The cancer has gone to my liver and I don't know where else.

"I don't have a ghost of a chance.

"It's too late for me. It may not be for you."

I want to tell you a little story about a boy I knew very well, my baby brother, as sweet a boy as I ever knew— kind, considerate of his mother, and loved by every member of the family. But he got into wrong company when he was just a little boy, and he started using cigarettes. He used to steal away and have his smoke, and then he got to smoking a little more and a little more, until he became a habitual smoker. He had four older brothers, and we tried to get him to quit smoking, to realize that he shouldn't be doing it.

He kept saying he was going to quit smoking, but a few years ago he died of lung cancer. And if anything makes you hate tobacco, it is to have a brother, one of the finest young fellows that you know, go to his death because he had that habit of smoking. He thought when he was a kid, "I can quit any time I want to." In fact, he used to say so, and he used to try to quit but he couldn't.

I want to tell you another story about a man whom I knew very well. He used to be one of the most successful oil well drillers in the Province of Alberta, a man who was well-respected, highly regarded, and a good citizen, but who, as many others, through social drinking, became an alcoholic. He was one of the fortunate ones who, with the help of Alcoholics Anonymous, and, as he said, with the help of the Lord, was able to overcome this dread disease.

One day, as I invited him to speak to a group of young people, his quick response was, "If I can help any youth to understand the evil of alcohol and what it will do to him, I am anxious to do it." This was his story:

"When I was in business, I used to drink with the boys at cocktail parties and at receptions, never thinking it was doing me any harm. In fact, I never worried about it at all. Even when I found myself taking a third or fourth drink, and wanting a drink during the day when I knew I should not be drinking, I had no idea that I was really becoming an alcoholic. I refused to accept the fact until I found myself literally in the gutter.

"The result was that my partner, my business associates, and all who knew me and even my wife and family found that they could not depend on me, and lost respect for me. As a result, I lost my wife. After pleading and working with me, she divorced me, and I found that I was alone. I had lost respect for myself, and had lost my home, family, everything.

"When I found myself in the gutter, helpless and alone, I was persuaded to go to Alcoholics Anonymous. With their help and my determination I was able to overcome the habit after months and months of severe struggle." Then he pointed out that only about one out of five is able to overcome this pernicious habit.

As he concluded, he said: "No man knows when he takes a single drink whether or not he will become an alcoholic. Therefore, no man, regardless of his wealth or position, can afford to take one single drink of liquor." He pled with every one of them not to touch it, and then emphasized that one out of every fifteen who drink will become an alcoholic, and often the brightest and most capable one, who least expects it, is the unfortunate one.

Just remember: if you are in a group where fifteen people are drinking socially, at least one of them will probably become an alcoholic. Every one of them will say: "How silly! It couldn't happen to me. I am just drinking socially. I am not going to drink much." And they continue to justify themselves until they are in the gutter.

I want to say to our youth: realize that you can't afford to play with these things that will take your life. You can't afford to do it anyway, because the Lord has said, "Don't do it." There is more and more proof that tobacco and alcohol are not good for us. To illustrate, may I refer to the following facts:

Alcohol—in liquors, beers, and all forms—has contributed more evil, sadness, and heartache to the world than will ever be imagined by our finite minds. Even in business its toll is tremendous. Experts claim that more than five workers out of every 100 are alcoholics, and these include men from the executive suite to the assembly line. They cost industry four billion dollars a year. One official, Lewis F. Presnall, director of the industrial services of the National Council on Alcoholism, says alcoholism among workers is a "huge problem and extremely costly to industry."

But alcoholism does more than hit industry in the pocketbook. It hits every citizen. In 1966 Senator Jacob K. Javits of New York introduced the Alcoholism Control Act in the United States Senate, and reported that some 15 percent of all new admissions to public non-federal mental hospitals in 1960 were alcoholics. It is calculated that over five million persons in the United States are alcoholics and that alcohol indirectly upsets another 20 million lives—persons such as family members, employers, and close associates. Two billion dollars each year are spent for the care and rehabilitation of alcoholics. Every taxpayer pays in increased taxes the cost of alcoholism.

National councils state that alcoholism has increased so rapidly that it now ranks fourth in the United States as a leading health problem. Only mental illness, heart disease, and cancer are more common. In our permissive society, the development of a state of mind conducive to the use of alcohol has been inevitable.

All of us need to be more vigilant in this matter, and especially Latter-day Saints who have the word of the Lord on this subject. Parents need to remember that their children associate with friends who are not aware of the dangers of alcohol, even with youth who themselves may be drinking. Dr. Frederick Hudson, director of an alcoholic clinic in San Francisco, claims that 70 percent of all alcoholics begin drinking as teenagers. These youths see the drinking of alcohol as a natural way of life among their parents and others. According to the 1963 White House Conference on Children and Youth, most youths who drink get their first drink in their own homes from parents who drink regularly.

I would like to refer to a story that I have often mentioned about the father who was called to the scene of a car accident in which his young daughter was killed. The group had been drinking, and the father in his anguish exclaimed: "I'll kill the man who provided this whiskey!" On returning home he found a note in his daughter's own handwriting in his liquor cabinet. It read: "Dad, I hope you don't mind our taking your whiskey tonight."

Since youth will not be able to avoid being exposed to alcohol, we need to encourage them to teach their friends the truth about alcohol. Parents may be interested to know that a special jury in St. Louis, Missouri, found that "almost 100 percent of the nighttime fatal accidents to teenagers in one year involved the use of alcohol." In fact, the U.S. Department of Health, Education, and Welfare has reported that more than 50 percent of all highway accidents are caused by drinking.

But alcohol's toll does not end on the highway. The Federal Bureau of Investigation has reported that almost 50 percent of those arrested were under the influence of alcohol. The *Quarterly Journal of Studies of Alcohol* reported that alcohol was involved in 64 percent of homicide cases, 70 percent of physical assault crimes, and 50 percent of shootings and other assaults. (Vol. 17.)

It is an established fact that much sex delinquency begins when one is under the influence of alcohol. Also, alcohol is the cause of more broken homes, frustrated and disappointed children, warped personalities, and dulling of minds than any other single cause. No one needs to question the inspiration of the instruction "wine or strong drink is not good." (D&C 89:5.)

In a similar way, mounting pressure continues to pile up against the use of tobacco. At first, isolated studies linked cigarette smoking with an increased risk of death from lung cancer. Then in 1962 the British Royal College of Physicians reported that some 500 Britons were dying each week from lung cancer and that 80 percent of these deaths were caused by cigarettes.

Besides being connected with lung cancer and pulmonary diseases, tobacco is also associated with deaths from peptic ulcers, stroke, and cancer of the larynx, mouth, pharynx, esophagus, and bladder, as well as other diseases. It is reported that each year tobacco is responsible for more than 11 million cases of chronic illness in the United States and 77 million days lost from work.

It is little wonder, then, that the Lord has said, "And again, tobacco is not for the body, neither for the belly, and is not good for man." (D&C 89:8.)

If we will continue to teach the facts about tobacco and alcohol, most of our people, we hope, will make the intelligent decision. According to research, teenagers are smarter than many adults in this respect. A U.S. Public Health Service survey reports that teenage smoking has dropped 10 percent in the last ten years throughout the United States, and that 80 percent of the teenagers who say they smoke also say they plan to quit.

In recent years we have all been shocked by the great increase in the use of drugs. Far too many of our own Latter-day Saints have experimented and continue to experiment with LSD and other mind-deadening and destroying drugs. They take drugs in opposition to known medical and scientific research and in opposition to sound thinking and moral teachings. Many reports of sad experiences with drugs, in which individuals involved now regret their actions, have come to our attention.

For example, LSD has been identified as a drug that "substitutes instant delirium tremens for the slower escapism of the whiskey bottle." It may cause the emotionally disturbed to go permanently insane. Harvard University has reported: "We now know that long-term subtle psychological damage can result from LSD. Numerous cases have been reported of prolonged psychotic reactions lasting from a few months to two years." The university also reports that the drug probably structurally damages the brain. What sane, intelligent person would want to damage his brain permanently?

Despite all that we know about the dangers of these drugs and their evil and shocking influence, many youths

—some of them Latter-day Saints—each year begin the drinking, smoking, and drug-use experience. Parents, teachers, and youth leaders must make a renewed and continual attempt to reach all of our youth—the religiously active as well as the inactive—concerning this message, and to encourage our youth and adults to be ambassadors in informing their associates of the dangers of these drugs. No good comes from them as they are currently used in contemporary society—only degeneration of physical and mental health.

All Latter-day Saints should read again that blessed revelation in the Doctrine and Covenants concerning our latter-day environment, as given in section 89:

Behold, verily, thus saith the Lord unto you: In consequence of evils and designs which do and will exist in the hearts of conspiring men in the last days, I have warned you, and forewarn you, by giving unto you this word of wisdom by revelation—

And all saints who remember to keep and do these sayings, walking in obedience to the commandments, shall receive health in their navel and marrow to their bones;

And shall find wisdom and great treasures of knowledge, even hidden treasures;

And shall run and not be weary, and shall walk and not faint.

And I, the Lord, give unto them a promise, that the destroying angel shall pass by them, as the children of Israel, and not slay them. Amen. (D&C 89:4, 18-21.)

We have not seen the end of these drugs and their devastating results. There will be more. And there will be continual pressure by the forces connected with the tobacco and alcohol industries. Yet, whatever the pressures, whatever our society may offer, Latter-day Saints need not succumb.

Our bodies are the temples of our personal spirits, and they are also the temples of the Spirit of God. Truly, the influence of the Spirit finds difficulty in penetrating a drug-dulled and drug-warped mind. May God bless us to seek after the good things of the earth, the good things of life. May all Latter-day Saints seek inspiration in their callings and encourage people everywhere to experience the full joy of mental, spiritual, and physical health that our Father in heaven has promised to those who follow his teachings. And may we all thank him for and determine to fully keep the Word of Wisdom. Never before has the divinity of its message been more apparent.

CHAPTER 23

Lead Them Not Into Temptation

One hundred forty years ago a prophet of God gave us a revelation that still applies to every man, woman, and child today, and that we should all heed:

A Word of Wisdom. . . . Given for a principle with promise, adapted to the capacity of the weak and the weakest of all saints, who are or can be called saints.

Behold, verily, thus saith the Lord unto you: In consequence of evils and designs which do and will exist in the hearts of conspiring men in the last days, I have warned you, and forewarn you, by giving unto you this word of wisdom by revelation. (D&C 89:1, 3-4.)

We, as members of the Church, have considered the Word of Wisdom as a direction from the Lord himself, with a warning and a promise. Today the whole world, with the scientific evidence now available to everyone, should, regardless of religion or race, observe this warning.

We read daily in newspapers and magazines such startling headlines as: "Cigarette Blamed in Apartment Fire and Death," "Youth Drug Craze Rises, Ending in Despair," "300 Pilot Deaths Laid to Alcohol."

These point up clearly the dangers of tobacco, drugs, and alcohol. Because of these great dangers, because of my own experiences and observations, and because of the real concern we have for our youth, who will determine the future of this great country and the world, I have chosen to discuss the evils of alcohol, drugs, and tobacco.

Before doing so, however, I should like to make it abundantly clear that throughout my life some of my close business associates have been men who used tobacco and alcohol. Many of them were very able and successful in business; they were community-minded and highly regarded, and I certainly do not wish to criticize or question the character of these or other users of tobacco and alcohol. I do most emphatically register my great concern about the dangers connected with their use. Many men have said, "I wish I had never touched the weed, or drink. They are really a curse."

Let me relate a few examples that have come to my attention recently concerning the wisdom of the Lord's counsel to us regarding these matters.

Not too long ago a bishop called me from California to make an appointment to bring in a young man from his ward who was involved with hippies. He felt I might be able to help him. They came in just after conference. His long hair, dress, and general appearance left no doubt that he was a hippie. I asked him to tell me his story. Briefly, this is what he said:

"I am a returned missionary, a married man, and I have a child; and here I am, a hippie, a drug addict, and I am guilty of many misdemeanors and even felonies. I am most unhappy. This is not what I want."

I asked him how it was that a man with his background ever got mixed up with these people. He said that one day when he was feeling despondent and discouraged, he decided that he wanted to be free, that he did not want to be bound by any traditions or Church restrictions in any way. He went out with some of these fellows in a spirit of rebellion, and then he said, "Here I am. Instead of being free, I'm a slave. In a way I am a fugitive. I wish you could help me. I just don't know what to do."

Before he left, he assured me that he would cut his hair and clean up and break away from these people, and that he would turn himself over to the law and do all he could to repent and live as he should. The following is a letter he wrote to me about six months later:

Dear President Tanner: I pray that you will know the true feelings of my heart at this time. I now live my life inside prison walls. It is my desire that others do not fall into the hands of Satan, as I did. If relating my experiences to other young people like myself can be of some worth in their lives, this is my hope. . . . I'm thankful that I was blessed with a bishop who has been my closest friend through all my trials. I'm grateful for your interest, President Tanner.

The reason I use this young man as an example is that his background should have given him the strength to resist or overcome, and it shows how dangerous it is for a man like him, let alone a youth who has no such ties or responsibilities, to even associate with those who tamper with drugs. His was a very sad case, and it touched my heart.

The next case I wish to share with you is similar to hundreds and hundreds of others. I have talked to the girl involved and to her parents; and though they know that many might recognize them as the ones about whom I am talking, they said if it will help someone they would be glad to have me use their story.

She comes from a very fine family. The father is a successful doctor, and the family has been active in the Church and the community. They have one son who has filled a mission, and another in the field now. They have an older daughter who is very highly regarded, active in the Church, and who was married in the temple. The girl about whom I am speaking is a fine, bright young girl, but she started chasing around with other girls and boys, some of whom were using cigarettes, alcohol, and drugs; and rather than be considered a "square," she began to indulge, finding it easier than resisting the pressure. In fact, she had no fear that she would ever become an addict.

Through lack of communication and failing to stay close to their daughter, and under the false assumption that all was well, her parents were not aware of her actions until they finally learned, to their great horror and sorrow, that she was using tobacco, alcohol, and drugs. Of course, they were heartbroken, and terribly embarrassed, as they realized there was nothing they could do but place her in an institution where they felt she could best be helped. She spent some time there, but through determination and a real struggle and with the help of the institution, she progressed to the point where she could come home weekends and be with her parents.

As I talked to her, her big concern, and the concern of her parents, was what she would do when she was released. Would she be free and feel secure? How would people accept her? She felt determined and sure that she would be completely cured. When I asked her if she would have the courage and strength to keep free of her former associates, she assured me she could, and sorrowfully said that several of them were either in institutions or prison. She also told me of some very sad cases in the institution— one, a 19-year-old boy, who was entirely helpless. We read also of others threatening and committing suicide.

Fortunately this girl was able to respond to treatment and return to a respectable place in society, but all too many cannot and do not.

Such experiences should help parents and youth to understand the problems confronting them. Parents, be alert and on your guard. One of these could be your own son or daughter.

Now here is another story I tell with the permission of the parents, who likewise expressed a real desire to do everything they can to help other youth to avert a tragedy such as that which happened to their son.

In a file they handed me was a newspaper clipping, written before his tragedy, showing the picture of a fine-looking lad who had just been elected president of the junior class in high school. The article said, "Wherever activity is bubbling or leadership is needed, that's where you'll find Jim. As a leading figure in school plays, student government, and class activities, his leadership abilities have always been outstanding."

Here was a boy with the promise of a happy and successful life. But one night, he did not come home as usual after closing up a service station where he worked. His worried parents started a search, which ended in the early morning hours with the father finding his son's beaten and bruised body in the back seat of a parked car. He had been dead for some time. Just imagine the shock and sorrow of his parents!

At the inquest the brokenhearted parents learned that Jim had joined a couple of the hometown boys and a couple from a neighboring town. After they had purchased and consumed liquor, a fight ensued between the local boys and the out-of-towners. Apparently someone knocked Jim down, ran into him with a car, and then placed his body on the back seat of the car where it was later found. The parents also learned that this was only the third time he had ever been drinking. He never dreamed that taking his first drink would lead to his untimely death.

We could go on and on and give statistics, facts, and figures to show that experiences similar to those I have related are happening by the hundreds and thousands. It is estimated that 60 percent of our adult population in the United States today consumes some quantity of liquor. There are some outstanding executives, business and professional men, who are successful and highly regarded, and for whom I have great respect, who indulge in the use of liquor in some degree.

I know too that their using alcohol will influence many of our youth to become social drinkers. It saddens me, however, to know that out of every fifteen of them, one will become an alcoholic. One's heart always goes out to a neighbor or friend and his family who have to endure the miseries of alcoholism.

I am convinced that our youth do not want to be bad. They do not set out to be alcoholics, nor to be drug addicts, nor to suffer and die with cancer of the lungs or some other pulmonary disease.

However, they see people drinking all around them—men and women who are leading citizens. They see it in their homes with no evident ill effects. They see it advertised in all the popular magazines, in the daily press, on every television set, in many movies, and on the billboards; and they hear it over radio. Yes, and these advertisements are shown with well-dressed, healthy-looking, successful businessmen, with big cars and fine offices, with young men and women engaged in all kinds of sports, attending socials where people are standing around with a cigarette in one hand and a glass in the other, all seeming to have a good time.

How can our youth resist without our help? These high-power advertising media never show a man or woman nursing a bad headache the morning after, nor do they show the crumpled cars, the mangled bodies, or the broken homes, or men lying in the gutter. Nor do they show a man facing a doctor who has just told him that he has cancer of the throat or lungs, or patients in a hospital being fed with a tube through the nostril because they cannot swallow.

I am sure that many will say, "Why all this gory stuff?" No, I have omitted much of the gory stuff, the many, many really sad and heartbreaking experiences happening to families every day. We must face the facts; we must do our part.

I have read with interest Dr. William Terhune's ten commandments on how to lessen the chance that we will become alcoholics. The last two of them are:

"Never take a drink to escape discomfort, either physical or mental," and "never take a drink in the morning, thinking it will offset a hangover."

I should like to submit one commandment as a substitute for his ten which would be much more effective, and that is: "Never take a drink." Alcoholism is one disease which no one needs to have. The only sure way to be free of it is to never take a drink.

On behalf of the First Presidency, and with their approval, I appeal to every member of the Church to keep the Word of Wisdom strictly, and to all responsible citizens to accept their responsibilities, to guard and protect our youth against the evils and designs of conspiring men who are determined by every available means to lead them to destruction. We cannot stand by and let our youth be destroyed because of our neglect. We must lead them not into temptation, but deliver them from evil.

There are those who argue that in the interests of tourism, liquor should be made more easily available. Surely every mother, father, and worthy citizen can see the folly of this and what it would do to our youth. We must not sell our heritage for a mess of pottage. There are better ways to encourage tourists.

I cannot imagine any father or neighbor wanting to contribute in any way to his or his neighbor's boy's becoming an alcoholic in order to get tourists into our area. Example is the greatest of all teachers. In the interests of our youth, I pray that we may all heed the warning of the Lord that alcohol is not good for man. We must take a stand against liquor by the drink and any and every other move that would make liquor more easily available.

It is the responsibility of every citizen and in the best interests of our youth and our future to see that enforceable restrictive legislation is enacted and enforced to keep our youth from this pernicious practice.

It is my testimony to all that those who heed the words of the Lord spoken through a prophet, and who keep his commandments, "shall find wisdom and great treasures of knowledge, even hidden treasures; And shall run and not be weary, and shall walk and not faint." And the Lord has promised "that the destroying angel shall pass by them, as the children of Israel, and not slay them." (D&C 89: 19-21.)

With the testimony I have that God lives and that Jesus is the Christ, the Savior of us all, and that they are interested in our welfare, I humbly pray that the Spirit and blessings of the Lord will help us to do all in our power to protect our youth against the evils and designs that do and will exist in the hearts of conspiring men, that we may lead them not into temptation but deliver them from evil, for his is the kingdom, and the power, and the glory forever.

CHAPTER 24

In the Lord's Service

It thrills me to see the marvelous work being done by our missionaries throughout the world. Sister Tanner and I have been privileged to visit many missions. In particular, I recall some of our experiences in the stakes and missions in the Orient, where we witnessed great growth among the Church members and the quality and devotion of our members.

Outstanding leaders were observed in every mission and stake, and great strides are being made. We had from 300 to 1,000 members and nonmembers attending each of our meetings, and one cannot help but have confidence in the future growth and strength of the Church there. We found a great spirit everywhere, particularly among our missionaries and servicemen.

Impressions I received while I was there were that these are devoted, able, humble, prayerful, effective missionaries; boys who have developed into men; men with courage, understanding, and leadership ability; ambassadors of the Lord, admired, loved, and respected by the members, carrying heavy responsibility, filling all or any leadership positions and training others to fill these positions, such as branch presidents, heads of auxiliaries, and teachers; baptizing, confirming, and ordaining, etc., encouraging and strengthening the weak, administering to the sick. One bore testimony of a miraculous healing that he experienced where he was the one who gave the blessing to his father.

They are men and women with testimonies who have met and overcome temptation and evil; men who will come home prepared and ready and able to accept any position in a ward or stake; men who have felt important and have been important; men who will strengthen, inspire, and give leadership to your wards and stakes and inspire your youth if you will just give them an opportunity to do so; men deeply concerned about inactive members; men deeply concerned about anyone who has a problem and who are trying to help him solve it. This is one group of men.

I would like to refer to the servicemen. We met some while we were in Korea and in Osaka, and many of these young men are doing a tremendous work in the Church.

Whenever I speak to newly called missionaries, I ask for all who are twenty-four years of age to stand, because that is the age Joseph Smith was when the Church was organized. Five stood at one such meeting, and I asked one of them to come up and tell us how he happened to come into the Church, and to bear his testimony. He said he was in the armed services in Vietnam, and that while there he met some of our young men, one in particular who was living and teaching the gospel, and as a result this young man is now a member of the Church. He explained the great difference it had made in his life, how he had repented of what he had done, and how he came to understand the purpose of life. And then I asked the other four. Two of them told the same thing in bearing their testimony —that they had joined the Church while in the armed services. It was a thrilling experience to realize the effect of young servicemen who were devoted, who had testimonies of the gospel and the courage to live and teach the gospel and bear testimony, while in the armed services.

It was thrilling to see in the stake and missions in the Orient how missionaries were able to bring people into the Church people who regard them very highly. One convert was a university professor; another, a successful businessman; two, outstanding doctors, one of whom was a heart surgeon. It was most humbling to see how these men praised the work of the young men who had brought them into the Church and influenced their lives, and they bore testimony of the great things that the gospel has done for them since they joined the Church.

I appeal to the bishops and stake presidents to see that these young men, when they return from their tours of duty, have an opportunity to serve.

And to the young men: Your study and your devotion and experience have prepared you for real service in the work of the Lord. Thank the Lord for the privilege you have had of testing in your lives and improving your testimony. Never feel that you have finished or completed your tour of duty in church service. You have only prepared yourself to be of further service in the work of the Lord. Seek and accept opportunities to serve. Never return to the old gang. Be an example. Let the young girls and boys see what a mission will do for a young man, and never let them down. These youth in the wards and stakes, when you return, will look up to you and expect great things of you; and if you live as you should, you will influence their lives for good, as much as you have the lives of those with whom you have come in contact when you were in the service—the service of your country or the service of the Lord.

Encourage these young men with whom you meet when you come home to prepare themselves for missions, temple marriage, and the blessings that are available to faithful members of the Church. Help them to overcome evil and temptations, to appreciate the priesthood that they hold, and to sustain their leaders. That is the thing I hope these returning men will do.

Magnify your priesthood at all times. Honor and uphold one another. Never, never submit to temptation.

Honor womanhood and virtue with your life, if necessary. Never become discouraged or quit. As you continue in active church service you will be more successful, more highly regarded, and happier than you will be in any other way. And I want to promise you, my young brethren, that if you will seek first the kingdom of God and his righteousness and be prepared to serve the Lord wherever you can, the Lord will bless you with greater success and happiness and contentment than you could possibly enjoy otherwise. You will do better in your school work if you will be active in the Church, and you will be an influence for good in the world.

A man with whom I am associated as a director in a large company said to me on one occasion (he is representing the government now, and he has been a very successful businessman in the lumbering industry): "We asked for applicants who were prepared to accept a certain job in the government. We had many applicants, and we got them down to ten, and as we were considering those ten, we noticed that one of them was a member of your church, and we took him just like that."

I said, "Why did you take him?"

He said, "Because we knew that he wouldn't be carousing at night; we knew that we could depend upon him, and we knew that he would do the work assigned to him." And I thought, what a tremendous thing if our young men would all just realize the importance of this.

The president of the Korea Mission, when I was over there, was telling me of the problems they have with young men in the service because the bishops were not sending the recommends for two or three months after they had arrived. He said that our servicemen do not enjoy —in fact, they resent—being there, and they become lonesome, and there are prostitutes there in great numbers. In fact, he told me that it was a common thing for these soldiers to have a prostitute companion.

He told me an experience where one of our priests who was lonely, who had not been too active, became involved with one of these prostitutes. And then one of our young men who was living the gospel and who was interested in trying to save these young men contacted him, worked with him, and finally got him to acknowledge the value of the Church, to repent of his doings, and to strive to work as he should to be worthy of the blessings of the Lord. And then he said if he could have just got hold of that boy when he arrived, he could have helped him and probably prevented this tragedy. He went on to tell of the experience with many of the young men there, and how many of them bear testimony that it was because somebody met them and worked with them, and gave them companionship and love, that they were able to withstand the temptations so prevalent there.

So we encourage bishops and stake presidents, when these young men leave home to go to school, to be sure that they send the recommends and the information they have regarding them to the university or college. When they go into the armed services, our priesthood leaders must, for the sake of these young men, be sure that they are not too busy and that their interest is keen enough to do all in their power to try to save these young men who are going into the armed services and to send information ahead of them to the group leaders or other proper people.

As for these missionaries, when they return, we must be close to them and let our influence be felt. Encourage them. They are on fire when they return from a mission. We must meet them, greet them, love them, and give them opportunities to serve. I have heard several examples of this, one just recently. A mother said to me, "When my boy returned from his mission, he wasn't given an opportunity to speak in the ward, he wasn't approached by the bishop other than to say, 'Hello, it's good to see you home,' and no one seemed to take an interest in him." Then she said, "I really had to work with that boy to keep up his interest and activity in the Church."

Brethren, you who are returning from these armed services and school and missions, report to your bishops and offer yourselves to be of service. And bishops, when these young people leave your ward, you send on information to the proper officials in schools, universities, and the armed services, so that they might know and be able to give the necessary help and encouragement when they arrive.

May the Lord bless us that we might realize the importance of a soul; that right in our midst we have people needing attention and help, and it is our responsibility to keep them active, to encourage them, and to reach them if they are having problems.

May we realize that the priesthood of God is the power of God given us to act in his name. May we do it wisely, humbly, effectively.

VI

Seek to Keep Faith
With Your Family

•

IV

CHAPTER 25

Keep Faith With Your Family

As a schoolteacher, Scoutmaster, and bishop, and as I have traveled from place to place and talked to different people, I find that many are worried about their children, their youth, are criticizing the youth of other families and blaming all kinds of conditions for their problems, and are wondering just what can be done or should be done to improve these conditions. On the other hand, I find many of our youth who are frustrated, who would really like to choose and do the right and be accepted, but who wonder just what it is all about, and what is important, and why so little emphasis is placed on the gospel of Jesus Christ. It is true that nothing brings greater joy and satisfaction and comfort to a parent than to see a child really develop into an honorable, respected, righteous citizen. The youth who develops into that kind of citizen is loved, respected, and admired by all. How can this be accomplished?

The other day I reread an article by the late J. Edgar Hoover of the Federal Bureau of Investigation entitled "Should I Force My Child," which reads:

Shall I make my child go to Sunday School and church? *Yes!* And with no further discussion about the matter. Startled? Why? How do you answer Junior when he comes to breakfast on

Monday morning and announces to you that he is not going to school any more? You know! Junior goes.

How do you answer when Junior comes in very much besmudged and says, "I'm not going to take a bath." Junior bathes, doesn't he?

Why all this timidity, then, in the realm of his spiritual guidance and growth? Going to let him wait and decide what church he'll go to when he's old enough? Quit your kidding! You didn't wait until you were old enough. You don't wait until he is old enough to decide whether he wants to go to school or not to start his education. You don't wait until he is old enough to decide whether he wants to be clean or dirty, do you? Do you wait until he is old enough to decide if he wants to take his medicine when he is sick—do you?

What shall we say when Junior announces he doesn't like to go to Sunday School and church? That's an easy one to answer. Just be consistent. Tell him, "Junior, in *our house* we *all* go to church and to Sunday School, and that includes you." Your firmness and example will furnish a bridge over which youthful rebellion may travel into rich and satisfying experience in personal religious living. The parents of America can strike a telling blow against the forces that contribute to our juvenile delinquency, if our mothers and fathers will *take* their children to Sunday School and church *regularly*.

There would be no need of forcing our children to attend Sunday School and church if we as parents attend regularly, because that would be just a part of their lives, and children like to be *with* their parents. It is difficult for children to understand why *they* should go to Sunday School or church when their *parents* feel it is more important or more interesting for them to go fishing or golfing. Our Lord and Master has said, "Thou shalt go to the house of prayer and offer up thy sacraments upon my holy day." (D&C 59:9.)

I thought a friend of mine showed a good example of this when his son came to him and said, "Dad, I don't want to go to church today." His dad replied, "My son, you have your free agency; you better hurry and get your coat or we'll be late." You notice the words "*We'll* be late," not "*you'll* be late."

How fortunate is the boy or girl who lives in a home where the parents believe in God, the Eternal Father, and his Son, Jesus Christ; who know within their hearts that the Savior came and brought the gospel of peace and goodwill and gave the plan of life and salvation whereby all mankind may be saved; who set about to so order their lives as to keep in tune with the spirit of their Heavenly Father; and who are prepared to keep his commandments. We have been admonished, "Counsel with the Lord in all thy doings, and he will direct thee for good." To join with the family in prayer every day—to talk to our Father in heaven, to seek his blessing, and to express our gratitude— will have a profound influence not only on the life of the child, but on the lives of members of the family as a whole. A feeling of love, unity, and of being in tune will be experienced by all. Also we should encourage them to go privately to the Lord in thanksgiving and supplication.

What strength and courage a young man receives as he goes out into the world when he comes from a home where there is no question in his mind that his parents feel and always act as Paul when he says, "I am not ashamed of the gospel of Christ: for it is the power of God unto salvation to everyone that believeth. . . . "(Romans 1:16.)

Great doubt is raised in the mind of a child whose parents profess one thing and do another; where they profess to be Christians and believe in God, but do nothing about it. Elijah came unto the people and said, "How long halt ye between two opinions? if the Lord be God, follow him: but if Baal, then follow him." (1 Kings 18:21.) The Lord has said, "If ye love me, keep my commandments." (John 14:15.)

Every day is full of choices. Our choices today determine our future and the future of our children. Such little questions as:: Will I be honest? Will I keep my pledge or commitment or promise? Will I prove dependable? Will

I go to church or will I go fishing? We cannot be *nearly* dependable, we cannot be *reasonably* honest, we cannot be diligent *sometimes,* we cannot *nearly* catch a plane and be where or what we wish to be.

Let us always remember and determine that the things which matter most must not be at the mercy of things which matter least. First we must choose what we want out of life and then if we wish to achieve it, we must abide by the rules, whether it be to gain a university degree, or to become an American citizen, or to reach the celestial kingdom.

As one of our poets wrote so well:

> Know this, that every soul is free
> To choose his life and what he'll be;
> For this eternal truth is given:
> That God will force no man to heaven.
>
> He'll call, persuade, direct aright,
> And bless with wisdom, love, and light;
> In nameless ways be good and kind
> But never force the human mind.
>
> Freedom and reason make us men;
> Take this away and what are we then?
> Mere animals, and just as well
> The beasts may think of heaven or hell.

Let each of us check and determine whether our innermost thoughts are holding us on the animal plane or whether they tend to lift us into the mental, moral, and spiritual realm. We become slaves as we break the laws of nature, as we become addicted to bad habits; or we remain free as we choose the right. The Lord has said, "Thou shalt have no other gods before me." (Exodus 20:3.) Some have as their gods money, political power, fame, false ideologies, idols, and even unknown gods.

Some years ago, while traveling with Lord Rowallan, Chief Scout of the British Commonwealth, I was thrilled with his comment as he led in the Scout promise. As he said, "On my honor I promise to do my duty to God," he stopped and said to the Scouters who were present, "As I make this promise I think of a God who can hear and answer prayers, who is interested in what we are doing, and who will guide us and bless us according to our needs and our faith." And then he said, "If any of you do not believe in such a God, you can serve better someplace else."

Selfishness, murder, hatred, and conquest are rampant throughout the so-called civilized world today. If each and every man could say and do as Joshua admonished, "as for me and my house, we will serve the Lord" and keep his commandments, we would have peace in the world. Yes, if the people in the world would begin today to love God and keep his commandments, we would have peace overnight. As someone has so aptly said, "Righteousness in the individual makes for harmony in the home, harmony in the home makes for order in the nation, and order in the nation results in peace in the world."

It would be most helpful if parents would sit down and discuss with the whole family what they want out of life; what they want to accomplish; and how they can help one another in doing it. After this decision is made, it will be necessary for all of them to answer the questions: Is it worth the effort, or am I prepared to do my part? Can I discipline myself, or have I the will power? Then, each and every one must make up his mind, accept his obligations, and go forward with determination, realizing that it will bring the greatest joy and satisfaction and success in life. When one begins to rationalize or try to explain why he does this or that which he knows is wrong, he is actually bringing his ideals down to his actions. On the other hand, though, if one repents and sets about to improve himself and keep the commandments, he is raising his standards or his actions up to his ideals.

What a marvelous thing it would be if we and our children could learn early in life the joy and satisfaction that come from living good, clean, honest, and upright lives all the time, and that there is no joy or satisfaction in sin. It is so important that we all try to enjoy living and that our young people have a good time. However, this good time should be such that in the future, whether it be a month, a year, or ten years from now, they can always look back on this as "a good time," realizing that a man of honor does not change his code of honor with passing circumstances. The greatest joy and happiness one can get out of living is to know that he has done and is doing right, and to be in the service of the Lord.

Children should be taught and trained to honor their father and their mother. Their parents gave them life and cared for them when they could not care for themselves. Every child of every age should love and honor his parents. It is much easier, however, for children to do this if the parents live worthy of the honor of their children and are always an example to them, and wield a real influence for good in their lives.

Parents have no responsibility greater than that of teaching and training their children to be honest, honorable, and righteous citizens; and there is no stronger, more effective way of doing it than for the parent to be what he would like his son or daughter to be. What a great day it will be for the world and the Church when every father and son will do and be what he would like the other to think he is. In other words, father should always try to put himself in the position where he would be glad to have his son say, "I do nothing save that which I have seen my father do." The same applies to mothers and daughters.

It is the manner of our living and not the words we use to explain it that makes up the moral fiber of the children God has given to us. We should never be surprised if our children grow up to be like us. Therefore, we must take the time to be the kind of people we would like our children to be. It is so important that the rush of the world and the pressure of business do not make fathers and sons, or mothers and daughters, strangers. When we say with a shrug of the shoulder, "Boys will be boys," maybe we should remember that boys will soon be men, and we should set about to help make them men. There is a point at which sympathy becomes coddling and kindness becomes indulgence, and they who are too busy, too lazy, or too soft-hearted to give children the example and discipline they need are being unfair to everyone and particularly to the children. It is most difficult for parents to discipline their children and expect them to do those things which are not important enough for the parents to do themselves.

Let us not forget that a young man or a young woman of character, industry, faith, intelligence, and loyalty will always be at a premium, and will always be able to find a good place or make one when he can truthfully say: "As for me and my house, we will serve the Lord," and truly seek first the kingdom of God and his righteousness, knowing that all things for his good will be added unto him.

CHAPTER 26

The Role of Woman in the Church

I should like to consider the role of womanhood in this church, where we have such a great body of wonderful women—wives, mothers, and single women engaged in the work of the Lord and in the service of their fellowmen. They are affiliated with the Relief Society, the principal women's organization; the Primary, where our children are instructed; the Sunday School, where the gospel is taught to all members; the MIA, which is the activity and social organization for youth and adults; and our women serve with dedication and skill in various other capacities.

After I had discussed business matters with some men the other day, the conversation took on a more personal informal note when one man said: "I have the most wonderful wife in the world." Another said: "That's what *you* think. I think *I* have the best." A third man said: "Isn't it a great blessing to have a wife you love, who loves you, one who is a good mother and homemaker, with high ideals, who believes in God and wants to help her family accept and live the teachings of the gospel of Jesus Christ."

What woman could want any greater glory or tribute than that which comes from an appreciative and loving husband? The applause and homage of the world fade into insignificance when compared with the approbation of God and expressions of love and appreciation that come from the hearts and lips of those who are nearest and dearest to her.

From the beginning God has made it clear that woman is very special, and he has also very clearly defined her position, her duties, and her destiny in the divine plan. Paul said that man is the image and glory of God; that woman is the glory of the man; and that the man is not without the woman, neither the woman without the man in the Lord. You will note that significantly God is mentioned in connection with this great partnership, and we must never forget that one of woman's greatest privileges, blessings, and opportunities is to be a co-partner with God in bringing his spirit children into the world.

It is of great concern to all who understand this glorious concept that Satan and his cohorts are using scientific arguments and nefarious propaganda to lure women away from their primary responsibilities as wives, mothers, and homemakers. We hear so much about emancipation, independence, sexual liberation, birth control, abortion, and other insidious propaganda belittling the role of motherhood, all of which is Satan's way of destroying woman, the home, and the family—the basic unit of society.

Some effective tools include the use of radio, television, and magazines, where pornography abounds and where women are being debased and disgracefully used as sex symbols—"sex-ploited," some call it. Immodest dress, drugs, and alcohol daily take a tremedous toll through the destruction of virtue and chastity and even lives. With modern electronic devices of communication and speedy transportation, much more is being heard throughout the world and by many more people than would be possible otherwise, and it is having its degrading influence and effect.

Yes, pornography, drugs, and alcohol are available to young and old in alarming quantity and are destroying the moral values and further deteriorating the minds and thought processes of those who succumb to these devilish wiles.

President Dallin Oaks recently said to the student body at Brigham Young University: "We are surrounded by the promotional literature of illicit sexual relations on the printed page and on the screen. For your own good, avoid it. Pornographic or erotic stories and pictures are worse than filthy or polluted food. The body has defenses to rid itself of unwholesome food, but the brain won't vomit back filth. Once recorded it will always remain subject to recall, flashing its perverted images across your mind and drawing you away from the unwholesome things in life."

It is so important that our young girls keep themselves from this kind of pollution. The girls of today will be the women of tomorrow, and it is necessary that they prepare for that role. Can you imagine the kind of world we will have in the future if the girls of today are weakened morally to the extent that virtue will not be taught in their homes, and if their children, if any, are not nurtured within the walls of homes sanctified by the holy laws of matrimony?

Marriage is ordained of God, and we must do everything we can to strengthen the ties that bind, to strengthen our homes, and to prepare ourselves by exemplary living to teach our children the ways of God, which is the only way for them to find happiness here and eternal life hereafter.

As we enumerate the many important responsibilities a woman has in connection with her duties as a wife, a mother, a homemaker, a sister, a sweetheart, or a good neighbor, it should be evident that these challenging responsibilities can satisfy her need to express her talents, her interests, her creativity, dedication, energy, and skill, which so many seek to satisfy outside the home. It is impossible to estimate the lasting influence for good a woman can have in any of these roles. Let me remind us of her primary responsibilities.

First of all, she is a co-partner with God in bringing his spirit children into the world. What a glorious concept! No greater honor could be given. With this honor comes the tremendous responsibility of loving and caring for those children so they might learn their duty as citizens and what they must do to return to their Heavenly Father. They must be taught to understand the gospel of Jesus Christ and to accept and live his teachings. As they understand the purpose of life, why they are here and where they are going, they will have a reason for choosing the right and avoiding the temptations and buffetings of Satan, who is so very real and determined to destroy them.

A mother has far greater influence on her children than anyone else, and she must realize that every word she speaks, every act, every response, her attitude, even her appearance and manner of dress affect the lives of her children and the whole family. It is while the child is in the home that he gains from his mother the attitudes, hopes, and beliefs that will determine the kind of life he will live and the contribution he will make to society.

President Brigham Young expressed the thought that mothers are the moving instruments in the hands of Providence and are the machinery that give zest to the whole man and guide the destinies and lives of men and nations upon the earth. He further said, "Let mothers of any nation teach their children not to make war, [and] the children would not grow up and enter it." (*Discourses of Brigham Young*, John A. Widtsoe, comp. [Deseret Book Co., 1954], pp. 199-200.)

When the Lord God said that it is "not good that the man should be alone; wherefore, I will make an help meet for him," he meant just that, and so presented Eve to Adam. We are taught that a man should leave his father and his mother and cleave unto his wife, and that they should be one flesh, and thus is described the relationship that should exist between husband and wife. It is said that behind every good man there is a good woman, and it is my experience and observation that this is generally true.

It is interesting to note that when the executives of companies look for new employees, or are planning promotions for their experienced ones, they almost always want to know what kind of wife a man has. This seems to be very important. In the Church when men are being considered for new priesthood offices, the question is always raised about the worthiness of the wife and whether or not she can give him full support.

Women, you are of great strength and support to the men in your lives, and they sometimes need your help most when they are least deserving. A man can have no greater incentive, no greater hope, no greater strength than to know that his mother, his sweetheart, or his wife has confidence in him and loves him. And men should strive every day to live worthy of that love and confidence.

President Hugh B. Brown once said at a Relief Society conference: "There are people fond of saying that women are the weaker instruments, but I don't believe it. Physically they may be, but spiritually, morally, religiously and in faith, what man can match a woman who is really converted to the gospel! Women are more willing to make sacrifices than are men, more patient in suffering, more earnest in prayer. They are the peers and often superior to men in resilience, in goodness, in morality, and in faith." (September 29, 1965.)

And girls, don't underestimate your influence on your brothers and your sweethearts. As you live worthy of their love and respect, you can help greatly to determine that they will be clean and virtuous, successful and happy. Always remember that you can go much further on respect than on popularity. I was reading the other day of a report of a conversation between two young prisoners of war in Vietnam. One said: "I am sick of war, bombers, destruction, prison camps, and everything and everybody."

"I feel much like that myself," said the other: "But there is a girl back home who is praying that I will come back. She cares, and it really helps me endure all these atrocities."

To mothers, daughters, and women everywhere, let me stress the fact that because of your great potential and influence for good in the lives of all of us, Satan is determined to destroy you. You cannot compromise with him. You must have the courage, the strength, desire, and determination to live as the Lord would have you live—good clean lives. Girls, keep yourselves virtuous and worthy of a fine young man who has likewise kept himself clean, so that together you can go to the house of the Lord to be sealed in the holy bonds of matrimony for time and all eternity, and prepare a home where God will be pleased to send his spirit children. Then you will be able to face your children secure in the knowledge that your own example is the way to happiness and eternal progression. They are entitled to this heritage. I humbly pray that you will so live as to give it to them.

The whole purpose of the creation of the earth was to provide a dwelling place where the spirit children of God might come and be clothed in mortal bodies and, by keeping their second estate, prepare themselves for salvation and exaltation. The whole purpose of the mission of Jesus Christ was to make possible the immortality and eternal life of man. The whole purpose of mothers and fathers should be to live worthy of this blessing and to assist God the Father and his Son Jesus Christ in their work. No greater honor could be given to women than to assist in this divine plan, and I wish to say without equivocation that a woman will find greater satisfaction and joy and make a greater contribution to mankind by being a wise and worthy mother raising good children than she could make in any other vocation.

The Lord has promised us great blessings if we will do our part in this divine plan. President Herbert Hoover gave this incentive: "If we could have but one generation of properly born, trained, educated and healthy children, a thousand other problems of government would vanish. We would assure ourselves of healthier minds, more vigorous bodies, to direct the energies of our nation to greater heights of achievement." (Quoted by President David O. McKay, *Conference Report*, April 1931, pp. 79-80.)

How fortunate we are to have the church of Jesus Christ established in these latter days, with a prophet of God upon the earth to receive divine revelation and direction for the children of men! We are blessed to know the personality of God, his attributes and characteristics. We have been given the plan of life and salvation. We are continually directed as to how we should live so we may have happiness here and eternal life hereafter. We have organizations set up to instruct and educate us in all matters pertaining to our temporal and spiritual welfare.

One of the finest programs the Church has instituted is what we call family home evening, where all members of the family are called together once a week. It is quite thrilling to me when I contemplate that each Monday evening, all over the Church throughout the world, our families are gathered together in their homes, and the father, where possible, as head of the house, is directing his family in a discussion of problems pertaining to their spiritual and temporal welfare, using a manual that has been carefully prepared and distributed to each family in the Church. Where these gatherings are held regularly and properly, they are of inestimable value to the family unit, as is evidenced by the many testimonies we receive. I wish to urge every family to follow this program, and I can promise you that as you do so, you will be greatly blessed in unity, love, and devotion and will be delighted with the outcome. Of course, family prayer should be a significant part of this evening, as well as regular family and individual prayer every day.

I can think of nothing sweeter than a home where a man is living his religion and magnifying his priesthood, with his wife supporting him in every way; where love and harmony exist; and where together they are trying to raise a family of righteous sons and daughters whom they can take back into the presence of their Heavenly Father. This may sound like an impossible dream, but I can assure you that there are thousands of such families within the Church, and it is something that can be a reality for every one of us as we accept and live the teachings of Jesus Christ. How fortunate a child is to live in such a home, and how great will be the joy of the parents in their posterity!

I repeat: Satan is trying to keep us from the full enjoyment which comes from keeping the commandments of God. We must never forget, and we must teach our children to know, that Satan is real and determined to destroy us. He knows the importance and significance of the family unit. He knows that entire civilizations have survived or disappeared depending on whether the family life was strong or weak. We can keep him out of our homes by living and teaching our children to live the principles of the gospel of Jesus Christ, thereby resisting temptation when it comes, as it surely will.

Girls, prepare yourselves to assume the roles of mothers by gaining knowledge and wisdom through a good education. We teach that the glory of God is intelligence, and so we must all be aware of what is going on around us and prepared to thwart Satan in his attempts to divert us from our divine destiny. With knowledge, wisdom, determination, and the Spirit of the Lord to help us, we can succeed.

We also believe that women should involve themselves in community affairs and in the auxiliary organiza-

tions of the Church, but always remembering that home
and children come first and must not be neglected.
Children must be made to feel that mother loves them
and is keenly interested in their welfare and everything
they do. This cannot be turned over to someone else.
Many experiments have been made and studies carried
out which prove beyond doubt that a child who enjoys
mother's love and care progresses in every way much more
rapidly than one who is left in an institution or with others
where mother's love is not available or expressed.

Fathers too must assume their proper role and responsibility. Children need both parents. While they are
at home fathers should assume with mothers the duties
attendant upon the young children, the discipline and
training of the older ones, and be a listening ear for those
who need to discuss their problems or who want guidance
and counseling. Through love establish a good relationship and line of communication with your children.

I would urge all husbands, fathers, sons, and brothers
to show our great respect and love and try to be worthy
of the women who are our wives, mothers, daughters,
sisters, sweethearts. There is no surer way for a man to
show his lack of character, of good breeding, and of quality
than for him to show lack of respect for woman or to do
anything that would discredit or degrade her. It is un-
christianlike, unfair, and displeasing to God for any husband or father to assume the role of dictatorship and
adopt the attitude that he is superior in any way to his
wife.

At the area conference in Munich, Germany, President Lee said: "If you husbands remember that the most
important of the Lord's work you will ever do will be
within the walls of your own home, you can maintain
close family ties. . . . If you will strengthen your family
ties, be mindful of your children, and be sure that home
is made a strong place in which children can come for
the anchor they need in this day of trouble and turmoil,

then love will abound and your joy will be increased."

As women realize the importance of the home and family, and with their husbands keep the commandments of God to multiply and replenish the earth, to love the Lord and their neighbors as themselves, to teach their children to pray and to walk uprightly before him, then will their joy be increased and their blessings multiplied to the extent that they will hardly be able to contain them.

These blessings will be joy and rejoicing in our posterity of healthy, happy children, which blessings those who reject this way of life will never know. There will be peace and satisfaction in the accomplishments of children who succeed and who in turn make their own contribution in making this a better world for generations yet unborn. What a joyous privilege and blessing it will be for those families who through obedience and love have prepared themselves to go back into the presence of our Heavenly Father and have it said of each of them: "Well done, thou good and faithful servant: . . . enter thou into the joy of thy lord." (Matthew 25:21.)

CHAPTER 27

Preparation Begins in the Home

The future and success of our youth—both boys and girls—depends in great measure on the way their parents live and the example they set for their children. Many—perhaps most, want to be like their dads and moms. Some would like their parents to be better, but they still want to be like their parents.

I received a letter from a missionary who said, "I wish you would take time to go and talk to my dad. See how he feels about the Church. See if he can be ready to go to the temple when I get home." It seems his dad is proud to have him serving a mission, very happy to support him there, but for some reason he is not prepared to do what he agreed to do—to keep the covenants he took upon himself when he was ordained an elder in the Church.

As parents we have responsibilities in the home. I would like to relate to you two or three experiences, and I hope you don't mind my using my own family. I am going to give you experiences that we actually had in family home evening programs, taken from three different families of my daughters and their husbands.

When Sister Tanner and I were at Waterton Lakes in Canada one summer, we had two or three families together. Do you know what those kids wanted to do? They wanted to have family night, and we did. One of the boys who is a deacon was asked to take charge, because the fathers were absent and he was the only deacon there in that group and there was no one who held higher priesthood. In the discussion the boy said, "What should you do when you are out with young fellows camping or with a group out away from home fishing or something, and when you go to bed you want to pray?"

Someone suggested, "Well, you might go outside and pray, outside the tent. Or if you're in a home, or a building where there is a bathroom, you might go in the bathroom and pray."

Another one said, "Well, couldn't you go to bed and pray?"

One of the girls of the same age spoke up and said, "Why can't you pray where you are? I have been out with a group of girls, and I have prayed with those girls there. All the girls pray, at least they did when I was with them. They knelt down and prayed when I did."

I thought that was a very fine answer, and I would like to give my experience, in addition to that. I have never found it embarrassing to kneel down to pray in the presence of other men. More than once I have seen men kneel down when I knelt down, or when I got up, I have found them kneeling down offering prayer. I am sure that every man, wherever he may be, though he doesn't pray regularly, would, if he found himself in very great danger or emergency, be glad to call upon God. We need not apologize for being one who calls on the Lord and knows he stands ready to answer our prayers.

Another family home evening experience: this time we had all the families together, and this is regarding a boy from one of the families. He was seventeen years of age. We had each participate one way or another in our little discussion. When we came to this young man, he said, "Grandpa, do you think it would be all right for me to give the first missionary discussion tonight?"

I said, "I think it would be fine."

He said, "Well, I have the material here and I would like this family to be the investigators, and I would like to give the first discussion."

Seventeen years of age, and he did it beautifully! Why? Because his family had set out to teach him that he should be prepared to go on a mission. Now there is a great difference in being prepared to go on a mission and being given the idea you should go on a mission. There is some social pressure being exerted when anyone tries to make someone feel that he should fill a mission because everybody is going on a mission. It is most important that our boys prepare to go and fill honorable missions realizing that they are going out as ambassadors of the Lord and not just to be like other boys.

I have heard parents say to their daughters, "Now you be sure that you get the right kind of husband. Don't ever marry anybody who isn't worthy of you." Well, I don't know whether my philosophy is good or not, but we have five daughters, and I said to those girls, "You be sure you are prepared for the best man you can get. That's the thing I want you to do, girls—be prepared to be the kind of mother you should be, the kind of wife you should be, the kind of member of the Church you should be—so that you are worthy of the best man available, and you will be much more likely to get that right kind of husband."

Here is an example of how another of the families is preparing: The two older boys were thirteen and fourteen when this took place. The mother arranged to get the phonograph recordings of the Book of Mormon. She said to these two boys, "Here is a copy of the Book of Mormon for each of you. We will play these records and you read the Book of Mormon while the record is playing. When you finish, if you finish by a certain time, I will give each of you ten dollars with the understanding that half of that ten dollars goes into your missionary fund."

I think that mother is helping to prepare her boys to go on missions. She is using the time profitably. It gives them an opportunity to discuss the Book of Mormon and for them to read it while they listen to it being read beautifully. As she reported on it, she said how profitable it had been to the boys and the whole family. The other children wanted to do the same thing when they heard the older boys. What a wonderful thing it is to teach the gospel to your children!

President Joseph Fielding Smith once told how his father gave him a copy of the Book of Mormon and asked him to read it, and he did read it, and it was very helpful to him. See how far he went in the Church, and how he became accepted as one of the greatest authorities on the scriptures.

Parents—and especially fathers—you are the heads of your homes. Be worthy of this trust. Make your family proud of you and their home. Live a life that is a worthy example to them that they might follow it, realizing that the greatest influence in the life of any individual is the influence in the home. May they gain testimonies of the the truthfulness of the gospel because we are members of the Church who hold and who honor the priesthood, and may the work of the Lord go forward.

CHAPTER 28

Vocational Training

The Church has always urged us as members to get a good education and to learn everything possible about ourselves, history and geography, science, the universe, and especially the gospel of Jesus Christ. The Prophet Joseph Smith said, "To be saved a man must rise above all his enemies, not the least of which is ignorance." (*History of the Church*, vol. 5, p. 392.)

In order to encourage adult education, he established the School of the Prophets. There the leading Brethren were encouraged to teach one another things pertaining to heaven and earth, history and current events, and also to study prophecy. Amidst their poverty, and in an endeavor to establish themselves in the Salt Lake Valley, the Saints founded the University of Deseret, later called the University of Utah. They established Brigham Young University, Ricks College, and many other Church-sponsored academies and schools.

Just a few years ago the First Presidency issued a statement on the subject of education, which stated: "The Church has long encouraged its members and especially its youth either to obtain a college education or to become well trained in some vocation."

In our fast-growing industrial society and scientific world, education has become a necessity. In order to obtain dignified and profitable employment, one must be well trained. It is becoming more and more difficult for the common laborer to find employment, and it is becoming more and more important that one be well trained in some field. We strongly urge all of our young people to continue in some form of study after leaving high school.

For some years, and especially since university education has become more common, many parents seem to have developed the feeling that it is necessary for their children to get a university education in order that they not be considered second-class citizens, and many parents have urged their children to attend a university even though they were not adapted to it or qualified or interested in a university education. This idea is entirely erroneous.

To correct these erroneous impressions, a fact-finding committee has reported the following findings with these recommendations:

Too many parents, counselors, teachers, principals, bishops, ministers, superintendents and school board members are academic-college oriented and tend to encourage all students to prepare for college.

Occupation and career guidance personnel should be better trained and more work oriented, and should stress entrance into occupations for which there will be jobs available and which are consistent with student interests.

The content, purposes and objectives of Vocational-Technical Education need to be thoroughly publicized so that all will know what can be gained from taking Vocational-Technical courses.

Efforts must be made to convince citizens that all work is honorable and that real success is doing well what one does best.

The society which scorns excellence in plumbing because plumbing is a humble activity, and tolerates shoddiness in philosophy because it is an exalted activity, will have neither good plumbing nor good philosophy. Neither its pipes nor its theories will hold water. (Dr. John W. Gardner, former Secretary of Health, Education, and Welfare.)

It seems that 80 percent of the employment opportunities now or in the future will require technically trained individuals, and those who engage in such employment are anything but second-class citizens. They are well respected, highly regarded, and badly needed, and training in these fields does not require a four-year college degree.

I heard a little story the other day about a plumber who went to do a job for a lawyer. After he had finished his job, the lawyer asked him for the bill. As he received the statement he said, "This is entirely ridiculous. It is twice as much as I get as a lawyer." The plumber then stated, "Well, it is more than I used to get as a lawyer too." Whether or not one gets more or less by following the trade to which he is adapted and that he will enjoy, it is important that he enjoys the work in which he is engaged. If he does it well, he is as highly regarded and respected as if he were engaged in any profession or other trade.

Today we find industry searching for well-trained technical students, while in many other professions it is most difficult to find employment. Let us remember and emphasize that attending a technical school is no reflection on anyone and that those who do so train are in very great demand.

Brigham Young, who was himself a painter and glazier, reportedly said: "I believe in education, but I want to see the boys and girls come out with an education at their fingers' end as well as in their brains."

Someone who had a great respect for titles once addressed a letter to him thus: "To his Excellency, Brigham Young, Governor of Utah, Indian Agent for the Territory and President of the Church of Jesus Christ of Latter-day Saints." When he later met the man, he told him he had left out the most important title he had been entitled to in his life and then he said, "The next time you shall put it in by itself, without the others. It will then read, right sprucely: 'For His Excellency, Brigham Young, Painter and Glazier.'"

Today our technical colleges provide training in drafting, electronics, farm technology, secretarial and office skills, technical and mechanical skills, medical assistance, photography, computer programming, and many other subjects. Then we have specialized schools offering training in art, music, drama, electronics, and business. In order to choose wisely the best academic program for the future, one should seek guidance from his parents and from a qualified counselor if one is available. He can also get good advice from talking to those who are engaged in the occupation that appeals to him. Having chosen, he should then select a good school that is recognized as such by industry.

I was interested to read of an occasion when a university professor addressed a group of students who had just closed their college life, and at a final dinner before separating to go their various ways, he said, referring to the furnishings and services which graced the banquet table, "Take this tablecloth. It is of most exquisite workmanship. It involved weaving, bleaching, smoothing, designing. It is damask linen. Is these anyone here who knows from personal experience anything about the labor involved? Have any of you ever contributed any labor to the manufacturing of table linen? Let me draw your attention to the samples of pottery here. Surely the men and women who produce such beautiful things are artists. What a joy it must be for a man to hold a thing in his hand—complete—and say, 'I made it.' Many forms of labor are involved here, also—digging the clay, carting, fashioning, painting, burning, baking, and finishing."

He then called attention to the cut glass, the silver, the rugs, the carpet, the curtains and drapery, and the mural decorations. He continued, "Here we are, then, a group of men on whom a university has set its stamp. We produce nothing to eat; we could not even lend a hand in the making of anything we see around us; and truth compels me to venture the suggestion that, in ninety-nine cases out of a hundred, the chief motive of a college education is to escape actual participation in just such work as gives, or ought to give, joy to the worker.

"I do not believe that a smattering of languages, of mathematics, and of history is education. I believe the system of cramming these things to pass an examination is pernicious." Then he said, "Why should men consider it degrading to handle tools and make useful and beautiful things?"

He concluded his remarks to his spellbound audience with these words: "Gentlemen, as one example, I wish it were possible for me to introduce to you a young Galilean carpenter, the master builder—Jesus of Nazareth."

To show how rapidly we are putting new inventions and discoveries into use today as compared with past history, I read to you from a table showing the progress in technology and the lapse of years in certain fields from discovery to commercial use.

Photography	112 years
Radio	35 years
Radar	15 years
Television	12 years
Atomic bomb	6 years
Transistor	5 years
Laser beam	1½ years

Think of the progress and of the great and exciting challenges that lie ahead.

Canada, with a population of approximately 15 million, is spending $400 million to expand her vocational-technical education programs in order to strengthen her ability to compete in this technological age. Most of the states of the USA are greatly expanding their programs.

William S. Knudsen, the president of General Motors Corporation, gave same excellent advice to young people at the time of an interview for a story in the *American* magazine. He came to America at twenty years of age and could not speak the language. He met and worked out many of the same problems that confront our youth today. In the interview he said:

If I were 21, I would try to get work in a machine shop. If that failed, I would try for a job in a filling station, or as apprentice to an electrician or a plumber. In short, I would work with my hands . . .

George Washington was a hard working surveyor; Thomas Jefferson was a gifted designer of useful appliances; Benjamin Franklin was a journeyman printer, an inventor, and the best electrician of his age; Abraham Lincoln split rails, kept a store, built and worked on flatboats. That these men knew how to work with their hands undoubtedly contributed to their hard, practical sense.

In reality, there is nothing "humble" about the position of a mechanic. The top-rank skilled mechanic is still the most sought-after and independent man you can find. The place of America today, the American standard of living, depends more on the skill of our mechanics than on any other one class. The genius of America is production; and many of our productive enterprises are headed by men who have come up from the worker's bench. . . .

And brain training is likewise an essential part of hand training. The best man is one who combines the learning of books with the learning which comes of doing things he can, as Charles F. Kettering, head of our research laboratories, says, "transfer the science of formula into the science of things." The young man who has that combination need not worry about getting along in the world today, or at any time.

Of course, I don't mean that everybody should go into mechanical work. But I am hitting at the false tradition of gentility which prevents any gifted youngster from following his natural bent. I want to tear down the idea that one honest job is more honorable than another. Honorable work is any work that you do well.

Again, I should like to say that the world is looking for well-trained individuals who are prepared to put their training to use. To enjoy life to the full, it is so important that we get understanding of the gospel, gain a testimony, and live according to its teachings. Nothing will bring greater joy, success, and happiness to an individual than to know that he is living according to the teachings of the gospel and that the Lord is pleased with his actions. With this in mind, the Church has provided and is providing institutes of religion in close proximity to universities, colleges, and technical schools where there are sufficient members of the Church to justify it, so that our students may gain their spiritual education. These institutes are directed by the priesthood. The First Presidency strongly urges the students to enroll in classes at the institutes so they can augment their secular learning with a religious education and spiritual experience.

Some time ago I was talking to the employment counselor for one of the large universities. He told me that recruiting officers for many of the companies give preference to a member of the Church who is living his religion and even greater preference to a returned missionary. Still or even with all this background of opportunities and training which the Church provides, one cannot overstress the importance of preparation through education for his chosen vocation.

There are questions every young man should ask himself, such as: What are my natural abilities and trends? What do I enjoy doing most? What kind of vocation would make me most happy? Which vocations offer the greatest opportunity for service and growth? How can I best prepare myself to be of greatest service?

Preparation is essential to success. It contributes as much as, if not more than, anything else to a useful citizen in every field of endeavor. As Ralph Waldo Emerson said, "The future belongs to him who prepares for it." Regardless of the opportunities around us, the only way we can take advantage of them is by and through preparation.

If our youth wish to improve their position, they must improve themselves. Too many hope and want to do the first, but not the second. Companies are always looking for men who are honest, dependable, trained, and prepared to accept responsibility, persons with prospects to move up to higher positions that require more than technical ability alone. Too many young people today are trying to find the easiest way of getting their degrees and are prepared to cheat wherever possible. Those who do this are a menace rather than an asset to their community. There are those whose only interest is making money and those who are prepared to go the extra mile.

It is so important that every single young person take advantage of every opportunity to improve and prepare himself so that he might contribute most and be in greatest demand in whatever vocation he chooses.

I have often been asked which vocation I would recommend for a young man to follow. My answer has always been that it matters not what vocation you choose but how well you do the job, and providing you also live your religion. The man who is trained and dependable and determined to give his best in the work he has chosen, and who stands by his standards, is always in demand.

I should like to give you an example of this by relating an experience I had when I was Minister of Mines in the Province of Alberta. One afternoon during a session of the legislature, I called in the head accountant of the department and asked him to prepare some information for me so I might answer questions that had been asked in the legislature. I told him I needed the information by three o'clock the next afternoon. He said, "It will take some doing, but we will do what we can."

The next morning when I arrived at the office he was standing at my door with the information in his hand. I said, "I thought you said this would take some doing." He replied, "The three of us stayed here all night to get this material for you."

I had noted before how devoted he was and how anxious he was to be of service, but this was proof without doubt of his integrity and devotion and of his willingness to go the extra mile. It was not long before he was made Assistant Deputy Minister of the department, then Deputy Minister, then chairman of the Conservation Board of the

Province, and then chairman of the Energy Board for all of Canada. All this because he was prepared to do his work and then some. Men and things automatically find their places according to their size. A change in size and qualifications will automatically result in a change of place.

I well remember, when I was a young boy, my father taking a wagon load of potatoes to town—a distance of seven miles—to sell to a merchant. The merchant looked at them and said what a fine load of potatoes it was and bought them. Father unloaded them and went home. The next time the merchant saw father he accused him of dishonesty in that he had put his largest potatoes on the top. The fact of the matter is that as he took the potatoes over this rough road of seven miles, there was a great deal of shaking and all of the potatoes had found their proper place with the big ones at the top and the little ones at the bottom. This is generally true throughout life. Take a glass jar and put a dozen or so beans in the bottom and a handful or two of rice on top, shake the jar, and you will see the beans come to the top and the rice to the bottom. You can rearrange it as often as you wish and the same result will be obtained as the jar is shaken. This same kind of shaking and jarring is going on in life, and people find their proper places according to their size or qualifications. The same shake or test is good luck for some and bad luck for others, because the big ones always come to the top and the little ones find their proper place down in the bottom. There are always many more at the bottom because more people prepare themselves for the places at the bottom.

When I was president of the Trans-Canada Pipelines, we had a messenger boy but needed a second one. The new boy, a widow's son, was a bright young fellow who was interested in all that was going on and always had his eyes open to see how he could be helpful. He wanted to serve and assist others and learn what he could about the business. He was not trying to be president of the company, but he was trying to be the best messenger boy it was possible to be and attended night school to be better educated. Everybody liked him. He had only been there a few months when one of the supervisors who had observed him wanted him to come with him, so he was advanced to a more responsible position. Before the end of the year he had another advancement, and he will continue to advance because of his attitude. He was prepared to go the extra mile. He was interested in his company and wanted to be of service and was dependable in every way. The other messenger boy was still there as a messenger boy when I left. Of course, he felt that the company didn't appreciate him and his ability. This type of individual usually complains and asks why he is treated so shabbily and why the management doesn't appreciate him and treat him more fairly.

One cannot overemphasize the importance of being honest and being prepared to stand by your standards. A young man who is a member of the Church cannot be strictly honest and break the Word of Wisdom or do any of those things that are contrary to the Church standards.

When I was in Berchtesgaden in Germany attending the Servicemen's Conference, I was most interested in hearing a very outstanding surgeon, who had had years of technical training and was recognized in his field, bear his testimony as to the power of the priesthood and the efficacy of prayer. He said that when he had a very difficult case to diagnose or a very serious operation to perform, he would always go to the Lord fasting and praying that the Spirit of the Lord might direct him in his decisions and in his operation. He said that on different occasions he had been led by the Spirit of the Lord and the power of the priesthood to make a diagnosis beyond his natural ability and training, and that in some of his operations he was directed; his hands were steady and he was given hidden treasures of knowledge. What a great privilege and blessing it is to be able to call on the Lord knowing that he is interested in your welfare and stands ready to answer a call!

It is so important that a young person early in life determine in his own mind, and with the counsel and advice of others, just what kind of person he is going to be, and then set about to do those things which will prepare him.

There are always two great forces at work. The Lord has said, ". . . this is my work and my glory—to bring to pass the immortality and eternal life of man" (Moses 1:39), and he has shown the way. On the other hand, Satan has pledged himself to destroy man, and he and his cohorts are determined to do this. We must make up our minds as to what we will do and let nothing interfere.

President David O. McKay always emphasized that one could not enjoy a true education without learning to be honest, virtuous, temperate, and show brotherly love. He said that "education seeks to make men and women prize truth, justice, wisdom, benevolence, and self-control as the choice acquisitions of a successful life." (*Improvement Era*, September 1967, p. 3.)

It is well to remember that the Lord said through Joseph Smith:

> Whatever principle of intelligence we attain unto in this life, it will rise with us in the resurrection. And if a person gains more knowledge and intelligence in this life through his diligence and obedience than another, he will have so much the advantage in the world to come. (D&C 130:18-19.)

To be successful and happy in this life and to gain eternal life, one must prepare himself through training for his chosen vocation. He must be competent, honest, truthful, willing, and a good citizen. He must have faith in God. The Lord has promised, ". . . seek ye first the kingdom of God, and his righteousness; and all these things shall be added unto you." (Matthew 6:33.) We must also accept and live the 13th Article of Faith:

We believe in being honest, true, chaste, benevolent, virtuous, and in doing good to all men; indeed, we may say that we follow the admonition of Paul—We believe all things, we hope all things, we have endured many things, and hope to be able to endure all things. If there is anything virtuous, lovely, or of good report or praiseworthy, we seek after these things.

VII

Seek to Emulate the Lives
of Great Men

CHAPTER 29

Joseph Smith, the Prophet

No greater man other than Jesus Christ himself has ever lived upon this earth or contributed more to man's welfare and the spiritual side of life, and whose influence has been and will be felt throughout the world, than Joseph Smith the Prophet.

Sometimes we hear people say, "If I had lived at the time of Christ, I would have accepted his teachings." But people did not accept him in his own time—and many do not accept him today. Yet now that he has gone, millions do accept him as the Son of God, the Savior of the world.

The world as a whole has not accepted Joseph Smith as a prophet of God, but he has influenced the lives of millions of people. Over three million people living in the world today are members of The Church of Jesus Christ of Latter-day Saints and have accepted and enjoy the blessings of being members of Christ's church. There are many others I know who have been more or less converted who know that the gospel of Jesus Christ is true but who have not seen fit to become members of the Church.

Now I have a very close, tender feeling about the Prophet Joseph Smith. You know, he lived in this dispensation. He isn't somebody who lived in an earlier dispensation.

His influence has been felt in my family ever since the Church was organized.

As I indicated in Chapter 2, my great-great-grandfather, John Tanner, was healed of an affliction through administration of the elders who taught him the gospel and baptized him. This was just two years after the Church was organized, and shortly after his baptism he met the Prophet Joseph Smith at a time when the Church was experiencing financial difficulty. Being well-to-do, John Tanner sold everything he had and turned it over to the Prophet in order to take care of the indebtedness of the Church. Such was his love for Joseph Smith and his dedication to the work of the Lord.

As I visualize Joseph Smith as a boy fourteen years of age, I can see a young man reading the scriptures because there was much excitement regarding religion, and many were saying, "Come with us," and others, "Lo, this is the way," and so on. And as he was reading the scriptures he read in James, "If any of you lack wisdom, let him ask of God, that giveth to all men liberally, and upbraideth not; and it shall be given him. But let him ask in faith, nothing wavering. For he that wavereth is like a wave of the sea driven with the wind and tossed." (James 1:5-6.)

Joseph was reared in a religious family, and he thought that if anybody needed wisdom and help, he did. He had never prayed vocally to the Lord before; but he went into a grove near his home and looked around to see if anyone were present. Then he kneeled down to pray, and he says that as he began to call upon his Heavenly Father—

. . . immediately I was seized upon by some power which entirely overcame me, and had such an astonishing influence over me as to bind my tongue so that I could not speak. Thick darkness gathered around me, and it seemed to me for a time as if I were doomed to sudden destruction.

But exerting all my powers to call upon God to deliver me out of the power of this enemy which had seized upon me, . . .

just at this moment of great alarm, I saw a pillar of light exactly over my head, above the brightness of the sun. . . .

. . . When the light rested upon me I saw two Personages, whose brightness and glory defy all description, standing above me in the air. One of them spake unto me, calling me by name and said, pointing to the other—*This is My Beloved Son. Hear Him!* (Joseph Smith 2:15-17.)

Can you imagine Joseph's feelings in the presence of these two heavenly Personages as they spoke to him? As soon as he could speak he asked them which church he should join.

I was answered that I must join none of them, for they were all wrong; and the Personage who addressed me said that all their creeds were an abomination in his sight; that those professors were all corrupt; that: "they draw near to me with their lips, but their hearts are far from me, they teach for doctrines the commandments of men, having a form of godliness, but they deny the power thereof." (Joseph Smith 2:19.)

Joseph learned two very important things as a result of this experience: first, that one can call upon God and receive an answer to his prayer; and second, that though he had been taught that God was a spirit or a force or an influence, he knew as he left that grove as well as he knew that he lived that God lives; that Jesus, who had been crucified and was resurrected, is a living being; and that they had heard his prayer and had talked to him.

As he related his experience to the preachers and others, he said that he was treated with great contempt and was told that there were no such things as visions in these days, and that revelation had ceased.

. . . and though I was an obscure boy, only between fourteen and fifteen years of age, and my circumstances in life such as to make a boy of no consequence in the world, yet men of high standing would take notice sufficient to excite the public mind against me, and create a bitter persecution; and this was common ai iong all the sects—all united to persecute me.

. . . I was led to say in my heart: Why persecute me for telling the truth? I have actually seen a vision; and who am I that I can withstand God, or why does the world think to make me deny what I have actually seen? For I had seen a vision; I knew it, and I knew that God knew it, and I could not deny it, neither dared I do it. . . . (Joseph Smith 2:22, 25.)

He suffered this ridicule and persecution for a period of three years. He had no Sunday School, no seminary nor institute classes, no sacrament meeting, no priesthood meeting to attend. In fact, he was left alone. Yet in spite of all the persecutions and ridicule by those who should have been his friends, he continued with this testimony: "I saw a vision. God knows that I saw it, and I cannot deny it."

Now, do you think that young lad made up that story, and after three years of persecution still maintained that it was true? Joseph says that having been all alone, and "left to all kinds of temptations; and, mingling with all kinds of society, I frequently fell into many foolish errors, and displayed the weakness of youth. . . ." (Joseph Smith 2:28.)

As a result, he seriously felt the need of calling upon the Lord for forgiveness and for further direction. As he prayed to the Lord, the Angel Moroni appeared and said that he was a messenger sent from the presence of God. He told Joseph that God had a work for him to do, and that his name should be known for good and evil among all nations and among all people. He told him about the gold plates upon which the record of God's dealings with the ancient American people had been inscribed, and that these contained the gospel in its fullness as taught by the Savior to the people on the American continent. He showed him in a vision where he, Moroni, had hidden the plates in the Hill Cumorah. After talking to Joseph, and quoting from Malachi and Isaiah, he instructed him to meet him at the spot where the records were concealed.

On the following day Joseph met the angel as instructed and was shown the plates, but he was not permitted to take them. He was instructed by the angel to meet him at the same place, at the same time each year for four years thereafter. Imagine that young man when he went to the Hill Cumorah and opened that stone box and saw those plates. When he met the angel each year thereafter for four years, he was taught and instructed by Moroni, the same man who had placed those plates in the Hill Cumorah.

At the end of this time, when Joseph was but twenty-two years of age, he was permitted to take the plates and was told to guard them carefully. You know the persecutions he suffered and the great opposition he had while translating those plates. Remember, he was a young man of humble circumstances without wealth or position and little scholastic education when called to do this important work. But as he said, "By the spirit and power of God was I able to do it."

While translating he came to a passage referring to baptism. As a result, he and Oliver Cowdery decided to ask the Lord about baptism and how it should be performed. As they were calling upon the Lord, John the Baptist appeared to them—the same individual who baptized Jesus Christ. Imagine this lad now with his companion, Oliver Cowdery, having this heavenly being come and place his hands upon their heads and confer upon them the Aaronic Priesthood. He then instructed them to baptize and ordain each other. He told them at that time that Peter, James, and John had instructed him, and that they later would appear and confer upon them the Melchizedek Priesthood. Imagine Peter, James, and John, the three senior apostles who had labored and traveled with the Lord and into whose hands the work of the church had been committed when the Savior left them, appearing to Joseph and Oliver and placing their hands upon their heads and conferring the Melchizedek Priesthood, the power of God delegated to man to act in his name. They were later ordained apostles of the Lord Jesus Christ.

In spite of all of the opposition they received, the Book of Mormon was translated in just a little over two years. No one has been able to prove it wrong. The Book of Mormon is not in conflict in any way with the Bible, but is a new witness for Christ. The Jewish people—those who accept the Bible—accept the Old Testament as the word of God. The Catholics and the Protestants accept the Old Testament and the New Testament as the word of God. The Latter-day Saints accept the Old Testament and the New Testament as the word of God as literally as, if not more so than, any other church, but they also accept the Book of Mormon as the word of God, the gospel in its fullness as taught by Jesus Christ on the American continent. And all those who have tried to prove the Book of Mormon wrong—its religious teachings or its history—have failed to do so.

Now I see that young man, when he was twenty-four years of age, standing up before a small group of people and saying to them, "I have been chosen and ordained an apostle, a prophet, a seer, a revelator, and a translator and First Elder of the Church of Jesus Christ."

No man in all history has made the claim that this young man made as he stood there and said, "God the Father and his Son Jesus Christ appeared to me and they talked to me. The Angel Moroni appeared and talked to me. John the Baptist appeared and conferred the Aaronic Priesthood upon me. Peter, James, and John came and conferred the Melchizedek Priesthood upon me." No greater claim was ever made.

I think of him translating that Book of Mormon under the spirit and power of God and coming to a passage that said there was a wall around Jerusalem, and telling his wife Emma, "You know, I never knew there was a wall around Jerusalem." And when he came to Third Nephi and realized that Jesus Christ had actually appeared to the people on the American continent after his resurrection, I can imagine him saying, "Well, I didn't know that Christ ever appeared to the people on the American continent. I didn't know that he gathered the people around him and that he took the children upon his knee and that he prayed with them and he wept with them." Of course he didn't know. And he learned many other things from the Book of Mormon that he did not know before.

Now, let me ask, could he make this claim and suffer all of this persecution and come forward with the translation of the Book of Mormon with all of the opposition that he had experienced if it hadn't been that he did so by the power and Spirit of God and through revelation as he said he did? It would just be impossible.

As I see this church being organized, as he stood before this small group and said, "It's our responsibility to take this message to the whole world," I imagine they felt the weight of that responsibility on their shoulders. But he wasn't discouraged. Even while he was translating the Book of Mormon and before the Church was organized, he had over twenty recorded revelations that now appear in the Doctrine and Covenants. During the first two years after the Church was organized, he had fifty-three recorded revelations. Think of Joseph Smith and the things he did, the things he accomplished, and the contributions he made to the world. The Spirit of the Lord, the power of God, and revelation were given to him that he might accomplish these things.

In reviewing some of his accomplishments, I should like to refer first to the Book of Mormon, a history of a people covering a thousand years of their travels, their everyday life, their wars, and other experiences. It occupies 522 pages. It is the only bona fide record of the early people, now known as the American Indians, on the American continent. Remember the promise given by Moroni regarding the Book of Mormon:

> And when ye shall receive these things, I would exhort you that ye would ask God, the Eternal Father, in the name of Christ, if these things are not true; and if ye shall ask with a

sincere heart, with real intent, having faith in Christ, he will
manifest the truth of it unto you, by the power of the Holy
Ghost. (Moroni 10:4.)

No greater promise is made regarding any book. How
would Joseph Smith dare state that promise if it were not
there in the original? Many, many people have asked God
and have proven that promise to be true and have learned
as a result that the gospel is true. Remember that this work
was done by a young man with no formal education, who
worked for his neighbors for a living, who was opposed
and tormented and persecuted from the time he was fourteen years of age—and all this was accomplished by the
time he was thirty-eight, when he was martyred.

Then we have the Pearl of Great Price, where we
find the stories of Moses and Abraham and their teachings. We have the great Doctrine and Covenants, con-
taining 136 revelations. We have also seven volumes of
history of the diaries and journals and records and writings of Joseph Smith. Now, can you realize what this
young man accomplished during just a few years? This
was all accomplished from 1820 until his martyrdom in
1844.

We learn from the teachings as recorded in the Book
of Mormon, the Doctrine and Covenants, and the Pearl of
Great Price about man's relationship to God, our preexistence, the council in heaven when every one of us
was there and in which all of us took part. All of us voted
for Jesus Christ as the leader. This knowledge is available
to the world only through the revelations of Joseph Smith.
We are taught about the resurrection. Read Alma in the
Book of Mormon and learn about the resurrection. No
other place in the world do we find such clear teachings of
this important event, nor does the world understand it as
we understand it as a result of these teachings.

We are taught also how we can work for our dead,
thereby making available the blessings of the gospel to

millions of our ancestors who died without a knowledge of it. We have the principle of celestial marriage and eternal progression. What a wonderful thing it is to know that I can be sealed to my wife for time and all eternity, and she to me, and that we can carry on as a family unit throughout eternity and continue in eternal progression.

We have the restoration of the priesthood. Think of the young missionaries going out into the world, clothed with the authority of the priesthood. Each has the power of God which has been delegated to him to act in His name, and as the missionary teaches the people and baptizes them, what does he say? "Having been commissioned of Jesus Christ, I baptize you in the name of the Father, and of the Son, and of the Holy Ghost." (D&C 20:73.) Every person whom he baptizes is just as much baptized as was Jesus when John the Baptist baptized him. Then as the elder, having been given the authority, lays his hands upon the head of the new male convert and confirms him a member of the Church and then later ordains him a deacon, teacher, priest, or elder, it is of the same force and effect as if one of the apostles had performed these ordinances.

These are but a few of the teachings, accomplishments, and contributions of Joseph Smith, the Prophet. Now let me refer to Nauvoo, Illinois. I have read with interest the history of Nauvoo and the experience of our Saints there. I know the question has been asked time and time again, "If this is the church of Jesus Christ, why did the Lord allow those people to suffer the persecutions they did and be driven from place to place?" Let us remember that the Lord told Joseph Smith that if the Saints would live according to the teachings of the gospel, and if they remained true and magnified their callings, the work would progress. But the Lord has also said he will have a tried people.

As we all know, there was much unrest in the Church, and many proved unfaithful and turned against the Prophet, some of whom he trusted fully and who were holding high office in the Church. As a result there was great persecution. The faithful, however, remained true, the work of the Lord went forward, and the Church was purged of the weak and rebellious.

In Nauvoo during the six years they were there the Saints built beautiful homes, built a city larger than any other in Illinois, built a city hall, a university, and were even able to build a temple to God. Imagine this great accomplishment under the direction of this young man and in the face of great opposition and persecution! And while all of this development was taking place, the Church also sent many missionaries to preach the gospel to the world. Nine of the Twelve Apostles were sent to England at one time or another.

Before Joseph Smith was martyred and long before the great persecution of the Saints in Nauvoo, he prophesied that the people would be going to the Rocky Mountains. In fact, he had prepared a company to go and examine and study conditions there, but he was martyred before that company began its study.

Then as I think of the Saints crossing the plains and coming into a desert in the Salt Lake Valley, and making it blossom as a rose, where nobody had been able to make it fruitful before, it is a testimony to me that the gospel is true and that the Lord's blessings will attend those who are faithful to him and will magnify their callings.

To me, the story of Joseph Smith and the restoration of the gospel is the greatest story of modern times. If the world knew these truths and would accept them, then the purpose of Christ's mission would be fulfilled, because he said, ". . . this is my work and my glory—to bring to pass the immortality and eternal life of man." (Moses 1:39.)

And through our prophet today the Lord has asked us each to be a missionary to help the world realize that this is the gospel of Jesus Christ, the plan of life and salvation, which, if accepted, will bring peace to the world, joy to mankind, and make it possible for us to enjoy immortality and eternal life.

CHAPTER 30

David O. McKay, the Man

My first association with President David O. McKay was when he was a counselor to President Heber J. Grant in the First Presidency and I was bishop of the Cardston First Ward in Canada. I met with him at stake conference and then at an outing at Waterton Lakes, where I was able to observe him in a capacity other than in church administration and saw how he enjoyed nature and fishing with the boys. He was a real sport.

When I went to Edmonton as a member of the Alberta government, I realized that there was very little missionary work being done in western Canada, and since President McKay was in charge of the missionary work of the Church, I began to correspond with him regarding the need of a mission being established in the western provinces.

My correspondence with him at that time helped me realize how keenly interested he was in mankind and their welfare and, as anyone would expect, in the building of the kingdom of God. A mission was finally established with headquarters in Edmonton, and I continued to correspond with him and talk to him as it was getting established.

My call as a General Authority, and then particularly as a counselor in the First Presidency, gave me an exceptional opportunity for close association with him, to partake of his spirit, and to see how the Lord worked and directed the Church through him as his mouthpiece. This was a privilege and honor extended to few men, and one for which I am most humbly grateful and appreciative.

In order to understand the man, I think it is essential that we know something of his boyhood and family life. He was born September 8, 1873, at Huntsville, Utah, a son and one of ten children of David and Jennette Evans McKay. His parents were devoted members of the Church who taught their children obedience and faith in the Lord Jesus Christ and the importance of living according to the teachings of the gospel.

David grew up at Huntsville where, as a youngster, he worked at farm chores, delivered mail and newspapers, played the piano for the town band and second base for the town baseball team, and participated in all normal activities in the community.

In the home he was taught to pray privately and secretly to the Lord, and he participated with the family in family prayers. He learned to know beyond any shadow of doubt that the Lord can and does hear and answer prayers.

Let me share with you two little experiences that he has related. On one occasion when he was a little boy there was thunder and lightning, and he was frightened. After the storm was over and he was lying in his bed up in the attic, he heard a weird noise above his head that frightened him very much. He wanted to pray, but he did not know how to pray without getting on his knees, and he was afraid to get out of bed. Finally he mustered up courage enough to do this, and as he knelt by the side of his bed and prayed, he heard a voice distinctly say: "Don't be afraid. Nothing will hurt you." All fear left him and he went sound asleep.

Decades later, while he and Sister McKay were on an airplane soaring over Australia, a bolt of lightning slammed into the side of the plane, extinguishing the lights.

President and Sister McKay were completely calm and un-afraid, though fellow passengers were alarmed and chatter-ing excitedly. Such was his testimony that the Lord does hear and answer prayers. Throughout his life he always knew he could go to the Lord for strength, help, and guidance.

As a young boy he always had a great desire to have a testimony so he could, as he had heard his father and others do, bear witness to the truthfulness of the gospel, that God lives and that Jesus is the Christ. He said that at different times when he was riding on his horse out through the fields, he would stop by a tree or by a service-berry bush and kneel down and ask the Lord to give him a testimony, but each time he arose and found he was the same boy who had knelt down, and that the tes-timony had not come. But it did finally come, and in such a strong and mighty way that there was never any doubt in his mind. He bore his witness thousands of times as a special witness for Christ, and as he has said: "A testi-mony of the gospel of Jesus Christ is the most sacred, the most precious gift in our lives, obtained only by adherence to the principles of the gospel, not by following the paths of the world. You may get monetary pleasures by fol-lowing the enticements of the world." He would always emphasize that these are fleeting, and he often quoted from Robert Burns:

> But pleasures are like poppies spread,
> You seize the flow'r, its bloom is shed;
> Or like the snow falls in the river,
> A moment white—then melts forever;
> Or like the borealis race,
> That flit ere you can point their place;
> Or like the rainbow's lovely form
> Evanishing amid the storm.

From his boyhood and throughout his life, he always showed a keen interest in others and was willing to help and lift them whenever possible. Typical of this is the story told of a little boy named Olvie Cramer who, with other members of the community, had gathered around an Indian woman, intently watching her weave and perform. Olvie was too small to see anything and was trying to squirm through the legs of the crowded onlookers. Suddenly he felt someone lift him high above the crowds, and a voice called, "Can you see the lady?" Olvie looked down to see who had lifted him above the heads and shoulders of the others, and it was a tall neighbor youth, David O. McKay. He spent his life trying to help other people to see things better.

He was a natural leader. At the age of twenty-four he was graduated from the University of Utah, where he was president and valedictorian of his class. The same year he left to fill a mission in Great Britain and was assigned to Scotland, where he became president of the Glasgow Conference. As a devoted missionary he often felt discouraged as he realized that many wonderful people in the land of his father were not heeding the message of the gospel. Then one day he read above the door of an unfinished building the following: "Whate'er Thou Art, Act Well Thy Part." This changed the course of his mission and influenced the rest of his life as he applied that motto in all he did.

While he was on his mission, as he was attending a very spiritual meeting, his mission president, James McMurrin, turned to him and said: "Let me say to you, Brother David, Satan hath desired you that he may sift you as wheat, but God is mindful of you." Then he added: "If you will keep the faith you will yet sit in the leading councils of the Church." Not many years passed until this prophecy was fulfilled. It might be interesting to note here how his mission president rated his work: "As a speaker: Good; As a writer: Good; As a Presiding Officer: Very Good; He has a good knowledge of the gospel. He has been energetic. He is discreet and carries a good influence. There is none better in the mission."

He returned from his mission in 1899, the year after I was born. The same year he became a teacher at the Weber Academy. He was ordained an apostle in 1906 by President Joseph F. Smith. It is interesting to know that David O. McKay was born while Brigham Young was presiding over the Church, that he remembered well the building of the Salt Lake Temple, and also the St. George, Manti, and Logan temples.

While an apostle he became Church Commissioner of Education. It is evident that he was always recognized as a leader of men. Also, while an apostle he was named assistant to the superintendent of the general board of the Deseret Sunday School Union. He later became the general superintendent and served in that position until 1934.

Let us chronicle some important events in his life. On speaking to a group of Saints in New Zealand, he was given the gift of tongues so that he could speak in tongues and all could understand him. This was in 1921. In 1922 he became a member of the Board of Regents of the University of Utah. He was then called to preside over the European Mission, following which he was elected president of the Weber State College Alumni Association. The next year he was elected chairman of the Utah Council on Child Health and Protection at the organization of this group, following a White House Conference on Child Welfare. In 1940 he was named to the Board of Trustees of the Utah State Agricultural College (now Utah State University).

President McKay was sustained as second counselor to President Heber J. Grant in the First Presidency in 1934. When President Grant died and President George Albert Smith became President of the Church in 1945, he again was called as second counselor in the First Presidency.

During his life he received honorary degrees from several universities in recognition of his outstanding ability and service. He also received every honor the American Boy Scout organization could bestow on an individual. In 1951, at the age of 78, he was chosen by the Council of the Twelve and sustained by the priesthood and general assembly of the Church as President of the Church. He was set apart and ordained by the Council of the Twelve under the hands of President Joseph Fielding Smith.

Under his administration the following temples were built and dedicated:

Swiss Temple	September 11, 1955
Los Angeles Temple	March 11, 1956
New Zealand Temple	April 20, 1958
London Temple	September 7, 1958
Oakland Temple	November 17, 1964

Plans were also underway for the erection of temples in Washington, D.C., and Ogden and Provo, Utah.

He traveled more than any other General Authority to extend missionary work and encourage the Saints throughout the world. While he was President of the Church he met and conferred with men from all walks of life, including presidents of the United States and presidents of large industrial corporations, some of whom called upon him for advice and counsel. In fact, from 1936 to 1963 he had a record of meeting and interviewing over 1500 distinguished persons from all parts of the world.

A leading official of the General Motors Corporation once made a courtesy call on President McKay. As he left the building, he turned to the gentleman who accompanied him to the office and said, "There is the most Godlike man I have ever met. If you wanted to make a man in the image of God, there is the pattern."

A leading medical man of this country wrote to President McKay, after having heard him deliver the commencement address at the Temple University in Philadelphia, and asked him for an autographed photograph. Upon receipt of it, the doctor wrote back to thank President McKay, saying: "Permit me to express my sincere thanks for your photograph, which fills a most prominent place in my 'Hall of Fame.' I shall ever appreciate your kindness, and as I look daily into the face of a great man of God, whose integrity and genuineness is unquestioned, perhaps I may receive additional strength to serve better humanity and the Great Physician above."

I had the great privilege of being present when President John F. Kennedy, President Lyndon B. Johnson, and President Richard M. Nixon made courtesy calls on President McKay, and noticed how keenly interested they were as they sat and discussed world problems and other matters of great importance with him, and how greatly impressed they seemed to be as a result of the counsel he gave and the wisdom with which he discussed these problems. Each time he taught some principle of the gospel as a solution to a particular problem.

I also had the cherished privilege of accompanying President McKay to Washington when he was invited by President Johnson to come there and discuss with him and seek his advice on problems that were causing him much concern. During the discussion President Johnson said that sometimes he felt as he did when he was a little boy. When he had more problems than he could handle, he would go to his mother and put his head on her breast and get a little sympathy. He mentioned that he had many problems today, and he felt the same way now that he had felt when he was a little boy needing help.

After a short visit in his office, President Johnson escorted the party to a private dining room. During the luncheon President Johnson turned to President McKay and said: "I feel that the spiritual and moral fiber of this country needs strengthening. We need it badly. I would like to ask you, President McKay, if you can tell me how we can get it. I have been out to see you on two or three occasions before, and each time I left you I came away inspired, and I feel I would like to have your advice on this."

I remember that President McKay answered him so well and thoroughly that you would have thought he had had time to consider the question for some days at least. He said: "Mr. President, I have read that you have said that you were first a free man; second, an American citizen; third, the president of the United States; and fourth, a Democrat."

President McKay then said: "I like that. Now you have asked me this question. I think you are an honorable man, and that you meant what you said about strengthening the spiritual and moral fiber of this country. I would say to you: Let your conscience be your guide, and let the people see that you are sincere in wanting to solve this problem, which is one that should be met. Lead out in it, and let the people follow."

I remember President Johnson looking at me and nodding his head, and then I said to him, "If the President had talked to you for an hour he could not have given you any better advice." President Johnson responded: "You are right."

This is another evidence of the very high regard in which men in high places held our President, David O. McKay, and listened to his counsel and advice. It is a great tribute to him. I often felt that as President McKay talked to these men he was inspired of the Lord and gave advice beyond his normal ability.

One cannot complete a sketch of the life of President McKay without noting his charming wit and humor. May I refer to one of his oft-repeated stories. He would say: "Too many of us are like that Scotsman of whom I told you, who had lost his wife by death. His neighbor came in, gave comfort, and said what a good neighbor she had been, how thoughtful of others, and what a good wife she had been to Jock, who was mourning. Jock said, 'Aye, Tammas, Janet was a guid woman, a guid neighbor as you say; she was a' you say an' mair. She was aye a guid, true wifey tae me, and I cam' near tellin' her sae aince or twice.'"

He was noted for his quick witty responses. On one occasion he was in the lobby of the Hotel Utah when a young man came up to shake hands with him and greeted him most cordially. President McKay then got on the elevator and went up to the eighth floor, where his apartment was. As he got off the elevator, this young man was there waiting for him, having run up all the stairs to get there. He said, "I just had to shake hands with you again before you die." President McKay quickly responded, "Well, I don't think you have to worry. Very few people die at age ninety-five."

It has been a signal honor, privilege, and blessing, and a most rewarding experience for me to have been called by the President of the Church and to act as one of his counselors, and for six glorious years to sit in counsel with him, to feel of his great spirit, and to have been taught and inspired by the Lord's anointed, his mouthpiece here upon the earth. The messages that he asked me to take to the members of the Church wherever I went and that meant so much to me were, "Remember who you are and act accordingly," and "Remember that you have an individual responsibility."

I should like to mention some personal observations about this great man. First, under his leadership the Church enjoyed unprecedented physical and spiritual growth. Shortly before he became President, the Church had 1,111,314 members; at the time of his death the membership stood at 2,800,000. The number of stakes increased from 184 to 500, and the missions from 43 to 88. The per capita payment of tithes and offerings increased materially, and the percent attendance at meetings increased at all levels, as the magnetic qualities of this good man inspired the Saints to set new goals and reach new heights.

I always found him to be a true exemplar of the life of Christ. He followed and lived by the two great commandments given to us by the Lord: "Thou shalt love the Lord thy God with all thy heart, and with all thy soul, and with all thy mind," and "Thou shalt love thy neighbour as thyself." (Matthew 22:37, 39.) I must say that this guided his whole life.

Let me give you some excerpts from a few of the many messages received from outstanding citizens throughout the United States and elsewhere at the time of his passing that are evidences of the high regard in which he was held:

"America has lost a foremost citizen and human being."

"His life work will be a sustaining force for long years beyond this day. His profound commitment to his fellow men and his faith inspired us to uplift our hopes and sights toward a better world."

"The world has lost one of its most effective spiritual leaders."

"He has been a symbol of integrity and moral strength to all people of the world."

"President McKay led the membership of the Church not by edict or command, but by the power of Christian example, which he manifested by love, meekness, kindness, and courtesy, all of which was delightfully expressed by his constant chivalry and his ever-present sense of humor."

"When in his presence, one always felt the spirit and power of this great man. He was always courteous, kind, and concerned for others through his excellent manners. He had an engaging smile, a twinkle in his eye, and a wonderful sense of humor."

President David O. McKay was a prophet of God through whom the Lord spoke. He knew and bore testimony that God lives and that Jesus is the Christ and gave his life for us. He believed it and he knew it as I know it, and I bear testimony to this effect. This is the Church of Jesus Christ, and if we follow our leaders and live the gospel as given to us in these, the latter days, we will enjoy immortality and eternal life, and while we are preparing ourselves, we will enjoy mortal life more nearly to the full and have greater success and happiness along the way.

CHAPTER 31

David O. McKay: A True Exemplar of the Life of Christ

We have met here today as an expression of our love and respect for our departed, illustrious, devoted, and beloved leader, David O. McKay—a prophet of God—and to his devoted wife and family.

It is a real honor and a humbling experience indeed to be asked by the family to speak at the funeral of their husband, father, grandfather, and brother, who was loved, respected, and adored by every one of them.

As I stand before you on this most solemn occasion, I feel so inadequate in trying to express my feelings, and humbly pray that the spirit and blessings of the Lord will attend each and every one of us and that what I may say might be of some comfort and solace to the family and encouragement to those who are paying homage to this great man.

He has spent his whole life in the service of his Lord and Savior and of his fellowmen. It has been a signal honor, privilege, and blessing and a most rewarding experience for me to have been called by the prophet as one of his

---

Address delivered at the funeral of President David O. McKay in the Salt Lake Tabernacle January 22, 1970.

counselors, and for six glorious years to sit in council with him, to feel his great spirit, and to have been taught and inspired by the Lord's anointed. I have continually prayed and shall continue to pray and strive to be worthy of this rare and wonderful opportunity and blessing, which is beyond compare.

I wish to express my appreciation for the opportunity I have had of becoming so well acquainted with his sweet and devoted wife, Emma Ray, whom I have always loved and respected, and also for the close and pleasant association I have had with Lawrence as superintendent of the Sunday School and in a business way, and with Edward, Robert, and with Conway Ashton, a son-in-law, and other members of this fine family whom I have learned to love and respect.

I should like personally to express my appreciation to the doctors and nurses for their true love, devotion, and kindness in caring for his every need, and which he appreciated so much.

After a normal lifetime of service, he was called at the age of seventy-seven as a prophet of God to preside over The Church of Jesus Christ of Latter-day Saints. Though he had passed the age when most men have finished their mortal life, he was hale, hardy, and alert, loving life and the challenges before him. He presided over the Church for nineteen years.

Under his leadership the Church has enjoyed unprecedented physical and spiritual growth. The missionary program has made greater progress, and we have seen more temple building than ever before. Priesthood programs and activity have been greatly enlarged, a successful correlation program inaugurated, and Regional Representatives of the Twelve have been called to assist in furthering the Church's worldwide program. In response to a growing need for an answer to some of the social problems confronting us, there has been greater emphasis on the importance of home and family relationships than at any other time.

His life of outstanding service and leadership has been acknowledged, and great tribute expressed, by newspapers, radio, and television from all over the continent, and elsewhere in the world, and by telegrams, letters, and phone calls from admirers far and near.

As one of the greatest prophets and leaders of this dispensation, his counsel has been sought and his influence felt by leaders in all walks of life, including presidents of the United States. He was loved and respected and revered by millions of people who now mourn his passing.

During his whole life he was a true exemplar of the life of Christ. He followed and lived by the two great commandments which the Lord gave to the lawyer, who asked him, tempting,

Master, which is the great commandment in the law?
Jesus said unto him, Thou shalt love the Lord thy God with all thy heart, and with all thy soul, and with all thy mind.
This is the first and great commandment.
And the second is like unto it, Thou shalt love thy neighbour as thyself.
On these two commandments hang all the law and the prophets. (Matthew 22:36-40.)

I should like to refer to one or two instances that seem to depict the love and harmony that existed in his home. When he was ninety years of age, Sister McKay, his lovely wife, wrote the following tribute:

I am very, very proud of my husband. He is just as lovely, just as courteous, just as polite, just as kind, just as sweet in our home as he is anywhere else, and I am proud of him. And I am very grateful for him. I cannot see a thing wrong with him. And I pray that our brethren will try to follow his example in every way, shape, and form.

There are two experiences which I have had, and which touch my heart, that I should like to repeat to you today. One morning, shortly after he had left the hospital following a slight stroke, I was in his study with him, and he said: "President Tanner, I had the sweetest experience last night. About 11 o'clock I got up to go to the bathroom, and had only gone two or three steps when Emma Ray was by my side, holding my hand." And I wondered how this little frail woman could assist this big man, but as tears came to his eyes, I knew that she had helped him through love and consideration for his well-being.

At another time I had him in his wheelchair and was wheeling him out to go to the meeting in the temple. I just got to the front door when he said, "Oh, I must kiss Emma Ray good-bye." Here he was in a wheelchair, on his way to a meeting, had only been married for sixty-five years, and felt it important that he should kiss his sweet wife good-bye. I turned his wheelchair around and wheeled him back through the hall, through the living room, to the bedroom, where he kissed Emma Ray good-bye. Then tears came to my eyes, and I thought what an example of love and affection, which, if practiced in every home, would contribute greatly to our joy and unity and progress.

His love of and devotion to the Lord cannot be questioned. Another experience I should like to repeat took place just before I was called into the First Presidency. We were sitting in a meeting of the First Presidency and Quorum of the Twelve discussing a very important matter, trying to determine what would be in the best interest of the Church and acceptable to our Heavenly Father. After the discussion had gone on for some little time, President McKay said, "Brethren, I think this is what the Lord would want us to do."

All of the brethren, though some strong views had been stated, realized that we should do as the President directed. I turned to a brother by whom I was sitting and said, "I never cease to marvel at the wisdom of that man, the keenness of his mind, how he can analyze a problem and come up with the right solution."

He turned to me and said, as he put his hand on my knee, "You are listening to a prophet of God." I was startled and a little chagrined, because I too knew that we were listening to a prophet of God, and that his answer would need to be correct and what the Lord would want us to do.

He believed, followed, and understood the gospel of Jesus Christ. He knew and taught that death was just passing from mortal to immortal existence to a life hereafter.

A little grandson of mine, eight years of age, who had leukemia and understood the seriousness of his condition, paid a great tribute to President McKay. His teacher had asked the class to write out what each would like to be more than anything else. Little Tommy wrote: "I would like to be President McKay because he is a prophet of God. When he dies he will go the celestial kingdom, and that is where I want to go."

Then he finished by saying, "Maybe I'll get there anyway." Such is the faith of a little child, and I am sure his wish has been realized. The Savior said: "Except ye be converted, and become as little children, ye shall not enter into the kingdom of heaven." (Matthew 18:3.)

Another little incident I should like to relate took place as President McKay's family were discussing the fact that he would be given a great welcome by the prophets and General Authorities who had preceded him, and by his father, his mother and brothers, and his many friends. His grandson Mark spoke up and said, "You know, it would really be interesting to be in on that celebration that is going on in heaven for Papa Dade. Boy! He's really got it made!"

How fortunate and blessed we are to know that we are the spirit children of God, that God lives, and that his Son Jesus Christ actually came to earth and gave his life that we might be resurrected and enjoy immortality and eternal life. This will make it possible for every one of us to go back into his presence if we will but follow the plan laid down by him.

President McKay has said much on this subject, and I should like to read at length some of the things he has said regarding life and the resurrection. He quoted John 3:16:

> For God so loved the world, that he gave his only begotten Son, that whosoever believeth in him should not perish, but have everlasting life.

Then President McKay goes on to say:

> As Christ lived after death so shall all men live, each taking his place in the next world for which he has best fitted himself. The message of the resurrection, therefore, is the most comforting, the most glorious ever given to man, for when death takes a loved one from us, our sorrowing hearts are assuaged by the hope and the divine assurance expressed in the words: "He is not here: for he is risen." (Matthew 28:6.) Because our Redeemer lives, so shall we. I bear you my witness that he does live, and I know it as I hope you know that divine truth.

Further quoting from President McKay:

> Resurrection and spring are happily associated, not that there is anything in nature exactly analogous to the resurrection, but there is so much which suggests the awakening thought. Like the stillness of death, old winter has held all vegetable life in his grasp, but as spring approaches, the tender, life-giving power of heat and light compels him to relinquish his grip, and what seems to have been dead comes forth in newness of life, refreshed, invigorated, strengthened after a peaceful sleep.
>
> So it is with man. What we call death, Jesus referred to as sleep. Indeed, to the Savior of the world there is no such thing as death—only life—eternal life. Truly he could say, "I am the resurrection, and the life: he that believeth in me, though he were dead, yet shall he live." (John 11:25.)
>
> With this assurance, obedience to eternal law should be a joy, not a burden, for life is joy, life is love. It is disobedience that brings death. Obedience to Christ and his laws brings life.
>
> The Church of Jesus Christ of Latter-day Saints stands with Peter, with Paul, with James, and with all the other apostles who accepted the resurrection not only as being literally true, but as the consummation of Christ's divine mission on earth. Christ broke the seal of the grave and revealed death as the door to immortality and eternal life. He is real. He lives. God help us to believe in him with all our souls, and to make him real in our lives.

President McKay then says:

The important question with each of us today, as it should be always, is: How well prepared are we to meet that eventuality in life, the inescapable experience called death? One man, contemplating this, tried to imagine what we could take with us when the end came. He wrote:

Supposing today were your last day on earth,
The last mile of the journey you've trod;
After all of your struggles, how much are you worth?
How much can you take home to God?

Don't count as possessions your silver and gold,
Tomorrow you leave these behind:
And all that is yours to have and to hold,
Is the service you've rendered mankind.

President McKay concludes:

When I first read that, I could not agree with him, nor do I today, unless he includes in that rendering of service, the development of spiritual gifts and attainments—the character that we have developed, the virtues which have been ours through righteous living in this mortal stage, and the credit of service to others.

During the months and years in which he was restricted in his activities, he carried on, giving leadership to the Church, and never at any time did I hear him complain. Last Friday morning as I called to inquire if he would like to see his counselors, the nurse replied that he was not able to see us. This Friday morning was the first time in months that he was not up, dressed, and in his study. He was determined and valiant to the very end. He was an inspiration and strength to all of us. And now he has gone to his great reward. What a glorious welcome he will receive from those who have gone on before him! Winston Churchill's statement when speaking of the late King George VI applies so well to our beloved President:

He was sustained not only by his natural buoyancy but by the sincerity of his Christian faith. During these last months the King walked with death as if death were a companion, an acquaintance whom he recognized but did not fear. In the end death came as a friend, and after a happy day of sunshine and sport. After "good night" to those who loved him best, he fell asleep, and as every man and woman who strives to fear God and nothing else in the world may hope to do.

I wish to bear my witness that God lives, and that Jesus is the Christ, the Savior of the world. He has given us the plan of life and salvation through his gospel, which, if accepted and lived, will make it possible for us to enjoy with our great leader, President David O. McKay, immortality and eternal life. May the Lord bless us all to this end, I pray, in the name of Jesus Christ. Amen.

CHAPTER 32

Joseph Fielding Smith:
A Man Without Guile

What a glorious tribute from his son-in-law, Elder
Bruce R. McConkie, and a message to all the world, through
the words of the prophets of old and our departed beloved
prophet, President Joseph Fielding Smith. I humbly pray
to the Lord, my brethren and sisters, that his blessings and
Spirit will attend us as they have so far in this meeting.

It is an honor indeed to be asked by the family to
speak at the funeral of the venerable patriarch of this
esteemed family—President Joseph Fielding Smith, a devoted man of God, one who has served so nobly both God
and his fellowmen and who has led by example his family
and all over whom he has been called to preside; one of
whom it can truthfully be said that he was a man without
guile and without pride.

It could never be said of him that he "loved the praise
of men more than the praise of God" (John 12:43); and,
with Tennyson, he would have said, "And may there be
no moaning of the bar, When I put out to sea."

This is not a time of sadness but a time of thanksgiving

*Address delivered at the funeral of President Joseph Fielding Smith in the
Salt Lake Tabernacle July 6, 1972.*

that we have had the benefit and blessing of his life and association, and the knowledge that he has gone to the great reward for which he was so well prepared.

What he said of President David O. McKay at his funeral services can well be said of President Joseph Fielding Smith:

> He exemplified perfectly the Old Testament standard: ". . . what doth the Lord require of thee, but to do justly, and to love mercy, and to walk humbly with thy God?" (Micah 6:8.) Wherever his voice was heard, there followed greater kindness among men, greater tolerance, greater love. Wherever his influence was felt, man and God became closer in purpose and in action.

And as he further said of President McKay,

> To my mind two statements made by the prophet Lehi exemplify his life. He was like a great river, "continually running into the fountain of all righteousness," and he was like a mighty valley, "firm and steadfast, and immovable in keeping the commandments of the Lord!" (1 Nephi 2:9-10.)
>
> I thank God for the life and ministry of this great man. He was a soul set apart, a great spirit who came here to preside in Israel. He did his work well and has returned clean and perfected to the realms of light and joyous reunion.

Since his passing, tributes have poured in from men in all walks of life and in high position in education, business, and government, including the president of the United States. Radio, television, and the press have been full of tributes and praise which have dealt extensively with stories of his life and accomplishments and his relationship to his family.

They, as we, have recognized his great love for people, particularly children. Typical of his thoughtful consideration and affection for his associates is an experience of last Friday as he left the office building with his secretary, Brother D. Arthur Haycock. He insisted on stopping to shake hands with employees on the basement floor of the building, including the telephone operators who were on duty.

His life-span covered the period from the covered wagon to the jet and space age. He took keen satisfaction in recounting the fact that as a boy he watched the quarrying, stone cutting, and transporting of the huge granite stones used in the building of the temple, and that he watched the construction of that great edifice.

Joseph Fielding Smith was called as an apostle of God and became a member of the Twelve about sixty-two years ago. He served with four Presidents of the Church and was the last of the General Authorities to bridge the gap between the days of Brigham Young and the present generation. Since he became a member of the Twelve, the number of stakes in the Church has increased from 62 to 581; the number of members from 393,000 to 3,090,953; the number of missions from about a dozen to 101. He has attended dedications of eleven of the thirteen temples, including the St. George and Salt Lake.

He passed on this heritage to his large, outstanding family, all of whom have been sealed in the temple of God for time and eternity. President Smith has eleven children (ten of whom are living), fifty-nine grandchildren, ninety-nine great-grandchildren—169 direct descendants.

It is interesting to note that this is more than twice the total population of the whole House of Israel in the day Jacob took his family into Egypt.

He has influenced the lives of hundreds of thousands of people as he lived and taught by word and pen every principle of the gospel. He left no doubt in the minds of anyone that he knew that God is a living God and that we are his spirit children; that Jesus Christ is the Only Begotten Son of God in the flesh; that he gave his life for us that we might enjoy immortality; and that by accepting and living the gospel we may enjoy eternal life. There was never any doubt in his mind that all mankind will enjoy a literal resurrection.

He bore testimony that he knew that God the Father and his Son Jesus Christ appeared to Joseph Smith; that the gospel has been restored in these the latter days; and that there is nothing in this world of as great importance to us as obedience to the principles of the gospel of Jesus Christ. He continued to cry repentance and encourage the people to live according to the teachings of the gospel.

As a young man I remember his series of "Questions and Answers" appearing in the *Era*, and reading some of his twenty-four books, notable among which are *Essentials in Church History, Man—His Origin and Destiny, The Progress of Man, Answers to Gospel Questions, Teachings of the Prophet Joseph Smith,* and *The Way to Perfection,* from which I taught many priesthood lessons. He has always been a great influence in my life.

It has been a great privilege and blessing for me to be so closely associated with him as President of the Church and prophet of God, and to see how the Lord works through his mouthpiece here upon the earth. I think my relationship with him has been unique and probably more varied than any other. As President of the Council of the Twelve, he welcomed me as an Assistant to that body and showed a great love and willingness to help me. He also welcomed me similarly as a member of the Quorum of the Twelve, where he was the senior and I was the junior member.

When I was called to the First Presidency, though he was the senior member of the Twelve and had been in office for over fifty years, he showed great respect for me in that position and gave me full support and confidence. During the two and a half years I have had the honor of being his second counselor in the First Presidency, he has shown every consideration and confidence and love. I thank the Lord for the great privilege and blessing it has been for me to have this opportunity of being so closely associated with him.

All of the members of his family have great love and respect for him, which they have expressed so many times in so many ways. May I read two statements. The first, from his oldest son, Joseph Fielding Smith, Jr.:

Father was always greatly appreciative of the Brethren, constantly expressing his great love for them and what they had done for him. He looked upon the Brethren with great affection and kindness, grateful for their loyalty, and said so often, "I love my brethren."

He was one individual who very definitely respected those in authority over him. He himself never criticized the Brethren, and we were taught in our home to love and respect the General Authorities.

I have never heard him use profane or abusive language. I have never seen him angry or display a temper. When he was disturbed, one could tell it by the expression of pain on his face. Any disobedience brought him great personal sorrow, which was all the punishment we needed.

The following tribute was written by his wife, Ethel Reynolds Smith, and published in the June 1932 issue of the *Improvement Era*: "You ask me to tell you of the man I know," writes Joseph Fielding Smith's wife, Ethel. She continues:

I have often thought when he is gone people will say, "He is a very good man, sincere, orthodox, etc." They will speak of him as the public knows him; but the man they have in mind is very different from the man I know. The man I know is a kind, loving husband and father whose greatest ambition in life is to make his family happy, entirely forgetful of self in his efforts to do this. He is the man that lulls to sleep the fretful child, who tells bedtime stories to the little ones, who is never too tired or too busy to sit up late at night or to get up early in the morning to help the older children solve perplexing school problems. When illness comes, the man I know watches tenderly over the afflicted one and waits upon him. It is their father for whom they cry, feeling his presence a panacea for all ills. It is his hands that bind up the wounds, his arms that give courage to the sufferer, his voice that remonstrates them gently when they err, until it becomes their happiness to do the thing that will make him happy.

The man I know is most gentle, and if he feels that he has been unjust to anyone the distance is never too far to go and, with loving words or kind deeds, erase the hurt. He welcomes gladly the young people to his home and is never happier than when discussing with them topics of the day—sports or whatever interests them most. He enjoys a good story and is quick to see the humor of a situation, to laugh and to be laughed at, always willing to join in any wholesome activity.

The man I know is unselfish, uncomplaining, considerate, thoughtful, sympathetic, doing everything within his power to make life a supreme joy for his loved ones. That is the man I know. (Bryant S. Hinckley, "Joseph Fielding Smith," *Era*, June 1932, p. 459.)

In conclusion I should like to refer briefly to two of his talks. In the very first address he gave at general conference following his appointment as a member of the Council of the Twelve in 1910, he said:

. . . it is a serious thing for any member of the Church to raise his voice against the priesthood, or to hold the priesthood in disrespect; for the Lord will not hold such guiltless; so He has promised, and He will fulfill. . . .

I say to you that the Lord blesses this people through the inspiration that comes to His servants, as they direct, and teach, and expound the scriptures. . . . I say to you that there is revelation in the Church. The Lord not only blesses the men who stand at the head and hold the keys of the kingdom, but He also blesses every faithful individual with the spirit of inspiration. He gives His people revelation for their own guidance, wherein they keep His commandments and serve Him. That is a blessing promised, and within their power to receive. We are blest with revelation; the Church is built upon that foundation. (*Conference Report*, October 1910, pp. 39-41.)

Then from his last talk at general conference in April of this year I read the following:

To the world I say: These are the last days. They are days of trouble and sorrow and desolation. They are days when Satan dwells in the hearts of ungodly men, when inquity abounds, and when the signs of the times are being shown forth.

And there is no cure for the ills of the world except the gospel of the Lord Jesus Christ. Our hope for peace, for temporal and spiritual prosperity, and for an eventual inheritance in the kingdom of God is found only in and through the restored gospel. There is no work that any of us can engage in that is as important as preaching the gospel and building up the Church and kingdom of God on earth.

And so we invite all our Father's children, everywhere, to believe in Christ, to receive him as he is revealed by living prophets, and to join The Church of Jesus Christ of Latter-day Saints. We call upon the world to repent, to worship that God who made them, and to believe the words of those whom he hath sent in this day to proclaim his gospel. . . .

To those who have received the gospel we say: Keep the commandments. Walk in the light. Endure to the end. Be true to every covenant and obligation, and the Lord will bless you beyond your fondest dreams. As it was said by one of old: "Let us hear the conclusion of the whole matter: Fear God, and keep his commandments: for this is the whole duty of man." (Ecclesiastes 12:13.)

To the youth of Zion we say: The Lord bless you and keep you, which most assuredly will be so as you learn his laws and live in harmony with them. Be true to every trust. Honor thy father and thy mother. Dwell together in love and conformity. Be modest in your dress. Overcome the world, and do not be led astray by the fashions and practices of those whose interests are centered upon the things of this world. (Ensign, July 1972, pp. 27-28.)

I pray that the Spirit and blessings of the Lord will attend and comfort the family in this, their hour of bereavement, and may we all, as a result of his life and teachings, be better prepared to meet our Heavenly Father when we are called home I pray in the name of the Lord Jesus Christ. Amen.

CHAPTER 33

President John F. Kennedy: A Memorial

President David O. McKay, who is now recuperating, would like to be with us in this memorial service. He sends his love and blessings and wants us to know that he is with us in spirit.

President Hugh B. Brown is representing the Church at the [Kennedy] funeral in Washington. In their absence it is my responsibility to conduct the service today.

All of the Brigham Young University stakes and wards are holding a memorial service in the BYU Fieldhouse, at which Elder Gordon B. Hinckley of the Council of the Twelve is the speaker.

We are glad to see so many here on this sad and solemn occasion, and to acknowledge the presence of all of the General Authorities who are in the city.

We who are gathered here join with shocked and bereaved people throughout the nation and the world on this day of mourning to do honor to our late beloved President, John F. Kennedy, who while in the service of his country was so brutally assassinated.

Remarks delivered in the Salt Lake Tabernacle Monday, November 25, 1963, at the first official function conducted by President Nathan Eldon Tanner after his call to the First Presidency. This tribute was followed by musical selections from the Tabernacle Choir and organist, and other brief expressions of sympathy.

Here in this historic Tabernacle we had the honor of his presence just a few weeks ago. He was permitted to serve this great country for less than three years, during which time he served capably, conscientiously, and with distinction. It is incredible to think that now we are called to mourn his most untimely and tragic passing.

We are all so deeply grieved and shocked by this terrible tragedy that it is impossible to find words to express our feelings.

In behalf of the First Presidency of The Church of Jesus Christ of Latter-day Saints and all members throughout the world, I wish to express sincere sympathy to Mrs. Kennedy and members of the family of our late beloved President.

The shocking and unbelievable event is not only humiliating to the United States where we knew such a thing could not happen, but is a tragedy affecting the whole world. We earnestly and sincerely appeal to Almighty God that we may all have the faith, the courage, and the fortitude to meet our responsibility, and that his blessings will attend and comfort the nation in this hour of grief.

On this occasion also, we pray that our new President [Lyndon B. Johnson], who has stepped into the leadership of the nation, may have divine guidance. We pledge to him our loyal support and pray that he may have the wisdom and courage to carry on with his new and heavy responsibility. He should be encouraged by the thought that the Almighty raises up men to meet emergencies, and to the degree that he places his trust in the Divine Providence, he will be made equal to what otherwise would be an insuperable task.

VIII

Seek Always to Serve and
to Give Thanks

CHAPTER 34

A Pledge to Serve

President McKay and brethren and sisters, I stand before you this morning in all humility. I wish to express my sincere appreciation of the confidence shown by the General Authorities, President McKay, and those associated with him, in calling one so unprepared to hold such a high office in this The Church of Jesus Christ of Latter-day Saints. No one with any less ability could be called to this position. I would like to assure President McKay and members of the General Authorities and you my brethren and sisters that I shall do my best and am prepared to dedicate my life and my best to the work of the Lord.

I know that this is the church of Jesus Christ, the kingdom of God here upon the earth, and I know that I shall need your faith and prayers, and I ask that I may have them, that I may carry on in a way that will become one in this responsible position, that I may represent the Church wherever I go in a way that will be pleasing to our Heavenly Father.

I should like at this time to express my sincere appreciation to my family. My paternal great-great-grandfather was a very close friend of Joseph the Prophet. And

Address delivered in the Salt Lake Tabernacle Saturday, October 8, 1960, when Nathan Eldon Tanner was called to serve as an Assistant to the Council of the Twelve.

on my mother's side, you have read of James Brown and his work, and you know Hugh B. Brown, who is my mother's brother. I want to thank all of them, especially my father, who was one of the finest men I ever knew, and my loving mother, and particularly I should like at this time to express my sincere and deep appreciation to Elder Hugh B. Brown for the influence that he has had on my life since I was a child. I have had the great privilege of associating closely with him throughout my life.

I should like to express my appreciation to my wife. Probably I could let you know the kind of woman she is by quoting my mother. She said to me one day, "You are fortunate, my boy, to have Sara as your wife. She has been a great support to you as a wife and a wonderful mother to your children. It is not everybody that could live with you as she has and put up with the things which she has to!"

We have five lovely daughters, and I should like to say to them that I appreciate how loyal and faithful they have been, how little worry and concern they have caused us, and how they are prepared to accept any call in the Church.

Speaking of my family, I suppose I should tell you that we have twenty-two grandchildren. I hope and pray that they will carry on in the Church.

President McKay, again I wish to thank you sincerely and those who are supporting you in this my call, and again I wish to say that I love the Lord with all my heart, and I pledge at this time that I will serve him and you with all my might, mind, and strength, and I pray for your faith and prayers and God's blessings, and I do it in the name of Jesus Christ. Amen.

CHAPTER 35

A Privilege and a Call

President McKay, brethren and sisters, in meekness and sobriety, and with a deep feeling of humility and inadequacy, I stand before you today in response to a call from a prophet of God to accept this honor and responsibility. Since he spoke to me I have slept little, but I have wept and prayed much. Because I know he is a prophet of God—our beloved President David O. McKay—of which I have borne testimony many times, I feel to accept this great call and responsibility, and I am prepared to dedicate myself and all that I have to this call. I shall continue to pray for the spirit and blessings of the Lord to attend me that I might have the wisdom and knowledge, the courage and strength, the desire and determination and ability to show my appreciation and prove worthy of the confidence of this, our prophet, these chosen men, the General Authorities, and you, my brethren and sisters, who raised your hands to sustain me in this calling.

I thank you from the bottom of my heart, and as your humble servant, the weakest of all, I beseech you to exercise your faith and prayers unitedly in my behalf, that I

Address delivered in the Salt Lake Tabernacle Saturday, October 6, 1962, when Nathan Eldon Tanner was sustained as a member of the Council of the Twelve.

might serve in a way that will be acceptable to our Heavenly Father.

I am so grateful to my devoted wife, for her love and affection, and that she has dedicated herself to the service of our Heavenly Father, and who will sustain me in anything that I am called to do in this the church and kingdom of God; and for my wonderful family, who too have accepted the call and say, ". . . choose you this day whom ye will serve; . . . but as for me and my house, we will serve the Lord." (Joshua 24:15.)

I wish also to express my apreciation to these great leaders for the support, the help, and encouragement they have given me during these two years of association with them, and for the help they have given me in years past. To see the devotion, the dedication, and the wisdom of these men, and to be associated with them, is a privilege, a pleasure, and a blessing that one cannot express.

We had the great privilege and pleasure of having President and Sister [Henry D.] Moyle and Brother [Gordon B.] Hinckley with us two months ago [in the West European Mission, where Elder Tanner was presiding], and to see how dedicated they are to this work. These two men, I believe, had fourteen consecutive meetings in fourteen consecutive days, in fourteen different towns in four or five countries. I do not see how they stood it, but if anybody ever forgot himself or lost himself in the service, this is an example of it. And I was so fortunate to have the opportunity and privilege of being with President McKay when he flew to Scotland to organize the Glasgow Stake. To see him at eighty-nine years of age leave his beloved, devoted wife, of whom he thinks so much, and whose health would not permit her to accompany him, and travel all day and all night in order to be there to organize that stake in that great country, the land of his progenitors, is a testimony indeed. It was a great blessing for those people to have a prophet of God in their midst.

The Scottish Mission was organized just eighteen months ago—with a membership of only 1,400 or 1,500 people—and today a stake is organized in the Glasgow area where there were only 400 or 500 members when the mission was organized, and today there are 3,500 members, 2,300 of which were taken into the stake, and the other 1,200 left in the mission. Due to the rapidity with which the growth has taken place, it was necessary to choose several men who have been in the Church just a few months to take the heavy responsibility of being counselors to bishops or act as ward clerks.

This is the result of the work being done by those devoted misisonaries, your sons and daughters. It is a great work that they are doing. It is not easy. It is a great challenge, and I appeal to you, my brethren and sisters, and all fathers and mothers, wherever they may be, to realize that it is not an easy thing for these young men to leave, as Brother [Theodore M.] Burton said, everything that they have and go out and devote two years to this missionary work. How blessed are those boys and girls who have come from homes where the parents are not ashamed of the gospel of Christ because they know it is the power of God unto salvation, where they are prepared and trained to live the gospel and make it a part of their lives every day. They are most fortunate when their parents have a testimony and are prepared to accept the call of our prophet—every member a missionary—realizing that this is the plan of life and salvation and the gospel of peace!

I want to bear you my testimony, my brethren and sisters, that if every member of this church would accept the call of our prophet today and live the gospel and keep the commandments of our Heavenly Father and become missionaries in very deed, we could contribute more to the cause of peace than all the power that might be gathered together by all the governments and all the men in uniform.

This is our privilege and our call, my brethren and sisters, and I hope and pray that we will have the courage, desire, and determination to accept it and live worthy of being members of The Church of Jesus Christ of Latter-day Saints. Let us live so that people can say, as the governor of Texas said at one time when introducing me to a group of oil men in Dallas, Texas: "The government is fortunate to have a man like Mr. Tanner." And when I finished speaking he said, "I want to tell you why I said that the government is fortunate to have a man like Mr. Tanner. I told you that Mr. Tanner was a bishop in the Mormon Church. And I want to say that any man who is worthy to be a bishop in that church needs no other introduction as far as I am concerned."

What a wonderful thing it would be if that could be said of every man who is a member of this church, and it should be thus. I want to bear you my testimony that I know that God lives; that Jesus is the Christ, and that he lives, though he gave his life for you and me; and that the gospel has been restored in fulness in this, the last dispensation; and that we have a prophet at the head of our church today to guide us, direct us, encourage us, instruct us.

May we accept this. May we prove worthy of our membership in the Church and kingdom of God is my prayer in the name of Jesus Christ. Amen.

CHAPTER 36

"I Will Go and Do the Things..."

My beloved President David O. McKay, President Brown, and brothers and sisters: It is with great difficulty and a feeling of deep humility that I stand before you in response to this high honor and heavy responsibility that has been bestowed upon me, one of the most humble servants, the weakest and least prepared of all. I humbly pray that the spirit and blessings of the Lord will attend me as I stand before you this morning.

I am sure that my call to this position must have been a shock to many of you, as it is to me. It is certainly another evidence of the fact that God moves in a mysterious way, his wonders to perform.

Only because these, my colleagues, have such a strong testimony that we are led by a prophet of God can they sustain me in this position. I humbly pray that as they sustain the Prophet in his decision, they, knowing my weakness, will continue to pray for me and give of their strength which I need so badly, and with that assurance, my brothers and sisters, I can say humbly as did Nephi of old:

Address delivered Friday morning, October 4, 1963, upon President Tanner's being called to serve as second counselor in the First Presidency.

I will go and do the things which the Lord hath commanded, for I know that the Lord giveth no comandments unto the children of men, save he shall prepare a way for them that they may accomplish the thing which he commandeth them. (1 Nephi 3:7.)

I humbly thank you all for your confidence and sustaining vote, and pledge to all of you and to these, my brethren and colleagues, whom I love so much, and whom I sustain with all my heart, and to you, President McKay, as the Lord's representative, and to God himself, everything with which the Lord has blessed me for the building up of the kingdom of God.

I thank God for my loyal and devoted wife and family whom I love so much and who have always sustained and strengthened me with their inspiration, loyalty, faith, and prayers and who will continue to sustain me in this new calling.

I thank my Heavenly Father for the wonderful privilege that I have had of associating with these fine men, for the influence they have had in my life, and for the encouragement and strength they have given me. And I thank God for the signal privilege I have had of associating so closely with, and feeling the great spirit and influence of, our beloved President David O. McKay. All that has been written and said about him, as he has just passed his ninetieth birthday, does not and cannot portray the greatness of him who has been chosen as a prophet of God and who is now President of The Church of Jesus Christ of Latter-day Saints—the kingdom of God here upon the earth. It is impossible to appreciate or estimate the tremendous influence for good that he has exerted upon all mankind. The closer that one is to him, and the more he is permitted to associate with him, the stronger one's testimony becomes that he is a prophet of God.

It is with sadness that I mention the absence of our beloved friend and colleague, President Henry D. Moyle, whom we all miss so much, and whose passing makes these changes necessary. His family, his friends, his church, his community, and his country have suffered a tremendous loss. He was a loving husband and father, a true and loyal friend, a thoughtful neighbor, a devoted member and capable leader of the Church. He was always working for the good of his country and the betterment of mankind. I wish to express my love and sympathy to Sister Moyle and her family and pray that the Spirit of the Lord will accompany and strengthen them and give them courage to carry on.

At this time, I should like to welcome Brother Thomas Monson [newly sustained to the Council of the Twelve], whom I sustain with all my heart.

I have not words to express my deep love for the Lord and my gratitude to him for his many blessings unto me and mine, and I sincerely pray for his continued guidance and strength, as I try to serve him. And I wish to pledge with you again that my life and all that I have will be completely devoted to the service of my Maker and to my fellowmen, always with a prayer in my heart that he will give me wisdom and knowledge, courage and strength, inspiration and determination and ability to keep his commandments and serve in a way that will be acceptable to him.

And I appeal to each and every one of you to exercise your faith and prayers in my behalf that I might lose myself in his service and go forward with an eye single to his glory.

I wish to bear my testimony that I know that God lives, that Jesus is the Christ who gave his life for you and me; that this is his church and kingdom; that we have at the head of our church this day a prophet of God who is led by him, and through whom we are led in the paths of truth and righteousness.

May we follow him, knowing that we will be led into immortality and eternal life, I humbly pray in the name of the Lord Jesus Christ. Amen.

CHAPTER 37

Rejoice, and Give Thanks

It is with joy and a deep feeling of gratitude that I bring to the Saints and people throughout the world greetings and best wishes from the First Presidency of the Church on this Thanksgiving Day.

Thanksgiving Day gives each and every one of us an invitation and wonderful opportunity to pause and count our many blessings and to give thanks to God and praise him from whom all blessings flow.

Let us acknowledge and thank him and show our love and gratitude for life itself, for the air we breathe, the food we eat and the health that we enjoy; for our eyesight and hearing and limbs; for our children and parents and husband or wife; for our friends and loved ones everywhere. Thank him for the freedom we enjoy in the free world and that we can worship God according to the dictates of our own conscience. Above all, let us thank God for his Son and the great sacrifice he made for you and me. We must not take these innumerable blessings for granted, but let us imagine ourselves being deprived of them, then let us stop and thank God again and show our gratitude for his blessings unto us. Let us call our family together in a

Address delivered over the Church-owned station WRUL November 28, 1963.

prayer of thanksgiving on this Thanksgiving Day, and every day throughout the year.

We of the First Presidency thank the Lord for, and send greetings and blessings and love to, our devoted mission presidents and missionaries, who, as ambassadors of the Lord, are taking the glorious message of peace and goodwill to the world; to the young men and women who are in the service of their country and who are prepared to give their all in the interest of liberty, freedom, and peace.

To our youth everywhere, we send love and greetings and continually pray for your health, welfare, and happiness and express our gratitude for you.

May we all make this a day of real thanksgiving and may we continue to show our gratitude to God by the way we live.

God bless you all.

Index

- A -

Aaronic Priesthood, conferred on Joseph Smith and Oliver Cowdery, 247, 248
Abel and Cain, 58, 84
"Abou Ben Adam," poem by Leigh Hunt, 46-47
Abraham, revelations to, 167-68
Activating members of church, 49-51
Adam and Eve, 22-23, 94, 130, 144-47, 155, 168-69
Adultery, woman accused of, 58
Aetna, Alberta, Canada, 10
Agnew, Spiro, 178
Agrippa, Paul testifies before, 25-26, 170
Alberta government, service in, 15-16
Alcohol, evils of, 65-66, 107, 183-86, 194-96
Alcoholic, government official who was, 183-84; ten commandments for, 196
Alcoholism Control Act, 184
Alcoholics Anonymous, 183
Ambition in work, examples of, 235, 236-37
Amendments to U.S. Constitution, 111
America, land choice above others, 92, 100; rights of citizens of, 102-103; democratic form of government in, 110
American continent, Christ appears on, 28, 131
American Council on Alcohol Problems, 66
Amos, prophet, 129
Angel Moroni, 132, 246-47
Antony, Mark, 160

Articles of Faith, 63, 91, 127, 139, 239
Articles of Faith (book), 140
Ashton, Conway, 266
Atonement, 152
Attorney General of Utah, quotation by, 110

- B -

Bach, Dr. Marcus, quotation by, 74-75
Bank manager, story about, 12-13
Baptism, 247, 251
Benjamin, King, visited by angel, 32-33
Berchtesgaden, Germany, servicemen's conference in, 237
Bible testifies of Christ, 22, 134; word of God, 128, 137, 248
Bill of Rights, 112
Birthright of citizens, 111
Bishop, importance of office of, 17, 290; tribute to, 50
Blessings, gratitude for, 159-60
Blood Indian Reservation, 77
Bodies are temples of personal spirits, 188
Bolton, New York, 7
Book of Mormon, testifies of Christ, 22, 24, 28, 169, 247; is record of Lamanites, 77, 80; tells of destruction of nonfollowers of Christ, 84; is word of God, 128; contains fullness of gospel, 135; testimonies of, 137; righteousness of people recorded in, 152; recordings of, given to young boys, 226-27; translation of, 248; history of, 248

Boy Scouts of America, 259
Brigham Young University, viii, 79, 178, 216, 228, 280
British Royal College of Physicians, 186
Brotherhood of man, 71-76
Brotherhood Week, 71
Brown, Hugh B., 72, 280, 286
Brown, James, 9, 286
Burns, Robert, poem by, 256
Burton, Theodore M., 289
Businessman's comments on hiring Mormons, 201

- C -

Cabinet of Province of Alberta, service in, 15-16
Caesar, Julius, 160
Cain and Abel, 58, 84
Cancer caused by smoking, 186
Cardston, Alberta, Canada, 9, 13, 15
Cardston First Ward, 254
Carter, Simeon and Jared, 7-8
Catholics accept Bible as word of God, 248
Celestial marriage, 251
Charity, 57
Chicago Democrat, 127
Chief Justice of Supreme Court in Ontario, Canada, 150
Children, parents to teach, 86-87, 207-13
Chinese proverb, 139
Choice (see Free Agency)
Christ (see Jesus Christ)
Christian living, true, 70, 74
Christianity, why people say it has failed, 139
Christmas, true spirit of, 35-36
Church, attendance, 68; growth of under David O. McKay, 262-63; growth of under Joseph Fielding Smith, 275
Church Commissioner of Education (David O. McKay), 258
Church's declaration of belief in government law, 100-101
Churchill, Winston, quotations by, 94, 271
Citizenship, rights of, 72-73
Civic responsibilities of citizens, 109-115
Cleveland, Grover, quotation by, 110
Columbus, Christopher, quotation by, 138
Commandments, keeping of, necessary for eternal life, 90-91, 92-95; of God, 119-23, 139-40, 143, 147; living, brings peace in world, 211

Community affairs, women's involvement in, 221-22
Compartmentalization in one's life, 68
Condemnation of hypocrites, 63-64
Conflict of good and evil, 150
Constitution, United States, 103, 104, 111, 112
Constitutional rights, 89
Cooper, Gordon, quotation by, 156
Cornelius, John C., quotation by, 101
Council in heaven, 83-84, 93, 144, 167-68, 250
Cowdery, Oliver, 134, 247
Cramer, Olvie, 257
Creation of earth, 144-48, 219
Crime, attacking, 89
Criticizing others, 53-61; Church leaders, 57-58
Crow Creek Indian Council, 79
Cumorah, Hill, 246, 247

- D -

Dallas, Texas, experience in, 16-17, 290
David chosen as king of Israel, 56; and Goliath, 137-38
Death, 165
Declaration of Independence, 110
Delinquency, juvenile, 105
Democratic way of life, 103
Dependability, 2
Deseret Sunday School Union, 258
Disobedience, no happiness in, 147
Doctrine and Covenants, 22, 249, 250
Drugs, evils of, 66, 187-88
Duty to study word of God, 149

- E -

Edmond, Paul, quotation by, 96
Edmonton, Alberta, Canada, missionary work begun in, 254
Education, importance of gaining, 140-41, 228-39
Eisenhower, Dwight D., quotation by, 156
Election campaigning, 60
Elijah appears to Joseph Smith and Oliver Cowdery, 134
Emerson, Ralph Waldo, quotation by, 234
England, early apostles sent to, 252
Enoch saw coming of Jesus Christ, 23
Entertainment of today, 88
European Mission, 258
Evans, Richard L., quotation by, 154
Evils in world today, 86, 88, 89, 120, 136

Example of parents, importance of, 207-13
Ezekial, revelation of, 132-33

- F -

Faith, live by, 166
Family, love in, 41-42, 60; brotherhood in, 73; prayer, 149; home evening, 220-21, 225-26
Fate, architect of own, 99
Father's advice and faithfulness, 1-2
Federal Bureau of Investigation, 186, 207
First Presidency statement on education, 228
Flood at time of Noah, 84-85
Forbidden fruits, partaking of, 147
Forgiveness, story about, 45-46; Jesus greatest example of, 59; pray for, 159; prayers, 161-62
Fosdick, Harry Emerson, 68
Franklin, Benjamin, quotation by, 155, 156
Free agency, 83-91, 92-99, 116-17, 208, 210
Freedom, quotation on, 104

- G -

Garden of Eden, 84, 94, 130, 146, 147, 168
Gardner, John W., quotations by, 104, 229
General Motors Corporation, 232, 259
Giant of the Lord (book), 9
Glasgow Conference of Scotland Mission, 257
Glasgow Stake, organization of, 288
God, description of in Article of Faith, 127
"God is dead" theory, 136
Goethe, quotation by, 96
Golden Rule, 40, 42, 44-45
Goliath slain by David, 137-38
Good Samaritan, 66
Gospel, only way to combat evils, 136, 152
Gossip, evils of, 57, 58
Government, Church belief in, 100-101; honoring and sustaining, 109
Grant, Heber J., 254, 258
Gratitude, 159, 294-95
Guest, Edgar A., poem by, 5

- H -

Hand, Judge Learned, quotation by, 107-108
Happiness, 48

Haycock, D. Arthur, 274
Health, law of, 120 (see also Word of Wisdom)
Hill Cumorah, 246, 247
Hill Spring, Alberta, Canada, 13-14
Hilton, Conrad, quotation by, 73
Hinckley, Gordon B., 280, 288
Hippie, story about visit of, 191-92
Holy Ghost comes to those who magnify priesthood, 175-76
Home, righteousness taught in, 149-50; importance of, 207-209; is basic unit of society, 215
Homestead of Tanner family, 10
Honesty, 62, 237
Honolulu Star Bulletin, article on smoking in, 181-82
Hoover, Herbert, quotation by, 220
Hoover, J. Edgar, quotations by, 141-42, 207-208
Hudson, Dr. Frederick, 185
Humility, 158
Hunt, Leigh, poem by, 46-47
Huntsville, Utah, 255
Hypocrite, definition of, 64; kinds of, 68

- I -

Immorality, 136
Inactivity in church, 48-52, 54, 69
Indian Placement Program, 77-80
Influence of Church members on others, 69-70
Integrity in government service, 114
Interpreter's Bible, 133
Isaiah, prophecy of, 23, 32
Israelites, 137-38

- J -

Javits, Senator Jacob, 184
Jefferson, Thomas, quotation by, 110
Jesse, house of, 55
Jesus Christ, divinity of, 21-31; scriptures testify of, 22-24; coming of, foretold by prophets, 22-23, 32-34; signs of the coming of, 24, 33-34; appears to Paul, 25-26; gives Sermon on Mount, 26; love of, for mankind, 26-27; crucifixion and resurrection of, 27-28; appears on American continent, 28, 248; appears to Joseph Smith, 29, 245; appears to Joseph Smith and Sidney Rigdon, 30; birth of, 34-35; gives second great commandment, 39-40; teaches about judging others, 55, 58-59; is greatest example of forgiveness, 59; teaches about evils

of hypocrisy, 63-64; teaches about brotherhood, 74; plan of, in council in heaven, 83-84, 93; admonishes parents to teach children, 86-87; reestablishes church on earth, 90; teaches about obedience to law, 102; described in Articles of Faith, 127-28; belief in is essential to salvation, 128; appears on American continent, 131; atonement of, 152; heals lepers, 160; sustained at council in heaven, 168; in Garden of Gethsemane, 168; was 24 when Church was organized, 199; mission of, 219
John the Baptist appears to Joseph Smith and Oliver Cowdery, 247
John the Revelator, 131
Johnson, Lyndon B., 71, 260-61, 281
Jones, Jenkin Lloyd, speech of, 85, 88
Joshua, taught about importance of choice, 92
Joy, men are to have, 90, 94
Judging others, 53-61
Juvenile delinquency, 105-106, 147

- K -

Kennedy, John F., memorial tribute to, 280-81
King George VI, 271
Kirtland Temple, 134
Knudsen, William S., advice to youth by, 232-33
Korea, servicemen in, 199
Korea Mission, 201-202

- L -

Lake George, 8
Lamanites, concern for, 77-80
Law, of Moses, 40; of land, 59-60; letter versus spirit of, 65; choosing to keep, 98; reverence for, 100-108; obedience to, 109-110, 111; of God, 117; natural, 98, 117; of chemistry, physics, gravity, 118
Lazarus, Emma, poem by, 72-73
Lazarus, in Bible, 165
Lee, Harold B., 91, 222
Lehi hears voice of the Lord, 131; advises sons, 172
Lepers, healed by Jesus, 160
"Let Each Man Learn to Know Himself" (hymn), 53
Letter from reformed hippie, 192
Liberty, quotation on, 108
Lincoln, Abraham, quotations by, 94, 102, 105, 138, 156
Liquor (see Alcohol)

Liquor laws, 65-66, 197-98
London Temple, 259
Los Angeles Temple, 259
Lost Sheep, parable of, 49
Love, 39-47, 123
Loyalty to country, 149
Lucifer, 83
Lung cancer, 186

- M -

Magnifying callings, 5
Malachi, revelation of, 133
Manning, E. C., Premier of Alberta, 114
Marriage, 41, 216, 218, 251
Mary, mother of Jesus, 24, 34
Mary, the other, 27
Mary Magdalene, 27
Mayflower, ancestors on, 7
Mayflower Compact, 155
McIntosh, Al, newspaper article by, 106
McKay, David, 255
McKay, David Lawrence, 266
McKay, David O., 54, 280, 285, 287, 288, 292; quotation by, 238; tribute to and life of, 254-64; sermon delivered at funeral of, 265-72; tribute to, by Joseph Fielding Smith, 274
McKay, Emma Ray, 54, 266, 267, 268
McKay, Jennette Evans, 255
McMurrin, James, 257
Melchizedek Priesthood, 247, 248
Merrill, Sara Isabelle (Mrs. N. Eldon Tanner), 14
Milton, quotation by, 96
Missionaries, advice to, 4; who baptized ancestors, 7-8; and love for the Lord, 42; and love for parents, 43; work of, 198-203; discussion of, at family home evening, 225-26
"Modern American Fable," 106
Monson, Thomas S., 293
Moral living, 4, 65
Mormon Battalion, 9
Moroni, Angel, 131; promise of concerning Book of Mormon, 163, 249-50; appears to Joseph Smith, 246-47
Morse, Samuel F. B., quotation by, 156
Movies, violence and immorality in, 88
Moses, protected and preserved by the Lord, 130, 137; revelations to, 167-68
Motherhood, 216-23
Moyle, Henry D., 288, 292
Munich, Germany, area conference at, 222
"Myself," poem by Edgar A. Guest, 5

- N -

National Council on Alcoholism, 184
Nauvoo, Illinois, 251-52
"Nay, Speak No Ill" (hymn), 43-44
Neighbor, love of, 39, 43-44, 59, 66, 75
Nephi told to write records, 148
New morality, 136
New Testament, 22, 25
New Zealand, David O. McKay in, 258
New Zealand Temple, 259
Newspaper reports on evils in world, 120
Nixon, Richard M., 89, 260
Noah, 85
Normal School, experiences at, 12-13

- O -

Oakland Temple, 259
Oaks, Dallin, 216
Obedience, 5, 116-23, 169
Ogden Temple, 259
Old Testament, 22, 248
Opposition in all things, 90
Orient, stakes and missions in, 198
Osaka, servicemen in, 199

- P -

Parable of lost sheep, 49; of rich man, 165-66
Parents told to teach children, 86-87, 122; responsibilities of, 149, 207-13, 217, 223; to teach youth about evils of alcohol, 185-86
Paul's vision and testimony of Jesus Christ, 25-26; advice to Timothy, 151; conversion, 169-70; appearance before King Agrippa, 170
Peace depends on keeping laws, 108
Pearl of Great Price, 22, 250
Percentages of church attendance, 49-50, 52
Persecution of Latter-day Saints, 251-52
Peter's testimony, 25
Peter, James, and John restore Melchizedek Priesthood, 247
Philistines, 137-38
Pornography, 88-89, 215, 216
Potatoes, story about delivery of, 236
Power, priesthood, 174
Praise of man, God, 142
Prayer, family, 11, 159, 161-63, 225; power of, 154-64; of Adam and Eve, 155; by Founding Fathers, 155; promises given to those who

pray, 157-58; for forgiveness, 159; reasons for, 159; parents to teach about, 161; promise of Moroni to those who pray, 163; discussion of youth on, 225; of David O. McKay, 255, 256
Preexistence, 165, 167
Prejudging others, 54-55
Premier of Alberta, 114
Preparation for life's work, 234
Presnall, Lewis F., quotation by, 184
Priesthood, keys of, 129; power and blessings of, 174-79, 237; magnifying, 175-76, 200, 221; oath and covenant of, 176; influence on world if magnified, 177; restoration of, 251
Primary teacher, advice of, 10
Prophets, testify of Jesus Christ, 22, 23, 32, 169, 171; revelation received through, 128, 166-69; pray for guidance, 157
Protestant churches, differences in beliefs of, 128-29, 248
Provo Temple, 259
Public service, 114-15

- Q -

Quarterly Journal of Studies of Alcohol, 186

- R -

Reformation, 129
Regional Representatives of the Twelve, 266
Relief Society, responsibilities of members of, 67, 218
Responsibility of Church members to bear testimony, 31
Resurrection taught by Alma in Book of Mormon, 250
Revelation, 127-35
Ricks College, 228
Rigdon, Sidney, 30
Righteousness, 142
Rockefeller, John D., creed of, 139
Rocky Mountains, Saints driven to, 252
Roman Empire, fall of, 85
Romney, Vernon B., quotation by, 110
Roosevelt, Franklin D., 73
Rowallan, Lord, 210

- S -

Sabbath day, 4, 121-22
Sacrifice, Adam and Eve told to offer, 169

Salt Lake Valley, 252
Salvation, plan of, 112, 145, 165-73, 220
Samuel, Lamanite prophet, 24
Samuel's experience in choosing king, 55-56
Satan's plan in council of heaven, 83-84, 93, 145-46, 151; tempts men, 178; and the Word of Wisdom, 180-81; seeks to destroy home, 215, 221
Saul rejected as king of Israel, 55
School of the Prophets, 228
Schoolteacher, understanding of, 54
Scotland Mission, 289
Scout promise, 210-11
Scriptures testify of Jesus Christ, 22-23, 166
Self-discipline, 86, 142
Self-respect, 6
Sermon on the Mount, 26, 63, 171
Service to others, 98, 113
Servicemen, 199, 200, 201-202
Servicemen's Conference in Germany, story told at, 237
Shakespeare, William, quotations by, 115, 160
Sin, no happiness in, 147
Slavery antithetical to free agency, 97
Smith, Emma, 248
Smith, Ethel Reynolds, article by, 277-78
Smith, George Albert, 258
Smith, Joseph, 7-9; visions of, 29-30, 244-45; called of God by revelation, 129; visited by Angel Moroni, 132, 246; visited by Elijah, 132; writes Articles of Faith, 127, 139; emphasis of, on education, 228; revelation of, on intelligence, 238; life and work of, 243-52
Smith, Joseph F., quotations by, 96-97, 113; ordains David O. McKay, 258
Smith, Joseph Fielding, given Book of Mormon by father, 227; ordains David O. McKay, 259; sermon delivered at funeral of, 273-79; writings of, 276
Smith, Joseph Fielding, Jr., quotation by, 277
Society, free, quotation on, 104
Sodom and Gomorrah, 85, 151
Standards of the Church, living, 237
Stapley, Delbert L., 79
Statue of Liberty, inscription on, 72-73
Stewart, Dr. William H., quotation by, 181

Strong, Patience, poem by, 75
Swiss Temple, 259

- T -

Talmage, James E., 140
Tanner, John, 7-9, 244
Tanner, N. Eldon, known as "Mr. Integrity," viii; described by A. Theodore Tuttle, ix; father of, 1-2, 11-12; gives advice to daughter, 3; slogan of, in mission field, 3-4; gives advice to youth, 4; ancestry of, 7-9; parents of, 9-10; education of, 10-13; borrows money for education, 12-13; principal of school, 13; opens general store, 14-15; serves in provincial government, 15-17; introduction of, by governor of Texas, 16-17; becomes U.S. citizen, 111; taught to pray by parents, 161-62; brother of, who died of lung cancer, 182; experience of, with grandchildren in family home evening, 225-27; advice of, to daughters, 226; experience of, as Minister of Mines in Alberta, 235; relates story about potatoes delivered to merchant, 236; experience of, in Trans-Canada Pipelines, 236-37; association of, with David O. McKay, 254; association of, with Joseph Fielding Smith, 276; address of, when sustained as Assistant to the Council of the Twelve, 285-86; address of, when sustained to Council of the Twelve, 287-90; address of, when called to serve in First Presidency, 291-93
Tanner, Sara Isabelle (Sally), 14
Teacher development training, 52
Technical training (see Vocational Training)
Technology, figures on, 232
Temple University in Philadelphia, 259
Temples dedicated in David O. McKay administration, 259
Temptation, overcoming, 150-51
Ten Commandments, 63, 119, 130, 139-40, 171
Tennyson, Alfred, Lord, quotation by, 154
Terhune, Dr. William, quotation by, 196
Testimony of Jesus Christ, 29
Texas, governor of, 16-17
Thanksgiving Day, 160, 294
Thomas, disciple of Christ, 27-28

Thurmond, Senator Strom, quotation by, 155-56
Times and Seasons, 127
Tobacco, evils of, 181-82, 186-87
Tourism, and liquor, 196
Traffic laws, disregard for, 107
Trust, poem on, 115
Truth, 166
Tuttle, A. Theodore, viii-ix

- U -

United States, rights of citizens of, 102-103
United States Public Health Service survey, 187
University of Utah (University of Deseret), 228, 257
Unrighteous judgment, examples of, 54
Unselfishness, 42
Utah Council on Child Health and Protection, 258
Utah State Agricultural College (Utah State University), 258

- V -

Vietnam, serviceman converted in, 199
"Vision, the" (poem), 75

Visions of Jesus Christ by prophets of old, 22
Vocational training, 228-39

- W -

Wanderers, search for, 48-52
Washington, D.C., temple in, 259
Washington, George, quotation by, 138
Waters, Mark, 181
Waterton Lakes, Canada, 224
Weber Academy (Weber State College), 258
Wentworth, John, letter to, 127
West European Mission, ix, 3, 288
White House Conference on Child Welfare, 258
Wife, tributes to, 214
Wilcox, Emma Wheeler, poem by, 73
Womanhood in the Church, 214-23
Word of Wisdom, 4, 50, 67, 120, 180-89, 190-97

- Y -

Young, Brigham, quotations by, 150, 217, 230-31
Youth, 49, 105-106, 178; stories of, involved with drugs, 191-94; criticisms of, 207